MEDIEVAL SINGLE WOMEN

Medieval Single Women:

The Politics of Social Classification in Late Medieval England

CORDELIA BEATTIE

OXFORD
UNIVERSITY PRESS

ST CHARLES COMMUNITY COLLEGE
LIBRARY

OXFORD
UNIVERSITY PRESS

Great Clarendon Street, Oxford OX2 6DP

Oxford University Press is a department of the University of Oxford.
It furthers the University's objective of excellence in research, scholarship,
and education by publishing worldwide in

Oxford New York

Auckland Cape Town Dar es Salaam Hong Kong Karachi
Kuala Lumpur Madrid Melbourne Mexico City Nairobi
New Delhi Shanghai Taipei Toronto

With offices in

Argentina Austria Brazil Chile Czech Republic France Greece
Guatemala Hungary Italy Japan Poland Portugal Singapore
South Korea Switzerland Thailand Turkey Ukraine Vietnam

Oxford is a registered trade mark of Oxford University Press
in the UK and in certain other countries

Published in the United States
by Oxford University Press Inc., New York

© Cordelia Beattie 2007

The moral rights of the author have been asserted
Database right Oxford University Press (maker)

First published 2007

All rights reserved. No part of this publication may be reproduced,
stored in a retrieval system, or transmitted, in any form or by any means,
without the prior permission in writing of Oxford University Press,
or as expressly permitted by law, or under terms agreed with the appropriate
reprographics rights organization. Enquiries concerning reproduction
outside the scope of the above should be sent to the Rights Department,
Oxford University Press, at the address above

You must not circulate this book in any other binding or cover
and you must impose the same condition on any acquirer

British Library Cataloguing in Publication Data
Data available

Library of Congress Cataloging in Publication Data
Data available

Typeset by Laserwords Private Limited, Chennai, India
Printed in Great Britain
on acid-free paper by
Biddles Ltd., King's Lynn, Norfolk

ISBN 978-0-19-928341-5

1 3 5 7 9 10 8 6 4 2

For Jeremy and Felicity

Acknowledgements

This book is dedicated to Jeremy Goldberg and Felicity Riddy who supervised my doctoral thesis on medieval single women at the Centre for Medieval Studies, University of York. I hope they enjoy what I have done with some of the earlier ideas and research.

Of course, this project has incurred numerous other intellectual and personal debts, and it is difficult to untangle them, but I am pleased to be able to acknowledge at least some of them here. Particular thanks must go to John Arnold, for being a reader and sounding-board throughout, regardless of the state of the text or of my mood. Judith Bennett has offered support from an early stage of this project and I am particularly grateful for the time she has spent writing letters of reference and commenting on the penultimate draft. I am also indebted to Steve Rigby and an anonymous reader for Oxford University Press for their feedback on the penultimate manuscript. Sharon Farmer, Lucy Grig, and Shannon McSheffrey all agreed to read draft chapters, and Pauline Stafford to act as a referee for my AHRC application. Indeed, I am grateful to the Arts and Humanities Research Council and the University of Edinburgh for supporting my research and, in particular, for granting me research leave, which allowed me to finish this study. The Carnegie Trust for the Universities of Scotland and the School of History and Classics at Edinburgh also provided funds for the final checking of archival material. Thanks must go to the staff of the various archives and libraries used and, at Oxford University Press, to Ruth Parr, Anne Gelling, and Rupert Cousens for their enthusiasm and efficiency. Countless people helped in various ways but I would like to single out the following: at Edinburgh, Pertti Ahonen, Donald Bloxham, Andrew Brown, Abigail Burnyeat, Kirsten Fenton, Francesca Locatelli, Sergi Mainer, Katie Stephenson, and Cheryl Ruiz; those who have continued to offer support beyond the York days, Debbie Cannon, Isabel Davis, Meg Gay, Joanna Huntington, Katherine Lewis, and Kim Phillips; and from school Latin classes to the present day, Jane Keating. I would, of course, like to acknowledge the love and support of my family: Judith, Derek, and my sisters, Emma and Naomi, who between them produced five children in the time it took me to produce this study.

Contents

List of Abbreviations xi
List of Tables xii

Introduction 1

Medieval classification schemes 2
'Single woman' as a category of difference 7

1. **Classification in Cultural Context** 13

Clean maids, true wives, and steadfast widows 15
Femmes Soles 24
Marriage, social change, and the politics of classification 31

2. **The Single Woman in Penitential Discourse** 39

Penitential discourse, women, and sexual sin 44
Fourteen degrees of active lechery 50
Seven states of chastity 56

3. **The Single Woman in Fiscal Discourse** 62

The schedule for the 1379 tax and the classification process 66
The Bishop's Lynn poll tax return of 1379 73
Widows, daughters, and work 83
Thinking with single women 93

4. **The Single Woman in Guild Texts** 96

Single sisters and the guild returns of 1388–9 99
Maidens and single men: the register of the Guild of the
 Holy Cross, Stratford-upon-Avon (1406–1535) 113

5. 'Singlewoman' as a Personal Designation   124

Early examples of 'singlewoman'   127
York's civic records *c.* 1475–*c.* 1540   130
From the medieval to the early modern   136

Conclusion: Cultural Intersections   144

Bibliography   149
Index   173

List of Abbreviations

BIHR	Borthwick Institute of Historical Research, York
EEBO	Early English Books Online, accessed via Edinburgh University Library
EETS, o.s.	Early English Text Society, original series
GL	Guildhall Library, London
MED	H. Kurath *et al.* (eds.), *The Middle English Dictionary* (Ann Arbor, MI: University of Michigan Press, 1956–)
SBTRO	Shakespeare Birthplace Trust Records Office, Stratford-upon-Avon
STC	Short Title Catalogue
TNA: PRO	The National Archives: Public Record Office, Kew
YASRS	Yorkshire Archaeological Society Record Series
YCA	York City Archives

List of Tables

2.1 The branches of lechery in two different traditions   49

3.1 The correlation of categories describing males in the 1379
      Bishop's Lynn poll tax return   75

3.2 The correlation of categories describing females in the 1379
      Bishop's Lynn poll tax return   77

3.3 The classification of females in the 1379 Salisbury poll
      tax return   84

3.4 The classification of males in the 1379 Salisbury poll
      tax return   85

3.5 The classification of males in the 1379 Derby poll
      tax return   90

3.6 The classification of females in the 1379 Derby poll
      tax return   91

. . . the analysis of language provides a crucial point of entry, a starting point for understanding how social relations are conceived . . . and how collective identity is established. Without attention to language and the processes by which meanings and categories are constituted, one only imposes oversimplified models on the world, models that perpetuate conventional understandings rather than open up new interpretive possibilities.

Joan Scott, 'Deconstructing
Equality-versus-Difference' (1988)

Introduction

In Shakespeare's *Measure for Measure* (*c.* 1604), the Duke of Vienna, petitioned as a dispenser of justice, asks Mariana, in turn, if she is married, a maid, or a widow. She answers negatively to each question, provoking the Duke's response, 'Why, you are nothing then: neither maid, widow, nor wife?' The fool Lucio interrupts, 'My lord, she may be a punk [harlot], for many of them are neither maid, widow, nor wife'.[1] Instead of being able to sum herself up in one word, Mariana has to explain her complex situation in order to avoid such negative labelling. She had been betrothed to the Duke's deputy, Angelo, but the marriage was never solemnized as she had lost her dowry. By pretending to be someone else, she subsequently had sexual intercourse with Angelo (and so she can no longer call herself a 'maid', with its associations of virginity). The sexual act following betrothal also makes them married in the eyes of Mariana and, probably, the law.[2] Mariana needs Angelo to recognize their marriage before she can lay claim to the category of 'wife', though, but he is still unaware that the woman he shared a bed with was Mariana. Her story explains where she fits in relation to the maid-wife-widow model: no longer a true maid, but not fully a wife. While none of the labels fit at this stage in Shakespeare's narrative, Mariana has to be seen to be heading towards one label at least.

All societies use classifications in order to understand and to impose order.[3] This is a book about social classification in late medieval England. It views classification as a political act, an act of power: those classifying

---

[1] Shakespeare, *Measure for Measure*, ed. N. W. Bawcutt (Oxford: Clarendon Press, 1991), pp. 211–12, ll. 171–80.

[2] See B. J. Sokol and M. Sokol, *Shakespeare, Law, and Marriage* (Cambridge: Cambridge University Press, 2003), esp. pp. 8–9, 26–8, 73–4.

[3] See G. Constable, 'The Orders of Society', in G. Constable, *Three Studies in Medieval Religious and Social Thought* (Cambridge: Cambridge University Press, 1995), p. 251; E. Durkheim and M. Mauss, *Primitive Classification*, trans. R. Needham, 2nd edn. (London: Cohen & West, 1969); G. C. Bowker and S. L. Star, *Sorting Things Out: Classification and its Consequences* (Cambridge, MA: MIT Press, 1999), pp. 1–4.

make choices about what divisions are most important or about who falls into which category, and such choices have repercussions. The subdivision of society into particular groups gives those groups a shared identity, which affects how they are perceived by others. The labelling of specific individuals identifies those individuals as members of a particular group, and thus assigns to them a place in the social structure. Not fitting into any of the named groups could also have ramifications. The power of classification, though, resides as much in language, in dominant cultural ideas, as with individual classifiers. Where is the pressure coming from to categorize Mariana in the opening story: the Duke, Shakespeare, or a ubiquitous cultural model that conceptualizes women as maids, wives, or widows?

This book focuses on the gendered aspects of classificatory schemes. When those classifying choose what defines a group or how an individual should be labelled, they are choosing between certain variables, such as social status, gender, marital status, or age, and deciding which to prioritize. Depending on the complexity of the classificatory scheme, more than one variable can be employed. Rather than isolate gender, the approach here is to examine how it relates to other social cleavages. The single woman has been chosen as the focus of enquiry precisely because it can be viewed as a troubling and disruptive category. Does the category encompass all unmarried women, thus constituting a huge subgroup which every female was part of at some stage in her life? Or, were the categories of 'virgin' and 'widow' so culturally significant in late medieval England that 'single woman' was a residual category for women seen as anomalous? Was the category 'single man' used in an equivalent way? It is intended, through a focused study on the category 'single woman', to illuminate the complexity inherent in categorizations and their usages.

MEDIEVAL CLASSIFICATORY SCHEMES

The classificatory schemes discussed in this book are of two key types: interpretative schemes, which divide society into various subgroups, and the labelling of named individuals. Otto Oexle defines interpretive schemes as 'terminological constructs intended to name, organize, and interpret social phenomena'.[4] A much-studied, medieval example is

---

[4] O. G. Oexle, 'Perceiving Social Reality in the Early and High Middle Ages: A Contribution to a History of Social Knowledge', in B. Jussen (ed.), *Ordering Medieval*

the trifunctional scheme of the three orders or estates: those who pray (*oratores*), those who fight (*bellatores*), and those who work (*laboratores*).[5] Similarly, the maid-wife-widow scheme referred to in *Measure for Measure* is often seen as the dominant one for medieval women, and it is a scheme that reappears in various forms throughout this book.[6] The second type concerns the use of personal designations, sometimes referred to as additions, such as 'knight', 'labourer', and 'widow'. The two classificatory schemes appear to be very different. The interpretive scheme operates at the level of the abstract and theoretical; it discusses types of person and sets out a normative model. While such schemes might give the impression of covering all of society, omissions are to be expected, whether for reasons of clarity or ideology. The labelling of named persons differs in that it focuses on the individual and concerns *real* people. And yet one should not exaggerate the differences. Interpretive schemes should not be treated as merely theoretical: they also had an effect on social reality and were affected by it in turn. Further, the labelling of individuals often involved choices about which labels to apply, labels that associate individuals with a wider group, and therefore should also be treated as value-laden schemes.

Interpretive schemes, whether threefold divisions or more elaborate ones, have a complex relationship with social reality, in their design and in their effect. Those that created or adapted an interpretive scheme might have been engaged in an attempt to understand, or explain, or affect social phenomena. Traditionally studies of such schemes have looked at political and religious treatises and sermons, largely written by monks, nuns, or clerics. Thus the schemes were in part the attempts of the religious to work out God's plan; as Giles Constable puts it, '[t]heir

Society: Perspectives on Intellectual and Practical Modes of Shaping Social Relations, trans. P. Selwyn (Philadelphia, PA: University of Pennsylvania Press, 2001), p. 92.

[5] See e.g. J. Le Goff, 'A Note on Tripartite Society, Monarchical Ideology, and Economic Renewal in Ninth- to Twelfth-Century Christendom', in J. Le Goff, *Time, Work, & Culture in the Middle Ages*, trans. A. Goldhammer (Chicago, IL: University of Chicago Press, 1980), pp. 53–7; G. Duby, *The Three Orders: Feudal Society Imagined*, trans. A. Goldhammer (Chicago, IL: University of Chicago Press, 1980); E. A. R. Brown, 'Georges Duby and the Three Orders', *Viator*, 17 (1986), 51–64.

[6] See e.g. C. Casagrande, 'The Protected Woman', trans. C. Botsford, in C. Klapisch-Zuber (ed.), *A History of Women in the West: II. Silences of the Middle Ages* (Cambridge, MA: Belknap Press, 1992), pp. 79–84; M. Hallissy, *Clean Maids, True Wives, Steadfast Widows: Chaucer's Women and Medieval Codes of Conduct* (Westport, CT: Greenwood Press, 1993), pp. 1–7; H. Leyser, *Medieval Women: A Social History of Women in England 450–1500* (London: Phoenix Giant, 1996), p. 93.

background and training accustomed them to look for deeper meaning in the observable world . . . and to apply to it the patterns they found in the Bible'.[7] In their writings they also attempt to explain to others how and why the world and its constituent elements function in particular ways. Further, they might try to set out how they thought things *should* be and so cause or prevent social change. Once in existence, a scheme could affect how others saw and interpreted social phenomena. Oexle reminds us of Georges Duby's observation that 'human beings do not orient their behavior toward real events and circumstances, but rather to their image of them'; that is, people apprehend reality through representations of reality, including interpretative schemes.[8]

Interpretive schemes are not just found in theoretical or sermonizing texts. While medieval *summae* are technically compendiums of theology, philosophy, and law, the tendency to organize things into neat categories was more widespread. Any text that presents society (or a subset thereof) as divided into various subgroups can be viewed as an interpretive scheme, even if it ostensibly did this for a specific purpose, such as to propose a system of taxation or seating arrangements.[9] Texts such as the sumptuary legislation of 1363 and the regulations for the graduated poll tax of 1379 have been analysed for what they reveal of 'how men of the time sought to reschematize the ordering of their changing society'.[10] Such texts, with evident pragmatic functions, have a more obvious relationship to a social reality. Nevertheless, they are not neutral descriptors of society but represent it from the observer's perspective. Both the 1363 sumptuary legislation and the 1379 poll tax schedule appear to be more at ease when dealing with the aristocracy than with urban society. Both use the former as the norm against which the latter

[7] Constable, 'Orders of Society', p. 254.

[8] Oexle, 'Perceiving Social Reality', p. 95, citing G. Duby, 'Histoire sociale et idéologie des sociétés', in J. Le Goff and P. Nora (eds.), *Faire de l'histoire*, 3 vols. ([Paris]: Gallimard, 1974), i, p. 148.

[9] Re. seating arrangements, see the 15th-century *Book of Nurture* in *The Babees Book*, ed. F. J. Furnivall, EETS, o.s. 32 (London: N. Trübner & Co., 1868), pp. 189–91, discussed in S. H. Rigby, 'Introduction: Social Structure and Economic Change in Late Medieval England', in R. Horrox and W. M. Ormrod (eds.), *A Social History of England, 1200–1500* (Cambridge: Cambridge University Press, 2006), p. 6. The classic example of this approach to pragmatic texts is Darnton's analysis of the ordering of an eighteenth-century civic procession: R. Darnton, *The Great Cat Massacre and Other Episodes in French Cultural History* (Harmondsworth: Penguin, 1985), pp. 113–21.

[10] M. Keen, *English Society in the Later Middle Ages, 1348–1500* (London: Penguin, 1990), pp. 8–9; see also P. Strohm, *Social Chaucer* (Cambridge, MA: Harvard University Press, 1989), pp. 3–10.

can be compared; for example, the sumptuary legislation of 1363 sets out that 'merchants, citizens, burgesses, manufacturers and craft masters of London and elsewhere who have goods and chattels worth more than £100 net per annum . . . may dress in the same way as esquires and gentlemen with land or rent worth £100 p.a.'.[11] Yet such urban groups were by no means new in the late fourteenth century. Perhaps these are illustrations of how earlier interpretive schemes affected how others saw and interpreted social phenomena. The aristocracy can be equated with the *bellatores* of the three-orders model. Some of the many adaptations of the three-orders model added a fourth estate, often to encompass urban society, and some subdivided the three or four divisions to distinguish, for example, between types of nobleman or urban dweller.[12]

The second type of classificatory scheme, the labelling of named individuals, is most commonly found in texts with a pragmatic function, such as tax or court records. Sometimes a text might assign an individual just one personal designation, such as an occupational status, or sometimes a person might be identified by a variety of labels, including marital status or a relational description to a named person. As individuals have more than one facet to their identity, this means that the classifier is usually making a choice as to which element is most relevant or important. While to some extent the use of labels is a bureaucratic procedure, one can still ask why particular labels are used and what they denote in a given context, and treat the texts as value-laden documents. Ellen Kittell's study of the documentary record for medieval Douai found that it was only when more distant authorities, such as royal French officials, intervened on a more consistent basis that uniform standards were adopted regarding the classification of individuals. Kittell comments that

In common with . . . royal officials, the historian shares a distinct remoteness from the webs of social relationships in terms of which medieval townspeople habitually identified one another. As the most distant of all authorities, the

[11] R. Horrox (ed.), *The Black Death* (Manchester: Manchester University Press, 1994), p. 341; see *Statutes of the Realm*, ed. A. Luders *et al.*, 11 vols. ([London]: [George Eyre and Andrew Strahan], 1810–28), i, pp. 380–2. See also Ch. 3, 'The schedule for the 1379 tax' below.

[12] See P. Burke, 'The Language of Orders in Early Modern Europe', in M. L. Bush (ed.), *Social Orders and Social Classes in Europe since 1500: Studies in Social Stratification* (London: Longman, 1992), pp. 5–6; S. H. Rigby, *English Society in the Later Middle Ages: Class, Status and Gender* (Houndmills: Macmillan, 1995), p. 308.

modern-day scholar is perhaps the most inclined of all to impose a grid of standard assumptions for the interpretation of personal reference in the documents.[13]

In this study, an analysis of texts that label named individuals, such as various registers and account books belonging to guilds or towns, tax returns, testaments, and court records, widens the social range of those doing the classifying. It is at the local level that the classification process most likely involved conversation between the person being labelled, the person responsible for the record in an official capacity, and a scribe, notwithstanding that the protagonists might already be known to each other.

While this study looks at medieval society and its constituent parts from the perspective of the classifiers, this is not about privileging a single view of society. Indeed, the approach taken deliberately seeks to broaden the vantage point, whilst acknowledging that the power to classify and record that process in written form was a socially limited one. First, it looks at classifiers from a range of social contexts: clerics who produced manuals related to confession and penance; the king's officials, from those in the Exchequer who drew up the 1379 tax schedule to the justices in the king's courts who adjudicated on appropriate additions (personal designations); local elites who ran guilds and provided the information for tax listings, and scribes who worked for church courts, civic governments, and parish guilds.

Second, it examines a range of texts and focuses on those that had an ostensibly pragmatic function, in other words those whose primary purpose was other than to describe or explain social divisions. The interpretive schemes analysed in this study are varied, and include parts of some pastoral manuals that seek to give guidance about confession and penance, the schedule for the 1379 poll tax, and some guild ordinances that set out a range of matters, such as subscription fees, members' rights and responsibilities, and prayers. A text that classifies sin, for example, did not have as its main intention an ordering of society into groups, but this might be a by-product if it classified that sin according to the status of the participants.

[13] E. E. Kittell, 'The Construction of Women's Social Identity in Medieval Douai: Evidence from Identifying Epithets', *Journal of Medieval History*, 25 (1999), p. 218. On classification and bureaucracy, see also J. C. Scott, *Seeing Like a State: How Certain Schemes to Improve the Human Condition Have Failed* (New Haven, CT: Yale University Press, 1998), esp. pp. 64–8.

Third, this study's focus on categories allows for consideration of how discourses intersect; cultural ideas are not confined to a particular realm but influence and inflect language use. Just as the creation of groups might be epiphenomenal, the selection of a particular category can have meaning, whether the classifier was conscious or not of why he chose the category or what its effect might be.[14] The text or texts selected as the initial case study in each chapter have all been chosen for their use of the category 'single woman', although they are sometimes compared with other texts that might not use the category.

'SINGLE WOMAN' AS A CATEGORY OF DIFFERENCE

An analysis of different medieval classification schemes shows that society could be divided up in different ways, depending on what factors were considered important. Gender is just one variable that could be drawn upon in classificatory schemes. Its role in the three-orders model, for example, is often not made manifest. When women are specifically mentioned, they, like the urban elements of society, might form a fourth estate, discussed separately from the knights, priests, and peasants, or might feature in the subdivisions, as female religious, or the wives of knights and ploughmen.[15] Thus they are either conceptualized as a separate group, which had its own subdivisions in terms of social status and so on, or they could be fitted into the functional division by virtue of their or their husband's status. Such schemes have fed into debates about whether women's social position was more affected by class or by gender.[16] They also support claims that men were more likely to be classified according to an occupational or social status, whereas women were generally classified by a marital or sexual status. The maid-wife-widow scheme has a similar prominence in discussions

---

[14] See e.g. S. Justice, 'Inquisition, Speech, and Writing: A Case from Late Medieval Norwich', in R. Copeland (ed.), *Criticism and Dissent in the Middle Ages* (Cambridge: Cambridge University Press, 1996), pp. 297–300.

[15] See Constable, 'Orders of Society', pp. 259–61; M. Corti, 'Models and Antimodels in Medieval Culture', *New Literary History*, 10 (1979), pp. 343–4; S. Shahar, *The Fourth Estate: A History of Women in the Middle Ages*, rev. edn. (London: Routledge, 2003), esp. pp. 1–4; M. W. Labarge, *Women in Medieval Life* (1986; repr. London: Penguin, 2001), esp. p. xiii; S. H. Rigby, *Chaucer in Context: Society, Allegory, and Gender* (Manchester: Manchester University Press, 1996), p. 127.

[16] See e.g. Rigby, *English Society*, pp. 244–5.

of how women were viewed as that of the knights, priests, and peasants model in discussions of medieval society more generally.

Rather than presenting an overview of this broader level of notionally all-encompassing models, this study takes as its focus the category 'single woman'. This apparently simple term in fact hides a multiplicity of possibilities and potential confusions, both medieval and modern. For the literary scholars Laurel Amtower and Dorothea Kehler, 'single' means unmarried and so the category includes all women at some stage in their lives. They posit that the 'sheer magnitude' of the category could be seen as threatening and perhaps explains its usual 'balkanization' into subcategories, such as maiden, widow, and prostitute, in pre-modern sources.[17] For the historians Judith Bennett and Amy Froide, the single-woman is never married (and they use this compound form to denote such a group), whether she might marry in the future (the life-cycle singlewoman) or not (the life-long singlewoman).[18] Yet some comment that it is difficult to find representations of singlewomen outside the dominant schema of maid-wife-widow. For example, Sharon Farmer found that thirteenth-century clerical elites conceptualized women as virgins, wives, widows, and, beyond that, as servants and prostitutes, but ignored those who lived and worked on their own in a whole range of occupations.[19] Thus a focus on the category 'single woman' entails thinking about how women are classified generally and, in particular, how the category relates to others such as 'maiden', 'widow', 'servant', and 'whore'.

[17] L. Amtower and D. Kehler, 'Introduction', in L. Amtower and D. Kehler, (eds.), *The Single Woman in Medieval and Early Modern England: Her Life and Representation* (Tempe, AZ: Arizona Center for Medieval and Renaissance Studies, 2003), quotation at p. xii. Historians also use the category in this way: the 1981 issue of *Annales de Démographie Historique* devotes a significant section to 'la femme seule', who is described as including 'célibataire, veuve, divorcée ou délaissée'. A. Fauve-Chamoux, 'Présentation', *Annales de Démographie Historique* (Paris: La Haye, 1981), p. 207.

[18] J. M. Bennett and A. M. Froide, 'A Singular Past', in J. M. Bennett and A. M. Froide (eds.), *Singlewomen in the European Past 1250–1800* (Philadelphia, PA: University of Pennsylvania Press, 1999), p. 2. This usage of 'never married' differs e.g. from that used by demographers where age is also important, but it is the one that will be used in this study. See M. Kowaleski, 'Singlewomen in Medieval and Early Modern Europe: The Demographic Perspective', in ibid., p. 40; S. C. Watkins, 'Spinsters', *Journal of Family History*, 9 (1984), p. 310, n. 1; O. Hufton, 'Women Without Men: Widows and Spinsters in Britain and France in the Eighteenth Century', *Journal of Family History*, 9 (1984), p. 357.

[19] S. Farmer, '"It Is Not Good That [Wo]man Should Be Alone": Elite Responses to Singlewomen in High Medieval Paris', in Bennett and Froide (eds.), *Singlewomen*, pp. 82–105. See also R. M. Karras, 'Sex and the Singlewoman', in ibid., p. 127, to be discussed in Ch. 2 below.

The competing and overlapping nature of social categories is an area that has already proved useful in relation both to the study of medieval society and to the study of gender. In relation to the question of whether women's social position was more affected by class or by gender, S. H. Rigby responds, '[t]he social position of an individual is the product of the meeting point of many different axes or dimensions of inequality. If gender was divided by class, then classes, in turn, were crucially divided in terms of gender.'[20] Rigby's 'axes of inequality' is a similar concept to Patricia Hill Collins' 'matrix of domination', which Sharon Farmer advocates as a conceptual tool for scholars of medieval gender. Genders are constructed within a range of 'interlocking inequalities' or, as Farmer puts it, a 'grid of . . . categories of difference', such as social status, ethnic or religious difference, and sexuality.[21] The point of these approaches, whether expressed in terms of axes, a matrix, or a grid, is to offer a multi-dimensional view of social identities and relations.[22] This book's approach, of using the category 'single woman' in order to illuminate the complexity inherent in categorizations, is in a similar vein. It is not just about single women as female and unmarried, although such a group would undoubtedly feature somewhere on the axes of inequality or within a matrix of domination. This study also seeks to explore the impact of other variables on social classification, such as sexual status, age, social status, occupation, and legal status.

Those scholars who have discussed the lack of representations in premodern texts of the single women they were interested in, sometimes discuss recovering single women from the 'white spaces' in texts, whereas others refer to the lack of a 'conceptual space'.[23] The approach taken here differs in that it begins with uses of the category 'single woman' in

[20] Rigby, *English Society*, p. 283.
[21] S. Farmer, 'Introduction', in S. Farmer and C. B. Pasternack (eds.), *Gender and Difference in the Middle Ages* (Minneapolis, MN: University of Minnesota Press, 2003), p. ix, citing P. H. Collins, *Black Feminist Thought: Knowledge, Consciousness, and the Politics of Empowerment* (New York, NY: Routledge, 1991), pp. 225–30; S. Farmer, 'The Beggar's Body: Intersections of Gender and Social Status in High Medieval Paris', in S. Farmer and B. H. Rosenwein (eds.), *Monks & Nuns, Saints & Outcasts: Religion in Medieval Society: Essays in Honor of Lester K. Little* (Ithaca, NY: Cornell University Press, 2000), p. 171.
[22] See also S. McSheffrey, 'Conceptualizing Difference: English Society in the Late Middle Ages', *Journal of British Studies*, 36 (1997), p. 136.
[23] Amtower and Kehler, 'Introduction', p. x; T. Sedinger, 'Working Girls: Status, Sexual Difference, and Disguise in Ariosto, Spencer, and Shakespeare', in Amtower and Kehler (eds.), *Single Woman*, pp. 167–74; Karras, 'Sex and the Singlewoman', p. 127; Farmer, 'It Is Not Good', p. 88.

medieval texts.[24] Rather than use the term 'single woman' to encompass any unmarried woman (including widows), or to refer to the never married only (or even the never married over a particular age),[25] this study explores how various medieval texts used the category. The Middle English 'sengle woman' can be found from the early fourteenth century, but for late medieval England one also needs to consider texts that use Latin or French and thus terms like *sola* or *femme sole*.[26] In a multilingual culture, it is possible that equivalences will be drawn between terms across a range of languages.[27] Indeed, some of the texts discussed switch between Latin and the vernacular, particularly in their use of personal designations.

As meaning is constituted within language, with words gaining their meaning through their difference from other words, this approach entails not assigning other categories, such as 'virgin', 'maiden', and 'widow', fixed meanings either. It is the shifting and varied meanings of categories with which this study is concerned. By thinking about how the category 'single woman' relates to other others, it is proposed that one can discover not only the concerns that produce the 'single woman' in a given text but those that led to the division of women into other categories. It is not a category that occurs in every discussion of women and so, when used alongside other categories, it can prompt a fresh look at the conceptualization of women more generally.

The emphasis on language means that the study goes into certain areas in depth, rather than attempt a broad survey of how the category 'single woman' was used in late medieval England. Each case study concerns the use of the category 'single woman' in a text or related set of texts, and all the chapters seek to situate the texts under discussion in their particular discursive contexts. But, as discourses do not operate in a vacuum, one must always be attuned to dominant cultural ideas, which can influence and inflect language use. Categories and specific terms can

[24] While this study does not follow any one theorist in approach, it was first influenced by J. W. Scott, 'The Evidence of Experience', *Critical Inquiry*, 17 (1991), 773–97.

[25] See n. 18 above.

[26] See B. Crespo, 'Historical Background of Multilingualism and its Impact on English', in D. A. Trotter (ed.), *Multilingualism in Later Medieval Britain* (Cambridge: D. S. Brewer, 2000), pp. 23–35.

[27] This is suggested in texts that use earlier etymological writings, such as that by Isidore of Seville, to read meanings into Middle English as well as Latin terms. e.g. see *On the Properties of Things: John Trevisa's Translation of* Bartholomæus Anglicus De Proprietatibus Rerum. *A Critical Text*, ed. M. C. Seymour *et al.*, 3 vols. (Oxford, 1975–88), i, pp. 301–2.

accrue associations through repeated use in particular contexts. Even when the context is different, these associations might *influence* the lexical choice of the classifier, consciously or not, or they can *inflect* the terms, thus affecting reception or future use, whether that is willed by the classifier or not. While one cannot recover what was in the minds of individual classifiers, Chapter 1 explores some of the key discourses and contexts that might have influenced a range of classifiers, including a religious discourse of chastity, a legal discourse about women's rights and responsibilities, and the social and political complexion of late medieval England.

While no one example can be taken as representative, because meanings must be understood in particular contexts, the case studies together cover a range of discourses, texts, classifiers, and subjects. Chapter 2 concerns the use of the category 'single woman' in some fourteenth- and fifteenth-century pastoral manuals, specifically its appearance in two different classificatory schemes: the first is the division of active lechery into fourteen degrees, predominantly according to the status of the participants, and the second is the division of chastity into seven branches, according to the states of those who are chaste. It enters a debate about whether, in relation to sex, medieval women were seen only as virgins, wives, widows, or whores, with the sexually-active single woman being elided with the commercial prostitute. It argues that while that might be the case in some texts, single women who have been sexually active, as marked out by the category 'single woman', also constituted a useful group in a religious discourse concerned with sexual sin and penance. Chapter 3 discusses the use of the category 'single woman' in the schedule for the 1379 poll tax and in some of the tax returns for that year. While some scholars have discussed the schedule as an interpretive scheme, this chapter argues that nominative tax returns can also be read as value-laden texts that are revealing of how certain groups conceptualized society and the people within it by analysing how the category 'single woman' is used in relation to other categories, such as 'widow', 'daughter', or an occupational designation. Chapter 4 analyses the use of the category 'single woman' in some of the guild ordinances contained in the 1388–9 returns; ordinances that subdivide guild members into different categories can also be read as interpretive schemes, albeit ones that are concerned with a particular subset of society. The category 'single woman' here largely operates in opposition to the category 'married woman' and, it is argued, shares some associations with the legal construct *femme sole*.[28] The chapter also asks why a guild register makes use of the category 'single man' but not the category 'single woman' in its classification of entrants to the guild in the fifteenth century, and examines what categories are used for unmarried women instead. Chapter 5 focuses on the use of the term 'singlewoman' as a personal designation in the fifteenth and early sixteenth centuries. It considers an array of texts, such as civic registers, testaments, and subsidy returns, in order to deduce whether there are chronological and discursive trends in which terms were used as personal designations. Each chapter thus takes a slightly different approach according to the nature of the source material with which it is dealing. The 'single woman' emerges *differently* as a category depending upon the context and purpose of a particular text. Taken as a whole they illustrate the complexity inherent in late medieval categories and their usages.

[28] See Ch. 1, '*Femmes soles*' below.

1

Classification in Cultural Context

Recent scholarship reminds us of the ways in which categories that we sometimes take for granted, such as 'widow' and 'virgin', are culturally constructed.[1] Bonnie Thurston, for example, contrasts the modern English association of the term 'widow' with 'a woman who has lost her husband by death . . . and has thereby acquired certain legal rights of inheritance', with the classical Hebrew and Greek words for widow, *almanah* and *chēra*, and their evocation of her as legally defenceless and economically vulnerable. The Hebrew *almanah* has the literal meaning of the 'silent one', from *alem* (unable to speak). This is a reference to her legal status. The Greek *chēra* literally means 'woman without', without a husband, but also without a source of social and financial support; the term might also be applied to a celibate person.[2] Similarly, in late antiquity the Latin term *vidua* ('deprived of') referred to a 'woman without a man', whether widowed, divorced, or never married.[3] For Bernhard Jussen, it is only when Christianity prompts a debate about

[1] See e.g. C. L. Carlson and A. J. Weisl (eds.), *Constructions of Widowhood and Virginity in the Middle Ages* (Houndmills: Macmillan, 1999). On virginity, see also K. C. Kelly, *Performing Virginity and Testing Chastity in the Middle Ages* (London: Routledge, 2000); S. Salih, *Versions of Virginity in Late Medieval England* (Cambridge: D. S. Brewer, 2001); J. Wogan-Browne, *Saints' Lives and Women's Literary Culture, c.1150–1300: Virginity and its Authorizations* (Oxford: Oxford University Press, 2001); A. Bernau, S. Salih, and R. Evans (eds.), *Medieval Virginities* (Cardiff: University of Wales Press, 2003); R. Evans, 'Virginities', in C. Dinshaw and D. Wallace (eds.), *The Cambridge Companion to Medieval Women's Writing* (Cambridge: Cambridge University Press, 2003), pp. 21–39. On widowhood, see also J. Bremmer and L. van den Bosch (eds.), *Between Poverty and the Pyre: Moments in the History of Widowhood* (London: Routledge, 1995), and the references below.
[2] B. B. Thurston, *The Widows: A Women's Ministry in the Early Church* (Minneapolis, MN: Fortress Press 1989), pp. 9–10 (quotation at p. 9).
[3] See B. Jussen, ' "Virgins-Widows-Spouses": On the Language of Moral Distinction as Applied to Women and Men in the Middle Ages', *History of the Family*, 7 (2002), p. 15; A. Roberts, 'Helpful Widows, Virgins in Distress: Women's Friendship in French Romance of the Thirteenth and Fourteenth Centuries', in Carlson and Weisl (eds.), *Constructions of Widowhood*, p. 25.

remarriage versus sexual chastity in the third century that widowhood itself became a significant social category.[4] The subsequent association with chastity meant that in the early middle ages *vidua* usually referred to a woman who had taken a vow of chastity rather than any widowed woman, who might be denoted by the term *relicta* instead.[5] These examples signal not only that categories are culturally constructed, but also that key factors affecting this construction include dominant religious and legal ideas in particular historical contexts. This chapter explores the associations that accrue to certain categories through their repeated use in particular contexts by influential cultural discourses, namely religious and legal ones; that is, it discusses the wider discourses that affect the more specific discourses upon which subsequent chapters focus. It also reviews some of the key socio-economic and political developments in late medieval England that might have had some bearing on the process of social classification. This chapter thus provides contexts for the case studies and evokes a sense of the interpenetration of medieval culture, but the case studies in turn will shed further light on the areas mapped out here.

The chapter has a threefold objective. First, it explores some of the key associations of the categories 'virgin' and 'widow' in religious discourses. The categories are, of course, used in different ways according to the genre and precise context of the text. There is clearly more than one understanding of the categories, with some texts distinguishing between different types of virgin and widow. Specifically, the life-stage virgin and widow (those who have not ruled out marriage) are often distinguished from the life-long virgin and widow (those who have ruled out marriage). The intention here is to lay the groundwork for an argument that recurs throughout this study: use of the categories 'virgin' and 'widow' in a religious discourse about chastity, a discourse which is widely disseminated and accepted, means that the categories often carry with them associations of chastity, which could influence their use in other discourses, or inflect their meaning, even when

---

[4] B. Jussen, 'On Church Organisation and the Definition of an Estate: The Idea of Widowhood in Late Antique and Early Medieval Christianity', *Tel Aviver Jahrbuch für deutsche Geschichte*, 22 (1993), pp. 26–7. See further B. Jussen, *Der Name der Witwe: Erkundungen zur Semantik der Mittelalterlichen Busskultur*, Veröffentlichungen des Max-Planck-Instituts für Geschichte, 158 (Göttingen: Vandenhoeck and Ruprecht, 2000).

[5] Jussen, 'On Church Organization', pp. 31–3; J. Crick, 'Men, Women and Widows: Widowhood in Pre-Conquest England', in S. Cavallo and L. Warner (eds.), *Widowhood in Medieval and Early Modern Europe* (Harlow: Pearson Education Ltd., 1999), pp. 34–6.

chastity is not an overt concern. Second, the chapter focuses on the category *femme sole* in legal discourse and the associations that it accrues. *Femme sole* is treated as a different category from 'single woman' not because it is in a different language, but because it has specific meaning as a legal construct in late medieval England; indeed, the construct does have Latin and Middle English variants, as we shall see.[6] The thesis, to be explored in some of the case studies, is that the associations of the *legal construct* might imprint themselves on the various terms even when the legal construct itself is not being intentionally evoked; that is, the legal construct *femme sole* could have an effect on the category 'single woman', whatever language is used. Third, it considers how contemporary perceptions and practice of marriage might have affected contemporary perceptions and practice of singleness, but also cautions that we should not assume that contemporaries had a unified sense of 'the single' and raises other factors that might have had a bearing on the creation of the category 'single woman'.

CLEAN MAIDS, TRUE WIVES, AND STEADFAST WIDOWS

The maid-wife-widow model is usually seen as the dominant classificatory scheme for medieval women.[7] Its ubiquity in part stems from the similarities shared by two different models which are both used in the medieval period: a life-stage model of maid-wife-widow and a hierarchical model of virgin-widow-spouse, which dates back to discussions of chastity in the writings of the early church fathers. The latter model, as used in the writings of Jerome, Ambrose, and Augustine, is a hierarchy of the saved based on a person's state of chastity at point of death; as John Baldwin has put it, the division is of those who never have done, those who have stopped, and those who do.[8] Based on the parable of the sower in Matthew 13: 3–23, virgins merit a hundredfold reward, widows a sixtyfold reward, and the married a thirtyfold reward. This model is about fixed states, the state of chastity

---

[6] This study contends that, in a multilingual culture, it is likely that equivalences would have been made across a range of languages: see p. 10 above.

[7] See the Introduction, 'Medieval classificatory schemes' above.

[8] Cited in Constable, 'Orders of Society', pp. 252–3.

that the person occupied at the end of his or her life; it is also a
model that might be applied to men as well as to women. In contrast
the maid-wife-widow scheme refers to female life-stages. The maid or
virgin (these terms and their variants are often used interchangeably in
medieval texts) in this model is the young woman who would usually
go on to marry and become the wife and then, if her husband pre-
deceased her, become the widow.[9] It is thus about transitional stages
in a woman's life. While such schemes look similar, they are in fact
classifying people from very different perspectives. Yet the two schemes
also intersect. As we shall see, later religious writings discuss the states
of chastity that people occupy at various points in their lives, and
thus they might also be seen as transitory stages. In such discussions
they distinguish between different types of virgin and widow. Further,
the maid-wife-widow model was not just a neutral description of the
female life-course, but usually contained within it the expectation that
women who were not currently married would not have sexual part-
ners. Although these models, particularly the life-stage one, can also
be found in the texts of secular writers, the focus here is on religious
texts.[10]

Christianity was a dominant cultural force in medieval society but, as
John Arnold asserts, '[d]ominant cultures are not passive, inert things.
They produce and reproduce themselves, to ensure continued communication and . . . maintain hegemony'.[11] While the writings of the
early church fathers were influential in the later middle ages, their
ideas, including that of a hierarchy of chaste states, were interpreted, adapted, and disseminated in a changed environment. The period
from the mid-twelfth century to the fourteenth century is particularly
important in Christianity's development, as it witnessed a concerted
effort in the new universities to try and reconcile a wide range of

---

[9] On the inter-changeability of terms, see Salih, *Versions of Virginity*, p. 16; F. H.
Stoertz, 'Young Women in France and England, 1050–1300', *Journal of Women's History*,
12/4 (2001), pp. 23–4; C. Taylor (ed.), *Joan of Arc: La Pucelle* (Manchester: Manchester
University Press, 2006), pp. 47–8. e.g. in Trevisa's discussion of *puella*, equivalences
are made between *puella*, 'maiden child', 'maiden', 'wench', and then between 'maid'
and *virgo*, and the passage suggests that all the various terms could suggest youth and/or
virginity: *On the Properties of Things*, ed. Seymour, i, pp. 301–2.

[10] For example, this section's subheading is a formulation used in Chaucer's *Legend
of Good Women*, G Prol. 282–3; L. D. Benson (ed.), *The Riverside Chaucer*, 3rd edn.
(Oxford: Oxford University Press, 1987).

[11] J. H. Arnold, *Belief and Unbelief in Medieval Europe* (London: Hodder Arnold,
2005), p. 28.

inherited texts, such as the writings of the early church fathers, papal pronouncements, and Roman law. By the mid-fourteenth century most religious texts were repetitive or heavily dependent on those of the preceding period. The University of Paris was at the centre of this theological activity, producing a number of treatises that were influential across western Christendom.[12] There was also an interest in reforming the state of the Western Church by educating both the clergy and the laity, through preaching and the production of pastoral literature: by the mid-thirteenth century the mendicant orders were predominant in the school of theology at Paris and were the main theorists and practitioners of the art of preaching, and, after the Lateran Councils of 1179 and 1215, there was an increased production of pastoral literature, from Latin *Summae* for confessors to vernacular manuals for parish priests.[13] This section therefore discusses the various ways in which the categories 'virgin' and 'widow' are used in a range of thirteenth-century religious texts, from a scholastic treatise to *ad status* sermon material to a vernacular pastoral manual.[14] First, though, the writings of the early church fathers require some elaboration.

The writings of the early church fathers were produced in a very different cultural context. An early use of the parable of the sower can be found in Cyprian of Carthage's *De Habitu Virginum* (*c.* 249): Cyprian asserted that martyrs would receive the hundredfold reward and virgins the sixtyfold.[15] It was when martyrdom became less common after the age of persecutions that it was increasingly displaced from the top of the hierarchy and, as virgins moved to the top, marriage became the

[12] See P. J. Payer, *The Bridling Of Desire: Views of Sex in the Later Middle Ages* (Toronto: University of Toronto Press, 1993), pp. 5–6, 9–10.

[13] See D. L. D'Avray, *The Preaching of the Friars: Sermons Diffused From Paris Before 1300* (Oxford: Clarendon Press, 1985), esp. pp. 13–28; J. Bird, 'The Religious's Role in a Post-Fourth-Lateran World: Jacques de Vitry's *Sermones ad status* and *Historia occidentalis*', in C. Muessig (ed.), *Medieval Monastic Preaching* (Leiden: Brill, 1998), pp. 209–29; L. E. Boyle, 'The Inter-Conciliar Period 1179–1215 and the Beginnings of Pastoral Manuals', in F. Liotta (ed.), *Miscellanea Rolando Bandinelli, Papa Alessandro III* (Siena: Accademia senese degli intronati, 1986), pp. 45–56; L. E. Boyle, 'The Fourth Lateran Council and Manuals of Popular Theology', in T. J. Heffernan (ed.), *The Popular Literature of Medieval England* (Knoxville, TN: University of Tennessee Press, 1985), pp. 30–43.

[14] As discussed in the Introduction above, no one example can claim to be 'representative', but the texts are used here as ways into particular genres and contexts.

[15] St Cyprian, 'The Dress of Virgins', in *Saint Cyprian: Treatises*, trans. R. J. Deferrari (Washington, DC: Catholic University of America Press in association with Consortium Books, 1958), p. 49 (ch. 21).

lowest of the three states from the fourth century onwards.[16] Jussen maintains that it was the writings of Jerome, Ambrose, and Augustine, as part of a dispute with a Roman ascetic called Jovinian, which not only used the virgins-widows-spouses formula but also built up 'a stock of rhetorical formulas and images of society, exempla, and associations' around it, with the result that it was 'treated for almost a millennium as the vocabulary of the moral order'.[17] Jovinian argued against this notion of hierarchy; for him, all baptized Christians, whether virgin, widowed, or married, were equal and would receive the same reward in heaven, whereas Jerome, Ambrose, and Augustine used the hierarchical model to present a case for total clerical celibacy.[18] The images of the intact virgin and the chaste widow were put forward as models to which the clergy should aspire.[19] For Jo Ann McNamara, it was the growing communities of female widows and virgins in the first three centuries, women who dedicated their chastity or virginity to God, which forced the early Church to promote first celibacy and then virginity, hence the predominantly feminine imagery in the writings of the church fathers.[20] But the intention of the model was to encompass all of the saved, male and female, and the debate was particularly concerned with the male clergy.

The period from the mid-twelfth century to the early fourteenth century differed in a number of ways. Chastity was now seen as a virtue to be promoted for all of society, whatever their chosen lifestyle.[21] As a result, chastity was discussed as temporary phases as well as life-long

[16] *Hali Meiðhad*, ed. B. Millett, EETS, o.s. 284 (London: Oxford University Press, 1982), p. xxxix; Millett suggests that Athanasius was the first writer to give virgins a hundredfold in his *Epistula ad Amunen monachum* of the early fourth century.

[17] Jussen, 'Virgins-Widows-Spouses', p. 15.

[18] See D. G. Hunter, 'Resistance to the Virginal Ideal in Late-Fourth-Century Rome: The Case of Jovinian', *Theological Studies*, 48 (1987), p. 51, citing Jerome, *Adversus Jovinianum*, 1.3. The passage is translated in St Jerome, *Jerome: Letters and Select Works*, A Select Library of Nicene and Post-Nicene Fathers of the Christian Church, 2nd ser., 6, ed. P. Schaff and H. Wace (Edinburgh: T. & T. Clark, 1996; reprint of Buffalo, NY: Christian Literature Company, 1892).

[19] See P. Brown, *The Body and Society: Men, Women, and Sexual Renunciation in Early Christianity* (New York, NY: Columbia University Press, 1988), pp. 341–64.

[20] J. A. McNamara, *A New Song: Celibate Women in the First Three Christian Centuries* (New York, NY: Institute for Research in History and Haworth Press, Inc., 1983). See also J. E. Salisbury, *Church Fathers, Independent Virgins* (London: Verso, 1991). This has perhaps led some to interpret the Jovinian debate as primarily about women too; e.g. G. Cloke, *'This Female Man of God': Women and Spiritual Power in the Patristic Age, AD 350–450* (London: Routledge, 1995), pp. 38–47; Payer, *Bridling of Desire*, p. 171.

[21] Payer, *Bridling of Desire*, p. 160.

states. In the universities the new disciplines of biblical studies, theology, and ecclesiastical jurisprudence led to attempts to make sense of inherited texts, such as those of the early church fathers, to co-ordinate them into systematic accounts, and to apply theological principles to the contemporary world.[22] For Pierre Payer, it was in the thirteenth century that theology 'came into its own', chiefly at the University of Paris under the influence of Albertus Magnus, Bonaventure, and Thomas Aquinas.[23] The treatises produced were influential across Western Christendom and in these one can find both the continuation of the tripartite, hierarchical model of chastity and further development, such as the elaborate subdivision of categories like 'virgin'. For example, Albertus Magnus in his thirteenth-century discussion of chastity divides it into the three states of virginity, widowhood, and marriage.[24] He considers all these states to apply equally to men as to women.[25] Virginity merits the most attention and is subdivided into four types: first, the innate virginity of infants before the age of reason; second, the virginity of individuals who have not taken a religious vow of chastity; third, virginity that is dedicated to God through a vow or firm proposal; and, fourth, that of foolish virgins (those whose behaviour is too extreme or their dress inappropriate).[26] Of these four, he says that only the third type is worthy of praise, although the first and second have 'bodily fairness'.[27] The conclusion is that virginity in its ideal form consists of physical integrity, the will to safeguard it, and the dedication of that resolve to God. He points out that 'if one inspects the original works (*originalia*) of the saints [Ambrose, Augustine, and Jerome] they will be seen only to speak of virgins who profess virginity for the sake of God'.[28]

---

[22] Ibid., p. 5; Arnold, *Belief,* p. 30. See further R. L. Benson and G. Constable, with C. D. Lanham (eds.), *Renaissance and Renewal in the Twelfth Century* (Oxford: Clarendon Press, 1982); J. W. Baldwin, *Masters, Princes and Merchants: The Social Views of Peter the Chanter and His Circle,* 2 vols. (Princeton, NJ: Princeton University Press, 1970); P. Biller, *The Measure of Multitude: Population in Medieval Thought* (Oxford: Oxford University Press, 2000), esp. pp. 31–2.

[23] Payer, *Bridling of Desire,* p. 10.

[24] See R. E. Houser, *The Cardinal Virtues: Aquinas, Albert, and Philip the Chancellor* (Toronto: Pontifical Institute of Mediaeval Studies, 2004), p. 230; on this treatise, *De bono,* see ibid., pp. 56–64. See also Payer, *Bridling of Desire,* p. 144; for other examples, see ibid., pp. 138–9.

[25] Payer, *Bridling of Desire,* p. 163; see ibid., p. 160.

[26] Ibid., p. 162; Kelly, *Performing Virginity,* p. 6.

[27] Payer, *Bridling Of Desire,* p. 162.

[28] Albertus Magnus, *Quaestiones de bono: De Castitate,* 3.3.4, ad 9, quoted in Payer, *Bridling of Desire,* p. 252 n. 32. See e.g. St Augustine, 'Of Holy Virginity', in St Augustine,

The life-stage virgin, then, is the second type, although if s/he did not act chastely, then even the virgin's 'bodily fairness' is blemished.

Some of the religious compilations and manuals of instruction for priests and the laity that proliferate after Lateran IV similarly make reference to the threefold model of chastity within more elaborate frameworks, and would have found a wider audience than those in the treatises of university masters.[29] The point can be briefly illustrated here with reference to Jocelyn Wogan-Browne's research on the late thirteenth-century Anglo-Norman *La Compileison*.[30] The text contains a chapter on 'the five degrees of chastity which are found in virginity and in widowhood'.[31](While this text feminizes the states of chastity, this is not the case in all such works.)[32] Of the five degrees of virginity, the first is 'promised by vow to God' and 'is the highest before God'; the second also relates to life-long virginity but unvowed.[33] The fifth is of the virgin who intends to marry and her degree before God is lower than that of a chaste married woman (*bone femme ki est marie*) in that 'she does not know whom she wishes to have and the woman who is married does not seek anyone other than him to whom she is joined'.[34] The third and fourth degrees relate to those who have not decided or have not yet considered whether they will marry or remain virgins. Vidual chastity is similarly elaborated upon; married chastity, as can be seen above, is referred to within the discussions of virginity and widowhood. While this text is interested in ranking types of virginity and chaste widowhood, it also makes it clear that not all types of virginity and chaste widowhood are better than married chastity. As in the writings of the church fathers, it is life-long virginity that is best and life-stage virgins are actually rated lower than the chaste married in this text: it is better to be a chaste wife than a flighty girl. This is not to say that the religious were not interested in life-stage virginity, but this positive treatment of marriage reflects a broader move in religious

On the Holy Trinity, Doctrinal Treatises, Moral Treatises, A Select Library of Nicene and Post-Nicene Fathers of the Christian Church, iii, ed. P. Schaff (Edinburgh: T. & T. Clark, 1956; reprint of Buffalo, NY: Christian Literature Company, 1887).

[29] Payer, *Bridling of Desire*, pp. 140–1. I shall discuss this practice in some Middle English manuals in Ch. 2 below.

[30] Wogan-Browne, *Saints' Lives and Women's Literary Culture*, pp. 44–6, 47; Hope Emily Allen has argued that the text was intended for both professed and lay people: ibid., p. 45 n. 93.

[31] Ibid., p. 44.   [32] See Payer, *Bridling of Desire*, p. 160; also see Ch. 2 below.

[33] Wogan-Browne, *Saints' Lives and Women's Literary Culture*, p. 45.

[34] Ibid., pp. 44–5.

discourse by the twelfth century to celebrate the role of marriage in earthly life.[35]

The next example differs in that it does not purport to be an explicit discussion of chastity, but advice to different groups of people. The text is Guibert of Tournai's *ad status* sermon collection. Guibert of Tournai was a prominent member of the Franciscan order, with connections to the University of Paris, and his sermon collection circulated throughout Europe; it was not until the fourteenth century that friars based in England played a major part in producing similar material.[36] One of the earliest *ad status* sermon collections is Alan of Lille's late twelfth-century *Ars praedicandi*, which offers summaries of appropriate sermon material, structured according to particular groups. It addresses the poor, the rich, soldiers, public-speakers, the learned, prelates, princes, cloistered monks and the religious, before turning its attention to the married, the widowed, and virgins. The emphasis in the sections for the latter three groups is on chastity: that for the married advises men to avoid sexual sin, even with their wives; that for the widowed advocates chastity for widowed women, and the sermon to virgins recommends life-long virginity to female virgins.[37] Guibert of Tournai's text differs in a number of ways, one of which is how he uses the categories of virgin, widow, and spouse. It is a more substantial collection, which offers eighty-eight full sermons, some of which he said were for men, some

---

[35] See M. Howell, 'The Properties of Marriage in Late Medieval Europe: Commercial Wealth and the Creation of Modern Marriage', in I. Davis, M. Müller, and S. Rees Jones (eds.), *Love, Marriage, and Family Ties in the Later Middle Ages* (Turnhout: Brepols, 2003), p. 20; J. Witte Jr., *From Sacrament to Contract: Marriage, Religion, and Law in the Western Tradition* (Louisville, KY: Westminster John Knox Press, 1997), pp. 22–30; Payer, *Bridling of Desire*, pp. 61–72.

[36] See D'Avray, *Preaching of the Friars*, pp. 144–7, 149–51, 160, 278; S. Farmer, *Surviving Poverty in Medieval Paris: Gender, Ideology, and the Daily Lives of the Poor* (Ithaca, NY: Cornell University Press, 2002), p. 167.

[37] Alan of Lille, *The Art of Preaching*, trans. G. R. Evans (Kalamazoo, MI: Cistercian Publications, Inc., 1981), pp. 148–9, 163–8. The material for the married is discussed in D. L. D'Avray and M. Tausche, 'Marriage Sermons in *ad status* Collections of the Central Middle Ages', *Archives d'histoire doctrinale et littéraire du Moyen Age*, 47 (1981), pp. 79–80, and that for widows in J. Longère, 'La Femme dans la théologie pastorale', in E. Privat (ed.), *La Femme dans la vie religieuse du Languedoc* (*XIIIᵉ–XIVᵉ S.*) (Toulouse: Privat, 1988), pp. 136–7. For Barbara Newman, the sermon 'to virgins' was aimed at nuns: B. Newman, 'Flaws in the Golden Bowl: Gender and Spiritual Formation in the Twelfth Century', in B. Newman, *From Virile Woman to WomanChrist: Studies in Medieval Religion and Literature* (Philadelphia, PA: University of Pennsylvania Press, 1995), p. 35. Alan of Lille also wrote a treatise on virtues and vices that used the threefold division of chastity: see Payer, *Bridling of Desire*, p. 139.

for women, and some for both sexes.[38] Those for women are divided into four categories: married women (three sermons), widows (one), virgins and young girls (nine), and nuns and female religious (one). The separation of religious from secular women means that Guibert's nine sermons *ad virgines et puellas*, the largest group of his sermons for women, appear to have been largely aimed at life-stage virgins (in contrast to Alan of Lille's material for virgins). In Jenny Swanson's words, 'Two of these [sermons] discuss the need for chastity . . . one discusses the value of literacy and basic medical knowledge, and warns girls against laughing in church, three discuss the perils of make-up and of the interest in fashion and perfume, one covers preparation for marriage, and one the dangers of wealth.'[39] The advice proffered, then, is about what conduct was desirable in a young, unmarried woman. The sermons to married women similarly cover practical matters such as managing the household as well as marital chastity, whereas the single sermon to widows focusses on chastity.[40] In this text, while the life-stage model seems to predominate for women, the moral associations of the categories maiden, wife, and widow, particularly the importance of chastity for all three categories, have clearly not been lost.

It is not that, over time, the hierarchical model was replaced by the life-stage model.[41] The two schemes are, at the theoretical level, very different, but the more that religious authors sought to interact with the world around them, the more the two intersected. In the texts produced from the mid-twelfth century onwards, religious authors wanted to recommend the virtue of chastity to all. Chastity was therefore discussed in relation to temporary phases in a person's life, as well as

---

[38] For Guibert's layout see C. Casagrande (ed.), *Prediche alle donne del secolo XIII: Testi di Umberto da Romans, Gilberto da Tournai, Stefano di Borbone* (Milan: Bompiani, 1978), pp. 146–7.

[39] J. Swanson, 'Childhood and Childrearing in *ad status* Sermons by Later Thirteenth Century Friars', *Journal of Medieval History*, 16 (1990), p. 322. His second sermon to this group is edited in Casagrande (ed.), *Prediche alle donne* pp. 105–8. See also Guibert de Tournai, *Sermones* (Louvain: Johannes de Westfalia, c. 1481–3).

[40] For his sermon to widows, see Casagrande (ed.), *Prediche alle donne*, pp. 97–105. On the sermons to married women, see D'Avray and Tausche, 'Marriage Sermons', pp. 86–117; the third sermon is edited in Casagrande (ed.), *Prediche alle donne* pp. 93–7.

[41] Cf. Jussen, 'Virgins-Widows-Spouses'. See further S. Salih, *Versions of Virginity*, p. 15, who questions 'whether a chronological narrative is an appropriate framework in which to describe varieties of virginity. It takes only a minor shift of perspective to see virginity as having always had multiple forms . . . although at any given moment some may be more accessible than others'.

states to be occupied until death. Yet in a society that had a patrilineal structure, there was more of a social premium on female chastity, and this association became so embedded that it operated even when property was not at stake.[42] Much advice on chastity, then, was tailored to a female audience. The examples discussed illustrate some of the ways in which Christianity sought to formulate and disseminate its ideas: at a learned level in universities through Latin treatises, at a pastoral level through vernacular manuals for parish priests and the literate laity, and to the person in the nave through sermons. They demonstrate that there is more than one understanding of the categories 'virgin' and 'widow', and that the life-stage virgin and the widow who might remarry could be conceived of differently to the life-long virgin and the vowed chaste widow.

The examples also prepare the ground for the argument, to be raised in some of the case studies, that the importance of the categories 'virgin'/'maid' and 'widow' in a widely accepted discourse about chastity means that these categories often carry moral overtones, which could influence their use in other discourses or inflect their meaning. A discourse that has certain specific intended effects and audience, and may deploy a vocabulary directed toward those effects, may nonetheless have additional and unforeseen effects in other discursive contexts. For example, a friar or priest giving a sermon about chastity might use the language of 'clean spousehood, widowhood and maidenhood' in order to reform the audience's sexual habits (or, perhaps more realistically, to make them feel guilty, in a *particular* way, about not behaving properly), but use of those categories in that setting means that when members of the audience encounter the same categories in a different context, such as in legal documentation for a property transfer, they may still bear echoes from that earlier context, even if the social logic of the new context is different.[43] Kim Phillips has questioned why deeds transferring the ownership of land sometimes begin with variations of

---

[42] See K. M. Phillips, *Medieval Maidens: Young Women and Gender in England, 1270–1540* (Manchester: Manchester University Press, 2003), pp. 146–53; Salih, *Versions of Virginity*, p. 18; Evans, 'Virginities', pp. 22–3.

[43] See e.g. ch. 58 of *Jacob's Well*: MS Salisbury Cathedral 103, fo. 119 (I am indebted to Professor P. H. Barnum for sending me her unpublished transcription). For the chapter heading see *Jacob's Well: An English Treatise on the Cleansing of Man's Conscience*, ed. A. Brandeis, Part 1, EETS, o.s. 115 (London: Kegan Paul, Trench, Trübner & Co., 1900), p. xv. This text is discussed further in Ch. 2 below. For the phrase 'social logic', see G. M. Spiegel, 'History, Historicism, and the Social Logic of the Text in the Middle Ages', *Speculum*, 65 (1990), 59–86.

'in my free power and virginity' ('in mea libera potestate et virginitate') or 'in my pure widowhood'.[44] It could be pertinent information: for example, some men's testaments left property to their wife on condition that she remain chaste, and if she remarried the property was to pass to another relative.[45] But, in general terms, it operates as an assertion of the woman's right to transfer property by virtue of her unmarried state; the statement 'in my free power and virginity' denotes both that the woman was of an age to make such a legal decision and that she was unmarried and so legally able to carry out the transaction.[46] Surely, though, such statements also signal the woman's good moral character and virtue, associations that maidenhood and widowhood acquire in a religious discourse of chastity.

FEMMES SOLES

The law was, of course, another dominant force in medieval society. Like Christianity, it was not fixed in one set of texts or a single institution: there were a whole host of overlapping legal jurisdictions. It was also not just about the goings-on at court. The law, for example, affected all day-to-day economic transactions; it was important to know who could be pursued for a debt and who could not, or whether a deal could be reneged upon. But it is clearly beyond the scope of this book to go into the full complexity of the position of women under the law.[47] The focus here is on the category *femme sole* and the associations it accrues in a legal discourse. As a legal construct

[44] K. M. Phillips, 'Four Virgins' Tales: Sex and Power in Medieval Law', in Bernau, Salih, and Evans (eds.), *Medieval Virginities*, pp. 93–5.

[45] See e.g. P. Fleming, *Family and Household in Medieval England* (Houndmills: Palgrave, 2001), p. 95; J. Kermode, *Medieval Merchants: York, Beverley and Hull in the Later Middle Ages* (Cambridge: Cambridge University Press, 1998), p. 94.

[46] For a summary of when females become 'of age' under common and customary law, see Phillips, *Medieval Maidens*, pp. 32–5.

[47] For explanations of why such a study has not been written see J. S. Loengard, ' "Legal History and the Medieval Englishwoman" Revisited: Some New Directions', in J. T. Rosenthal (ed.), *Medieval Women and the Sources of Medieval History* (Athens, GA: University of Georgia Press, 1990), pp. 210–36. See also J. S. Loengard, 'Common Law for Margery: Separate But Not Equal', in L. E. Mitchell (ed.), *Women in Medieval Western European Culture* (New York, NY: Garland Publishing, Inc., 1999), pp. 117–30; R. Kittel, 'Women Under the Law in Medieval England', in B. Kanner (ed.), *The Women of England from Anglo-Saxon Times to the Present: Interpretive Bibliographical Essays* (London: Mansell Information Publishing, 1980), pp. 124–37.

it operates as part of a binary with *femme coverte*, which refers to the legal position of the married woman under common law. Under common law, unmarried women (of age) could own land and chattels, sell and bequeath such property, and sue and be sued, whereas married women could not.[48] On marriage all of a woman's property (real estate but also other assets) came under her husband's control, with the exception of her 'paraphernalia' (personal clothes and jewels).[49] While some have referred to this as 'unity of person', it is better to view it as guardianship: the wife was still the owner of the property but, under common law, the husband was legally responsible for it.[50] Any actions to be taken at court were to be taken in both their names. It is because of this common law position that the married woman is referred to in various legal records as *coverte de baron* (covered by her husband) or as *femme coverte* (covered woman). In contrast, the unmarried woman is the *femme sole*, literally the woman alone.[51] As a legal term, though, *femme sole* denotes a 'woman not under coverture'; one might also think, for example, of under-age girls as under a form

---

[48] See F. Pollock and F. W. Maitland, *The History of English Law Before the Time of Edward I*, 2nd edn., 2 vols. (Cambridge: Cambridge University Press, 1911), i, pp. 482–5. Canon law did allow married women to make testaments, although under common law only those authorized by their husbands were considered valid: M. M. Sheehan, 'The Influence of Canon Law on the Property Rights of Married Women in England', in M. M. Sheehan, *Marriage, Family, and Law in Medieval Europe: Collected Studies*, ed. J. K. Farge (Cardiff: University of Wales Press, 1996), pp. 19–20, 25–30; R. H. Helmholz, 'Married Women's Wills in Later Medieval England', in S. S. Walker (ed.), *Wife and Widow in Medieval England* (Ann Arbor, MI: University of Michigan Press, 1993), pp. 165–82.

[49] See e.g. *Bracton on the Laws and Customs of England*, ed. George E. Woodbine, trans. S. E. Thorne, 4 vols. (Cambridge, Mass.: Belknap Press, 1968), ii, p. 179.

[50] See Pollock and Maitland, *History of English Law*, i, p. 485; M. H. Kerr, 'Husband and Wife in Criminal Proceedings in Medieval England', in C. M. Rousseau and J. T. Rosenthal (eds.), *Women, Marriage, and Family in Medieval Christendom: Essays in Memory of Michael M. Sheehan, C.S.B.* (Kalamazoo, MI: Medieval Institute Publications, 1998), pp. 211–12; C. Donahue, Jr., 'What Causes Fundamental Legal Ideas? Marital Property in England and France in the Thirteenth Century', *Michigan Law Review*, 78 (1979), pp. 64–6. Cf. J. H. Baker, *An Introduction to English Legal History*, 3rd edn. (London: Butterworths, 1990), pp. 550–1.

[51] See the entries under covert[2] [coverte de baron (law)]; femme [f. sule (law)], and sul (3) s.f. (law) in L. W. Stone and W. Rothwell (eds.), *Anglo-Norman Dictionary* (London: Modern Humanities Research Association, 1977–92), pp. 120, 299, 739, and the equivalent entries in J. H. Baker, *Manual of Law French* ([Amersham]: Avebury Publications, 1979), pp. 80, 111, 186. On the shift from Latin to law French in legal records see P. Brand, 'The Languages of the Law in Later Medieval England', in Trotter (ed.), *Multilingualism*, pp. 63–76; W. M. Ormrod, 'The Use of English: Language, Law, and Political Culture in Fourteenth-Century England', *Speculum*, 78 (2003), 750–87, esp. p. 753.

of coverture, the guardianship of a father.[52] Common law gives single women certain legal rights and responsibilities that married women do not usually have, with the result that the category *femme sole*, in whatever language used, takes on these associations of legal rights and responsibilities.

The argument that the category *femme sole* is imbued with the associations of legal independence can be most clearly demonstrated with respect to the custom of treating some married women as if economically and legally responsible, that is, as *femmes soles*, women not under coverture. This custom is well known by scholars (although some might question how widespread the practice was).[53] Indeed, it has led to the status of *femme sole* largely being discussed in relation to married women. Yet it should be borne in mind that what was being given were the legal prerogatives and obligations of a single woman. Most of the early evidence for the custom which allowed married women to act as if *femmes soles* comes from London. The practice might date back to the early thirteenth century but the first known record of it was in the now lost Darcy's custumal of the 1330s and 1340s;[54] John Carpenter, who borrowed extensively from Darcy's custumal, copied the pertinent customs into the city's *Liber Albus* in 1419, and they were also adopted by other towns.[55] Discussion of some of the *Liber Albus* customs, then,

[52] See Bracton on wardship and the *cura* of relatives and friends: *Bracton*, ed. Woodbine, ii, pp. 34–6, 188, 250–6. For the limited legal rights of the underage, see Phillips, *Medieval Maidens*, pp. 34–5.

[53] See e.g. Rigby, *English Society*, pp. 270–1; B. W. Gastle, ' "As if she were single": Working Wives and the Late Medieval English *Femme Sole*', in K. Robertson and M. Uebel (eds.), *The Middle Ages at Work: Practicing Labor in Late Medieval England* (New York, NY: Palgrave, 2004), pp. 43–4; M. K. McIntosh, 'The Benefits and Drawbacks of *Femme Sole* Status in England, 1300–1630', *Journal of British Studies*, 44 (2005), esp. pp. 412, 413.

[54] C. Barron, 'The "Golden Age" of Women in Medieval London', *Reading Medieval Studies*, 15 (1989), pp. 39–40; see also McIntosh, 'Benefits and Drawbacks', pp. 413–14.

[55] In the *Liber Albus* the customs are given in Anglo-Norman, with Latin headings, and they are included in York's Memorandum Book, with only minor differences in spelling (they are undated but follow an entry for 1436). Lincoln adopts two of the customs and, in its *White Book* of 1481, sets them out in Middle English so that the key term is 'sole woman'. Worcester summarizes them in 1467 as one ordinance, in Middle English, but does refer more specifically to a 'woman sole marchaunt' (see n. 60 below). See M. Sellers (ed.), *York Memorandum Book*, 2 parts, Surtees Society, 120 & 125 (Durham: Andrews & Co., 1912–15), ii, pp. 144–5; M. Bateson (ed.), *Borough Customs*, 2 vols., Selden Society, 18 & 21 (London: Bernard Quaritch, 1904–6), i, p. xxxvii, 226–7; J. T. Smith and L. T. Smith (eds.), *English Gilds*, EETS, o.s. 40 (London: N. Trübner & Co., 1870), pp. 382, 410.

will illustrate the point that the category's meaning is predicated on the legal position of the unmarried woman:[56]

The case of a wife trading alone [*Uxor quae sola mercandizat*]
And where a woman *coverte de baron* follows any craft within the said city by herself apart, with which the husband in no way interferes, such a woman shall be bound as a single woman [*come femme soule*] as to all that concerns her said craft. And if the husband and the wife are impleaded, in such case, the wife shall plead as a single woman in a Court of Record, and she shall have her law and other advantages by way of plea just as a single woman. And if she is condemned, she shall be committed to prison until she shall have made satisfaction; and neither the husband nor his goods shall in such case be charged or impeached.

Of hiring houses
Item, if a wife [*une femme*], as though a single woman [*come femme soule*], rents any house or shop within the said city, she shall be bound to pay the rent of the said house or shop, and shall be impleaded and sued as a single woman, by way of debt if necessary, notwithstanding that she was *coverte de baron* at the time of such letting, supposing that the lessor did not know thereof.

Of plea of trespass
Item, if plaint of trespass is made against a man and his wife for trespass committed by the wife only, then the woman shall make answer alone [*soule*] without her husband, if such a husband does not appear; and she shall have her plea as though she were a single woman [*come femme soule*]. And if she is attainted of trespass, she shall be condemned and committed to prison until she have made satisfaction.

The first entry is concerned with the wife who follows a different craft to that of her husband.[57] In such instances all obligations are hers alone and should have no impact on the husband. The second sets out that any woman, even the woman *coverte de baron*, who rents a property in the city will be held responsible for the payments. Again it concerns the woman who was making legal and financial commitments

[56] H. T. Riley (ed.), *Munimenta Gildhallae Londiniensis; Liber Albus, Liber Cus-tumarum et Liber Horn*, 3 vols. (London: Longman, Brown, Green, Longman, and Roberts, 1859–62), i, pp. 204–5, iii, pp. 38–9 (for the translation). On the custumal see W. Kellaway, 'John Carpenter's *Liber Albus*', *Guildhall Studies in London History*, 3 (1978), 67–84; Gastle, 'As if she were single', p. 52.
[57] In practice it seems to have been applied to all female traders, including those who ran an inn or alehouse; e.g. A. H. Thomas (ed.), *Calendar of Early Mayor's Court Rolls, Preserved Among the Archives of the Corporation of the City of London at the Guildhall, A.D. 1298–1307* (Cambridge: Cambridge University Press, 1924), pp. 214–15. See also McIntosh, 'Benefits and Drawbacks', p. 415.

independently of a husband. The third states that if a wife committed a trespass and her husband did not appear in court, she could be treated as though she were a single woman, that is, the case would not flounder in his absence, even if the husband had also been named in the plea. All three customs allow some married women to be treated in respect of economic and legal matters 'as a single woman' or 'as though she were a single woman' (*come femme soule*).[58] In the treatise's Latin table of contents the key phrase is 'ut sola mulier sine viro' (as though a single woman without a husband).[59] While one can view *femmes soles* as a particular subgroup of married women who had particular economic and legal rights and responsibilities, the language itself indicates that what was being given were the rights and responsibilities of the single woman.[60]

There are examples in court records of women using the *femme sole* position to denote their singleness, past or current, and the legal privileges and obligations that pertain to the unmarried state. Although one can find incidences in other courts, the following are all taken from London's records of 'Pleas and Memoranda', which chiefly consist of legal pleadings taken from the rolls of the Mayor's Court.[61] They can be divided into two types. First, there are a number of cases that refer to the woman as *sole* in order to signal that she had the ability to make and benefit from legal agreements concerning property. For example, Margery, widow of John Yakeslee, told London's Mayor's Court that she was a *femme sole*, a single woman, to denote that she was in a position to manage her late husband's property, the subject of an earlier action

---

[58] Another custom in *Liber Albus* uses the term *femme sole* when discussing the legal position of single women: see *Munimenta*, i, p. 219.

[59] Ibid., pp. 174–5. Although *sine viro* (without a husband) could refer to the married woman in court, see the Ipswich custumal which uses the formulation 'sole saunz baroun': Bateson (ed.), *Borough Customs*, i, pp. 223–4; discussed in Gastle, 'As if she were single', p. 49. Similar formulations in the Kingston-upon-Hull guild returns are discussed on p. 110 below.

[60] Perhaps once the custom was better established it could be referred to more directly, as in Worcester's 'woman sole marchaunt' or Winchelsea's 'marchaunt soule': Smith (ed.), *English Gilds*, p. 382; Bateson (ed.), *Borough Customs*, i, p. 227.

[61] See A. H. Thomas (ed.), *Calendar of Plea and Memoranda Rolls, Preserved Among the Archives of the Corporation of the City of London at the Guildhall, Rolls A1a–A9, A.D. 1323–1364* (Cambridge: Cambridge University Press, 1926), pp. vii–xi; McIntosh, 'Benefits and Drawbacks', p. 432. Variations on these cases can be found before the king's courts, but there a Latin equivalent is used, such as 'sola fuit' (was single). See e.g. M. S. Arnold (ed.), *Select Cases of Trespass from the King's Courts, 1307–1399*, 2 vols., Selden Society, 100, 103 (London: Selden Society, 1985–7), i, pp. 14 [1373], 81 [1334], 174 [1390].

in the court.[62] The rolls also record that in the late fourteenth century Alice, widow of Henry Smale, being *sole*, was gifted her father's goods and chattels in exchange for providing him with a bed, food, clothing, and so on, for the rest of his life. Prior to her husband's death the father had had a similar agreement with the couple.[63] Second, it might be that the woman's status as *sole* pre-marriage was an issue. In these cases married couples are pursued for debts, which the women had run up when single. The importance of the status is that, if the woman was *sole* at the time of the agreement, her husband would not have consented to the deal, but he would still become liable for it on marriage. For example, an action was brought against one Ralph Hamelyn and his wife Agnes to recover seven marks that Agnes had borrowed when she was *sole*.[64] Similarly, a case was brought against Thomas Charles and his wife Elisabeth for a debt she ran up when *sole*, that is, after the death of her former husband, Thomas Cokayn, but prior to her marriage to Charles.[65] This set of examples cautions that while an unmarried woman had the legal ability to borrow money in her own right, she might not be in a position economically to repay the debts while single. If we take all the cases together, they indicate that the position of *femme sole* had associations of economic and legal independence, but the latter examples also remind us of the social reality that such independence, or responsibility, was not an unqualified good.[66]

Another association of the position of *femme sole*, that of the woman alone, perhaps also accrues from the social reality of the legal arena. In some cases it was used by women in the hope that it would evoke sympathy for their disadvantaged legal position: with cost a factor, as was how powerful one's supporters were, women might adopt the position of the woman alone in order to signal a lack of support, financial and

[62] A. H. Thomas (ed.), *Calendar of Plea and Memoranda Rolls, Preserved Among the Archives of the Corporation of the City of London at the Guildhall, A.D. 1364–1381* (Cambridge: Cambridge University Press, 1929), p. 67 [4 Oct. 1366].

[63] Ibid., p. 294; the original agreement had been made on 1 October 1381, but it is not known when Henry died, although it was after 18 December of that year.

[64] A. H. Thomas (ed.), *Calendar of Plea and Memoranda Rolls, Preserved Among the Archives of the Corporation of the City of London at the Guildhall, A.D. 1413–1437* (Cambridge: Cambridge University Press, 1943), p. 144 [17 Jan. 1422].

[65] P. E. Jones (ed.), *Calendar of Plea and Memoranda Rolls, Preserved Among the Archives of the Corporation of the City of London at the Guildhall, A.D. 1437–1457* (Cambridge: Cambridge University Press, 1954), pp. 97, 101–2 [1447]; Thomas Cokayn was the city's Recorder in 1439: ibid., p. 161.

[66] Cf. the debate about young women and autonomy in Phillips, *Medieval Maidens*, pp. 7–8, 120–35.

personal. The clearest illustrations of this can be found in some late fifteenth-century chancery petitions. Chancery at this date operated as a court of 'conscience', a forerunner of the equity courts, and as such could take the full circumstances of a case into account rather than confine itself to common law rules. It would, for instance, accept petitions from those who claimed they were too poor or powerless to get a fair trial elsewhere.[67] The petition of one Alice Smyth, arrested in London for her late husband's debts, aimed to get her case moved to Chancery (she was petitioning from prison). The petition claims that 'she is a pore widowe and *sole woman* and hath litell goodes and fewe fryndes to helpe or labour for hir' (my italics).[68] This petition plays to Chancery's remit with the references to her lack of goods and supporters. The reference to Alice as a 'pore widowe' was presumably intended to portray her as vulnerable and in need of the Chancellor's pity; it is a Christian commonplace that poor widows were considered deserving of protection and charity.[69] That the category of 'pore widowe' is followed by that of 'sole woman' suggests that the latter might also be a position of pathos.

Another widow's petition to Chancery, that of Alice Wyndeler, also appears to use her 'sole' status to gain sympathy. According to the petition, her late husband had bought merchandise from one Thomas Elys of Clay worth £10 and had sealed obligations promising to pay in instalments at Michaelmas and Christmas. On his death he left Alice as his executrix and, although the relevant dates had not passed, Thomas had reclaimed the merchandise and was demanding 40s. from her. The bailiffs in Clay were pursuing Alice for the debt and so she petitioned Chancery that either Thomas keep the merchandise and cancel the

[67] For further discussion of the nature of the court and its petitions see C. Beattie, 'Single Women, Work and Family: The Chancery Dispute of Jane Wynde and Margaret Clerk', in M. Goodich (ed.), *Voices from the Bench: the Narratives of Lesser Folk in Medieval Trials* (New York, NY: Palgrave Macmillan, 2006), pp. 177–202; P. Tucker, 'The Early History of the Court of Chancery: A Comparative Study', *English Historical Review*, 115 (2000), 791–811; T. S. Haskett, 'The Medieval English Court of Chancery', *Law and History Review*, 14 (1996), 245–313.

[68] TNA: PRO, C 1/58/421 (1475–80 or 1483–5).

[69] See e.g. Thurston, *Widows*, esp. pp. 13–14; J. A. Brundage, 'Widows as Disadvantaged Persons in Medieval Canon Law', in L. Mirrer (ed.), *Upon My Husband's Death: Widows in the Literature and Histories of Medieval Europe* (Ann Arbor, MI: University of Michigan Press, 1992), pp. 193–206; B. A. Hanawalt, 'The Widow's Mite: Provisions for Medieval London Widows', in ibid., p. 21. Other Chancery petitions use the category 'poor widow', e.g. C 1/64/1130 (1475–80 or 1483–5). The category will also be discussed in Ch. 3, 'Widows', below.

debt or she be allowed to sell the merchandise to raise money to pay off the debt. As in the earlier example, the petition seeks to draw the court's attention to a wider context. It argues that Thomas has taken advantage of Alice's single status, here used to denote her vulnerability; his motivation is said to be his 'understondyng that your seid besecher is *sole* and hath little comforte and little help' (my italics).[70] The *femme sole* position is perhaps evoked for similar reasons in London's Mayor's Court in 1376. Ellen, widow of John Sage, haberdasher, was charged with seeking to sell on feast days, which contravened a recent ordinance concerning haberdashers. She was excused from paying the fine of 20s., both because she claimed to be unaware of the ordinance and because she was *sole*.[71] These examples suggest that, while the position of *femme sole* entailed legal rights and responsibilities, it might also be thought of as a vulnerable position, as a woman alone might lack the goods and powerful supporters to defend or pursue her rights at law.

The category *femme sole*, as used in legal discourse, has a range of associations: it denotes legal (and so economic) rights, but also legal (and economic) responsibilities, and it could signal a woman's position as a woman alone, lacking in support in both personal and financial terms. In the *Liber Albus* customs, *sola* and *soule* are also used to emphasize that a married woman could be called upon to answer in court *alone*, without the presence of her husband.[72] These associations in an important discourse could imprint themselves on uses of the term *femme sole*, or its variants in other languages, in other contexts even when the legal construct itself is not being intentionally evoked.

MARRIAGE, SOCIAL CHANGE, AND THE POLITICS OF CLASSIFICATION

Contemporaries' understanding of the categories discussed so far (virgin, widow, *femme sole*) hinged to some extent on their understanding

---

[70] TNA: PRO C 1/46/14 (1467–72, or possibly 1433–43). See also the petition of Katherine Bee: C 1/67/93 (1477–8); edited in A. R. Myers (ed.), *English Historical Documents [IV], 1327–1485* (London: Eyre & Spottiswoode, 1969), pp. 493–4. McIntosh cites a different Chancery example, that of Joan Lucas: McIntosh, 'Benefits and Drawbacks', p. 416 (C 1/211/42).

[71] Thomas (ed.), *Calendar of Plea and Memoranda Rolls . . . 1364–1381*, p. 213. This is also McIntosh's reading of the case: McIntosh, 'Benefits and Drawbacks', p. 416.

[72] See pp. 27–8 above.

of the purpose of marriage, which both affected and was affected by the social reality of marriage. The early church fathers' virgins-widows-spouses scheme, a hierarchy of chaste states, was interpreted and adapted in the changed environment of thirteenth-century Europe. These later, religious authors sought not only to understand but also to communicate with the wider world and they therefore offered a more positive view of the role of marriage. In late medieval England, the custom of treating some married women as *femmes soles* derived from a need to protect lenders and borrowers in an urban, commercial environment in which women took an active part.[73] The emphasis on unmarried women as 'women alone' in the legal arena probably also stemmed from a social reality in which being 'covered' (having a male supporter) could be an advantage. To some extent these are two different views of marriage: one is of marriage as sacrament and the other is about the control of property. Yet the two clearly intersect: marriage became the accepted institution for the necessary procreation of children and therefore it is about matters of sex and morality, but it is also about keeping property within the patrilineal family and thus ensuring legitimacy was imperative.[74] The dominant view is of marriage as the proper place for sex, the transmission of property, and (for certain sectors of society) the organization of labour within a household structure.[75]

The social reality of marriage (and thus of non-marriage) in late medieval England, in terms of its incidence and its connections with labour, warrants further discussion as some have seen this as crucial context for use of the category 'single woman' in contemporary texts.

---

[73] For a full discussion of the custom, see McIntosh, 'Benefits and Drawbacks'.

[74] See G. Duby, *Medieval Marriage: Two Models from Twelfth-Century France*, trans. E. Forster (Baltimore, MD: Johns Hopkins University Press, 1978), pp. 2–22; see also G. Duby, *The Knight, the Lady and the Priest: The Making of Modern Marriage in Medieval France*, trans. B. Bray (London: Allen Lane, 1983), esp. p. 19; C. N. L. Brooke, *The Medieval Idea of Marriage* (Oxford: Oxford University Press, 1989), pp. 119–43; D. Herlihy, *Medieval Households* (Cambridge, MA: Harvard University Press, 1985), pp. 82–8; Fleming, *Family and Household*, pp. 10–11; C. McCarthy, *Marriage in Medieval England: Law, Literature and Practice* (Woodbridge: Boydell Press, 2004), pp. 5–6; Howell, 'Properties of Marriage', p. 23.

[75] See e.g. P. J. P. Goldberg, 'Household and the Organisation of Labour in Late Medieval Towns: Some English Evidence', in M. Carlier and T. Soens (eds.), *The Household in Late Medieval Cities, Italy and Northwestern Europe Compared* (Louvain-Apeldoorn: Garant, 2001), pp. 59–70; P. J. P. Goldberg, 'Masters and Men in Later Medieval England', in D. M. Hadley (ed.), *Masculinity in Medieval Europe* (London: Longman, 1999), pp. 56–70.

For example, on the appearance of the term 'singlewoman' in York's civic records in the late fifteenth century, P. J. P. Goldberg remarks, '[t]he increasing importance of matrimony for women as job opportunities for the single female diminished is reflected in the changing convention of nomenclature'.[76] The use of the personal designations 'sengylwoman' and 'syngilman' in two early sixteenth-century testaments from Essex led L. R. Poos to comment, '[t]hus was contemporary Essex terminology of social typology extended to embrace those who passed their lives unmarried'.[77] For these scholars, the appearance of the Middle English, compound term 'singlewoman' was in large part linked to social changes. For Poos it is connected to the presence of the never married in society. For Goldberg it is about a heightened emphasis on marriage in a changed economic environment, in which unmarried women would have found it harder to support themselves outside of marriage and in which they could be seen as competing for work with the single man.[78] Both arguments are part of a prevalent historiographical tradition, which sees single women as key indicators of the demographic and economic situation in late medieval England, at least from the Black Death onwards.[79]

Demographic historians are interested in the single, particularly the single woman, as they are the key indicators of marriage patterns and birth rates.[80] The dominant consensus is that late medieval England, from at least the late fourteenth century, was characterized by the 'northwestern European marriage pattern': men and women marry 'late' (in their mid to late twenties) someone of their own age; they set up their own household on marriage; before marriage they often circulate between households as life-cycle servants, and a significant proportion

[76] P. J. P. Goldberg, *Women, Work, and Life Cycle in a Medieval Economy: Women in York and Yorkshire c.1300–1520* (Oxford: Clarendon Press, 1992), p. 278.

[77] L. R. Poos, *A Rural Society after the Black Death: Essex 1350–1525* (Cambridge: Cambridge University Press, 1991), p. 157. Cf. Froide's argument for use of the term in the early modern period: A. M. Froide, *Never Married: Singlewomen in Early Modern England* (Oxford: Oxford University Press, 2005), pp. 159–60.

[78] See e.g. the Bristol weavers' ordinance of 1461: *The Little Red Book of Bristol*, ed. F. B. Bickley, 2 vols. (Bristol: W. Crofton Hemmons, 1900), ii, p. 127.

[79] For an overview of the debates about population and economic change, with attention to the role of women, see Rigby, 'Introduction', pp. 10–30.

[80] See R. B. Litchfield, 'Single People in the Nineteenth-Century City: A Comparative Perspective on Occupations and Living Situations', *Continuity and Change*, 3 (1988), p. 83; Kowaleski, 'Singlewomen', pp. 39–41; M. Bailey, 'Demographic Decline in Late Medieval England: Some Thoughts on Recent Research', *Economic History Review*, new ser., 49 (1996), p. 2.

never marry (the group referred to by Poos).[81] Whether this pattern was triggered by the population loss of the Black Death of 1348–9 (thought to be between one third to a half of the population) or not, the regime itself is seen as vital to explaining why it perhaps took until the early sixteenth century for population levels to recover.[82] Population levels are dependent, of course, not just on mortality rates (and England did experience recurrent plague epidemics), but also on birth rates. If women marry later, and some do not marry at all, one can assume that this would have a depressive effect on population replacement rates. Thus the presence of large numbers of single women are seen to hold the key to population trends in late medieval England. Maryanne Kowaleski's recent review of this field suggests that the never married accounted for approximately thirty to forty per cent of all adult women in urban areas and large parts of rural England.[83] We also need to add to that figure widows: while some women would have been widowed young and subsequently remarried, it is also possible that greater land availability after the Black Death meant there was less of a drive to marry widows for their land.[84] Indeed, the numbers debate must be considered in conjunction with that about opportunities, about why people made the 'choices' that they did, such as to defer marriage.

The linked argument focuses on the economy and in particular on the labour market. In relation to women, the debate is about whether the population losses of the Black Death, and a resultant fall in the

---

[81] See R. M. Smith, 'Hypothèses sur la nuptialité en Angleterre aux XIIe–XIVe siècles', *Annales: Economies, Sociétés, Civilisations*, 38 (1983), 107–36; R. M. Smith, 'Some Reflections on the Evidence for the Origins of the "European Marriage Pattern" in England', in C. Harris *et al.* (eds.), *The Sociology of the Family: New Directions for Britain* (Keele: University of Keele, 1979), pp. 74–112; Goldberg, *Women, Work, and Life Cycle*, pp. 203–76; Poos, *Rural Society*, pp. 141–58. For an overview of the debate, see M. Kowaleski, 'Singlewomen', pp. 41–51.

[82] There are problems in gauging population levels from the extant source material; see the useful discussion in C. Klapisch-Zuber, 'Plague and Family Life', in M. Jones (ed.), *The New Cambridge Medieval History*, 6 (Cambridge: Cambridge University Press, 2000), pp. 124–54.

[83] Kowaleski, 'Singlewomen', pp. 45–6, 50–1.

[84] See B. A. Hanawalt, 'Remarriage as an Option for Urban and Rural Widows in Late Medieval England', in Walker (ed.), *Wife and Widow*, pp. 141–64; M. Mate, *Women in Medieval English Society* (Cambridge: Cambridge University Press, 1999), pp. 34–8; Rigby, 'Introduction', p. 20. The adding back in of widows here seems ironic as sources such as the late 14th-century poll tax returns do not clearly distinguish between the never married and the widowed and so the figures for the never married are based on various hypotheses, including subtracting 'probable widows': see e.g. Kowaleski, 'Singlewomen', pp. 71–2, n. 39.

pool of available labour, opened up their working opportunities.[85] The focus is largely on the unmarried, female worker, in part because the married woman was more likely to be engaged in unpaid labour within the household and beyond this her work is often obscured by her legal coverture.[86] Also, in terms of establishing the existence of the northwestern European marriage pattern, scholars are interested in finding evidence of significant numbers of unmarried women who live in service or work independently.[87] The optimistic view is that women chose to delay marriage, or perhaps even never marry, because of access to a greater variety of jobs.[88] The counter-argument is that nevertheless women's status, relative to men's, remained the same: for example, women took up unskilled positions as unskilled male workers largely took over the skilled positions, women's wages went up but so did those of men, and women in general continued to earn less than men with less job security.[89] There is a consensus, though, that opportunities that arose from the problems caused by population losses, would lessen if the economic situation changed (although there are different views as to when and where this happened).[90] As the earlier quotation from Goldberg signals, job opportunities for the single female diminished

---

[85] For summaries of the debate see Mate, *Women*, pp. 27–61; S. H. Rigby, 'Gendering the Black Death: Women in Later Medieval England', *Gender and History*, 12 (2000), 745–54; McIntosh, 'Benefits and Drawbacks', pp. 411–12; M. K. McIntosh, *Working Women in English Society, 1300–1620* (Cambridge: Cambridge University Press, 2005), pp. 29–33.

[86] See J. M. Bennett, 'Medieval Women, Modern Women: Across the Great Divide', in D. Aers (ed.), *Culture and History 1350–1600: Essays on English Communities, Identities, and Writing* (London: Harvester Wheatsheaf, 1992), pp. 147–75; McIntosh, *Working Women*, pp. 7–8, 15–16.

[87] See R. M. Smith, 'Geographical Diversity in the Resort to Marriage in Late Medieval Europe: Work, Reputation, and Unmarried Females in the Household Formation Systems of Northern and Southern Europe', in P. J. P. Goldberg (ed.), *Woman is a Worthy Wight: Women in English Society c. 1200–1500* (Stroud: Alan Sutton, 1992; reprinted as *Women in Medieval English Society*, 1997), pp. 27–46; Goldberg, *Women, Work, and Life Cycle*, pp. 158–202; Poos, *Rural Society*, pp. 181–206. Cf. Bailey, 'Demographic Decline', pp. 5–14.

[88] See e.g. Goldberg, *Women, Work, and Life Cycle*, pp. 339–40.

[89] See Bennett, 'Medieval Women, Modern Women'; S. Bardsley, 'Women's Work Reconsidered: Gender and Wage Differentiation in Late Medieval England', *Past and Present*, 165 (1999), 3–29. See also M. Kowaleski, 'Women's Work in a Market Town: Exeter in the Late Fourteenth Century', in B. A. Hanawalt (ed.), *Women and Work in Preindustrial Europe* (Bloomington, IN: Indiana University Press, 1986), pp. 145–64.

[90] Goldberg's thesis about the late 15th century is largely based on the York evidence. Barron, for example, suggests that such a shift might not have affected London until some time in the 16th century. See Goldberg, *Women, Work, and Life Cycle*, esp. pp. 336–61; Barron, 'Golden Age', p. 48.

when the economy experienced a downturn and local authorities might well have been concerned about women living outside of marriage.[91] In a comparable debate, service is sometimes viewed as a beneficial experience in that it enabled women to leave the natal home, to socialize with people of their own age, and to work towards a dowry or a fund that would help them establish themselves independently.[92] Yet others stress that it also worked to the advantage of the employer: servants who worked in return for bed and board and a final settlement in cash or goods were a cheap source of labour in a period when labour costs were rising.[93] Thus women might have not so much chosen a working life in preference to marriage, but rather needed to work to support themselves, perhaps because *men* were choosing to delay marriage, or never marry, or to save for the future because the cultural expectation was that men and women would be in a position to set up their own households on marriage.[94]

These are significant debates and the single woman in late medieval England is clearly an important subject for research. But the debates also raise a number of questions about how we interpret evidence. For example, can we easily distinguish between the never married and the widowed and what other distinctions might be lost in the process? How far can we attribute motives to a group of people that are made into a group by virtue of scholars' interests? This study therefore takes a different approach. We can assume that there were large numbers of unmarried women in late medieval English society at any given time, although one might argue about proportions and particularly about how many were never married rather than widowed, and about

[91] See e.g. P. J. P. Goldberg, 'Coventry's "Lollard" Programme of 1492 and the Making of Utopia', in R. Horrox and S. Rees Jones (eds.), *Pragmatic Utopias: Ideals and Communities, 1200–1630* (Cambridge: Cambridge University Press, 2001), pp. 97–101. Most similar evidence of concern dates from the late 16th century, though: see Froide, *Never Married*, pp. 19–22; M. K. McIntosh, *Controlling Misbehavior in England, 1370–1600* (Cambridge: Cambridge University Press, 1998), pp. 110–11; C. Peters, 'Single Women in Early Modern England: Attitudes and Expectations', *Continuity and Change*, 12 (1997), p. 329.

[92] See e.g. P. J. P. Goldberg, 'Female Labour, Service and Marriage in the Late Medieval Urban North', *Northern History*, 22 (1986), pp. 26, 24.

[93] Rigby, 'Introduction', p. 16. See also Phillips, *Medieval Maidens*, p. 131.

[94] See M. E. Mate, *Daughters, Wives and Widows After the Black Death: Women in Sussex, 1350–1535* (Woodbridge: Boydell Press, 1998), pp. 21–31; C. Donahue, Jr., 'Female Plaintiffs in Marriage Cases in the Court of York in the Later Middle Ages: What Can We Learn from the Numbers?', in Walker (ed.), *Wife and Widow*, pp. 183–213. On assessing motivations see also Bennett and Froide, 'A Singular Past', pp. 21–3.

how many might remain single throughout their lives. But rather than taking unmarried women as a coherent group, or selecting some of these women as a subgroup (the never married), this study asks how contemporaries viewed unmarried women; that is, it analyses how contemporaries divided up society, particularly in relation to gender, and why, and thus reveals *which* unmarried women were a source of concern in different contexts. It looks at classifiers from a range of social contexts so that it does not privilege a single view of society, although admittedly the power to classify and record that process in written form was a socially limited one. Were classifiers concerned about all unmarried women or were they concerned about particular subtypes of unmarried women for particular reasons? Beyond gender and marital status, what role did other factors play, such as social status, age, sexual behaviour, who unmarried women lived with, and what work they did? By exploring how various medieval texts used the category 'single woman' in relation to other categories, one can better evaluate what contemporary concerns were and what lay behind them.

This study bears in mind, though, that concern about women was not the main driver behind the creation of the texts to be discussed: they all have an ostensibly pragmatic function, and some are affected by broader social and political developments. For example, the purpose of the 1379 poll tax schedule was to set out how much taxpayers should pay according to their social, occupational, or marital status, and the property that they owned. It has been discussed as an attempt 'to reschematize the ordering of their changing society', with equivalences made between types of nobleman or urban dweller.[95] Further, the tax itself derives from a need to raise revenue for the war with France (see Chapter 3). Similarly, the guild returns of 1388–9 were sought partly because of the government's need for revenue for the war effort, partly because of concern about collective activities in the wake of the Peasants' Revolt of 1381, and possibly because of anxiety about heresy at a time when fear of Lollardy was on the increase (Chapter 4). The tension between a desire to inform the laity of the key tenets of the Christian faith and the potential for error and heresy, particularly once religious texts circulate in the vernacular, is the backdrop to the texts discussed in Chapter 2, pastoral manuals, and a Bishop's Register. For Goldberg and Poos the appearance of the term 'singlewoman' in late fifteenth- and early

---

[95] Keen, *English Society*, pp. 8–9. See Introduction, 'Medieval classification schemes' above.

sixteenth-century civic records and testaments was linked to changes in marriage and work patterns. Yet changes in nomenclature could also be the product of bureaucratic changes, such as changes in the language of record-keeping and from attempts to standardize personal designations in certain types of record (as demonstrated in Chapter 5). This is not to say that the selection of a particular category does not have meaning or a subsequent effect, but that we also need to keep such broader factors in mind.

2

The Single Woman in Penitential Discourse

On the 3 June 1389, William Ramsbury, a layman of modest learning, came before John Waltham, Bishop of Salisbury, accused of preaching and teaching heresies and errors to people in the diocese.[1] One of the opinions which Ramsbury was said to hold was that it was not a sin to know carnally a nun; another was that 'it is permitted for any priest or other man to know carnally any women, even nuns, virgins, and wives, and this in order to increase the human race'.[2] Added to the latter opinion is the assertion that Ramsbury 'has known carnally virgins, wives, and other single women since he held these opinions'.[3] As presented in the Bishop's Register these opinions are illuminating not only of the views of a potential heretic but also of the orthodox position. The entry signals that there could be some dissent from the Church's teachings, but the layman's challenge also suggests that such teachings were widely known. By the late medieval period, the Church held that only sexual intercourse between a husband and a wife for the purposes of procreation or to prevent one's spouse from falling into sin was permissible (as long as the participants did not enjoy it).[4] It also taught that the sin could

---

[1] Most of the entry from the Register of Bishop Waltham is transcribed in A. Hudson, *Lollards and their Books* (London: Hambledon Press, 1985), pp. 120–3; it is calendared in *The Register of John Waltham, Bishop of Salisbury, 1388–1395*, ed. T. C. B. Timmins, Canterbury and York Society, 80 (Woodbridge: Boydell Press, 1994), pp. 169–70.

[2] 'licitum est cuicumque sacerdoti et alij cognoscere carnaliter quascumque mulieres eciam monialas, virgines et vxores, et hoc propter multiplicacionem generis humani': Hudson, *Lollards and their Books*, p. 121.

[3] 'cognoscendo virgines, vxores et alias mulieres solutas a tempore quo dictas opiniones tenuit': ibid.

[4] See R. M. Karras, *Sexuality in Medieval Europe: Doing Unto Others* (New York, NY: Routledge, 2005), pp. 30, 72; J. A. Brundage, *Law, Sex, and Christian Society in Medieval Europe* (Chicago, IL: University of Chicago Press, 1987), pp. 260–2, 278–87; T. N. Tentler, *Sin and Confession on the Eve of the Reformation* (Princeton, NJ: Princeton University Press, 1977), pp. 168–86.

be increased according to the status of the person involved. Confessors were asked to extract the following information from sinners: 'who, what, where, with whom, how often, why, in what way, when'.[5] In the example from Waltham's Register men are divided into priests or others, the status of priest being one that would also increase the severity of the sin, and women into nuns, virgins, wives, and other single women. The phrase 'other single women' (*alias mulieres solutas*) is used for those women who did not increase the sin beyond that of, what is known as, 'simple fornication'. While this suggests a lower level of concern about sex and the 'single woman', this chapter contends that 'single woman' was a useful category in a religious discourse concerned with sexual sin and penance. The focus here is on pastoral texts that use the category in their discussions of the sin of lechery (lust), and in their discussions of the opposing virtue, chastity. The chapter explores what the category denotes, why it was included, and how it relates to other categories such as 'virgin', 'widow', and 'whore' in these texts.

The argument revises that of Ruth Karras, who has argued, in an important and influential work, that 'there was no conceptual space in the medieval scheme of things for a sexually active singlewoman who was not a prostitute'. In relation to a fourteenth-century preacher's manual in particular, the *Fasciculus Morum* ('Little Bundle of Morals'), she concludes that, 'If not a wife, virgin, widow or concubine, a woman was a prostitute; there was no other category'.[6] The approach taken in this study differs from previous discussions of medieval single women. It does not proceed from a prior definition of a group applied to the evidence (in Karras's essay, the 'singlewoman' is never married), but from the examination of uses of the category 'single woman' in medieval texts. Through looking at a text that, unlike *Fasciculus Morum*, does classify women as 'single' (as well as categorizing them as maids, wives, widows, and prostitutes) we can see how the addition of the first category affects the meaning of the other categories. This allows one to consider what is meant by frequently used categories such as 'maid'

---

[5] See M. C. Woods and R. Copeland, 'Classroom and Confession', in D. Wallace (ed.), *The Cambridge History of Medieval English Literature* (Cambridge: Cambridge University Press, 1999), pp. 393–4.

[6] Quotations from Karras, *Sexuality in Medieval Europe*, p. 104, but this was also the argument in Karras, 'Sex and the Singlewoman'. For the influence of her argument see e.g. A. M. Froide, 'Marital Status as a Category of Difference: Singlewomen and Widows in Early Modern England', in Bennett and Froide (eds.), *Singlewomen*, p. 263 n. 22; J. M. Bennett, 'Writing Fornication: Medieval Leyrwite and its Historians', *Transactions of the Royal Historical Society*, 13 (2003), p. 156; Arnold, *Belief and Unbelief*, p. 146.

and 'widow' in a *particular* context.[7] The *Fasciculus Morum* is however drawn upon for its discussion of lechery, which can be compared with those in the pastoral texts selected. Thus, while some texts did portray all sexually-active, unmarried women as whores, this chapter seeks to further the debate by discussing why single women who have been sexually active might also constitute a useful group in a penitential discourse.[8]

The text that this chapter initially focuses on is the discussion of active lechery in a Middle English treatise known as *Jacob's Well*.[9] Although it was probably composed in the early fifteenth century, like many other treatises from this period it reuses material from other sources. *Jacob's Well* sets out fourteen degrees of lechery in deed, increasing in sinfulness from the first to the fourteenth, which are common to texts derived from Lorens d'Orléans's *Somme des vices et des vertus*, better known as *Somme le Roi*.[10] In most of the *Somme*-derived texts the conventional metaphor of branches on a tree is used for the different degrees of lechery, but *Jacob's Well* refers to different depths in a stagnant pit.[11] The fourteen degrees of active lechery are defined by the status of the participants, with the exception of the act of sodomy, which is ranked fourteenth and so the most sinful.[12] In the other high levels the key elements are religious office or ties of kinship; for example, the eleventh

---

[7] Cf. the religious texts considered in the previous chapter in which the various schema employed did not allow for the sexually-active single woman.

[8] See e.g. Thomas Aquinas's *Summa Theologica*, 2a 2ae, qu. 154, art 6, resp. ad 1: 'fornicatio est concubitus qui fit cum meretricibus, idest mulieribus jam corruptis' ('fornication is intercourse which is done with whores, that is with women who are already corrupted'): St Thomas Aquinas, *Summa Theologiae*, 60 vols. (London: Blackfriars in conjunction with Eyre & Spottiswoode, 1964–75), xliii, p. 228; the translation is my own.

[9] *Jacob's Well*, ed. Brandeis, pp. 160–2.

[10] An edition of *Somme le Roi* has not been published yet (one is apparently in progress by Dr E. Brayer), but for a summary of the fourteen degrees from this text, see *Book for a Simple and Devout Woman: A Late Middle English Adaptation of Peraldus's* Summa de Vitiis et Virtutibus *and Friar Laurent's* Somme le Roi, ed. F. N. M. Diekstra (Groningen: Egbert Forsten, 1998), p. 506. For the *Somme*-derived texts, see n. 14 below.

[11] The language of 'branches' is used as sins are often depicted as trees: see R. Newhauser, *The Treatise on Vices and Virtues in Latin and the Vernacular*, Typologie des sources du moyen âge occidental, 68 (Turnhout: Brepols, 1993), pp. 160–1. The allegory used throughout *Jacob's Well* is that of the sinful body of man as a stagnant pit, which must be purified through the sacrament of penance: see *Jacob's Well*, ed. Brandeis, pp. v–vi; L. M. Carruthers, 'The Liturgical Setting of *Jacob's Well*', *English Language Notes*, 24/4 (June 1987), pp. 8–19.

[12] As Payer comments, 'sodomy' in such discussions often encompasses 'all same sex relations, bestiality, and the use of inanimate objects': P. J. Payer, 'Confession and the

degree is between a secular man and a woman of religion, whereas the thirteenth degree is between a woman and a prelate. In the lower levels, though, it is the woman's sexual status that is key. In *Jacob's Well* the male is described as a 'syngle man' in all of the first five levels and therefore it is the woman's status which increases the degree of sin.[13] The woman is described as 'syngle womman', 'comoun womman', 'wydewe', 'mayden', and 'wyif'. Analysis of these divisions of lechery, therefore, not only enable one to deduce who is denoted by the term 'syngle woman', but also who is included in the other categories, and why women were divided up in this particular way. Other texts that also derive from *Somme le Roi* in some way, namely, *Ayenbite of Inwyt*, the *Book of Vices and Virtues, Speculum Vitae*, and a *Myrour to Lewde Men and Wymmen* are discussed for comparative purposes.[14] For example, *Speculum Vitae* and the *Myrour* use very similar categories in the first five degrees.[15]

Jacob's Well only exists in one manuscript, made in the 1440s, although this appears to be a copy of an earlier exemplar, probably composed in the first quarter of the century, and its author is unknown.[16] Although the text itself probably had limited circulation, there are two ways in which its ideas could have disseminated more widely. First, in oral form, as there is internal evidence that the text was intended to

Study of Sex in the Middle Ages', in V. L. Bullough and J. A. Brundage (eds.), *Handbook of Medieval Sexuality* (New York, NY: Garland Publishing, Inc., 1996), pp. 10–11.

[13] *Jacob's Well*, ed. Brandeis, p. 160, ll. 9–24; although, in the fifth degree of lechery, if the man is also married this makes the sin 'more grevouse': ibid., l. 30.

[14] *Dan Michel's* Ayenbite of Inwyt *or Remorse of Conscience*, ed. R. Morris and rev. P. Gradon, 2 vols., EETS, o.s. 23, 278 (Oxford: Oxford University Press, 1965–79); *The Book of Vices and Virtues: A Fourteenth Century English Translation of the* Somme le Roi *of Lorens D'Orléans*, ed. W. N. Francis, EETS, o.s. 217 (London: Oxford University Press, 1942); *A Myrour to Lewde Men and Wymmen: A Prose Version of the* Speculum Vitae, *ed. from B. L. MS Harley 45*, ed. V. Nelson (Heidelberg: Carl Winter, 1981); J. W. Smeltz, 'Speculum Vitae: An Edition of British Museum Manuscript Royal 17.C.viii', Ph.D. thesis (Duquesne P, 1977). On this tradition, see R. R. Raymo, 'Works of Religious and Philosophical Instruction', in A. E. Hartung (ed.), *A Manual of the Writings in Middle English 1050–1500*, 10 vols. (New Haven, CT: Connecticut Academy of Arts and Sciences, 1967–98), vii, pp. 2258–61.

[15] Smeltz, '*Speculum Vitae*', pp. 440–3; *Myrour*, ed. Nelson, p. 165.

[16] L. Carruthers, 'Where did *Jacob's Well* Come from? The Provenance and Dialect of MS Salisbury Cathedral 103', *English Studies*, 71 (1990), pp. 335–6. Carruthers argues that the author was probably a parish priest or a canon: Carruthers, ' "Know thyself": Criticism, Reform and the Audience of Jacob's Well', in J. Hamesse *et al.* (eds.), *Medieval Sermons and Society: Cloister, City, University* (Louvain-La-Neuve: Fédération Internationale des Instituts d'Études Médiévales, 1998), pp. 219, 232; cf. Raymo, 'Works', p. 2262, which argues that the author was a Franciscan friar.

be read in church over a period of ninety-five days.[17] There are also references within the text to the intended audience, which suggest that the author envisaged an audience listening in church as well as a clerical audience.[18] For example, its sermon fifty-seven, 'On the continence of widows and virgins', contains a direct address to young girls to guard their modesty: 'Þou mayden, bere noȝt þis laumpe of þi body often & openly in towne, in weyes & open stretys, in marketys, at feyris & in styraclys [shows] & among gret multitude of peple . . . þerfore ȝe maydenys kepe ȝe out of þe wynde of pride'.[19] The maidens addressed must be lay people, as nuns would not be cautioned about traipsing around town. Second, the treatise itself was largely composed from other texts, some of which are known to have had a wider circulation. After the first nine chapters, the material is largely taken from two sources.[20] The *exempla* (moral stories) seem to come predominantly from the *Alphabetum narrationum*, a Latin compilation of tales.[21] The doctrinal information, including the division of active lechery into fourteen degrees, is from *Speculum Vitae*, a popular poem written between 1349 and 1384.[22] It exists in thirty-eight manuscripts and two fragments, which date from the late fourteenth and fifteenth centuries.[23]

[17] See e.g. *Jacob's Well*, ed. Brandeis, p. 1; the text is divided into 95 chapters but only the first 50 are edited.

[18] Carruthers, 'Liturgical Setting', pp. 24; Carruthers, 'Know Thyself', p. 221.

[19] MS Salisbury Cathedral 103, fos 118v–119r, quoted in Carruthers, 'Know Thyself', p. 228; for the chapter heading see *Jacob's Well*, ed. Brandeis, p. xv.

[20] Although the allegorical structure belongs to the author, only the first two chapters which explain the allegory appear to be wholly his own. Chs. 3 to 9 recount the sins and offences punishable by excommunication, which canon law required priests to read out four times a year. Shaw argues that the list was 'a commonplace that appeared frequently in the bishops' statutes', and the author has either copied one of these or used a canonical compilation: J. Shaw, 'The Influence of Canonical and Episcopal Reform on Popular Books of Instruction', in Heffernan (ed.), *Popular Literature*, p. 50. Cf. Carruthers, 'Liturgical Setting', pp. 16–17.

[21] J. Y. Gregg, 'The Exempla of "Jacob's Well": A Study in the Transmission of Medieval Sermon Stories', *Traditio*, 33 (1977), 359–80. Carruthers claims that, in elaborating on the deadly sins, *Jacob's Well* uses *A Lityl Tretys On the Seven Deadly Sins*, a short work written in Suffolk by a Carmelite *c.* 1390, but this text divides lechery into eight branches: Carruthers, 'Where did *Jacob's Well* Come from?', p. 340; *A Litil Tretys On the Seven Deadly Sins by Richard Lavynham*, ed. J. P. W. M. van Zutphen (Rome: Institutum Carmelitanum, 1956), pp. 22–5. On this text, see also Newhauser, *Treatise on Vices and Virtues*, pp. 144–5.

[22] Carruthers, 'Liturgical Setting', p. 13; *Myrour*, ed. Nelson, pp. 36–9.

[23] See Raymo, 'Works', p. 2261; *Myrour*, ed. Nelson pp. 9, 10 n. 8, 24–5. It is not used here as one of the main case-studies as its rhyming couplets do not lend themself to concise quotations and it is not yet available in an edition that compares different manuscripts. The *Myrour*, which exists in four 15th-century manuscripts owned by pious

In turn, *Speculum Vitae* was a translation and rearrangement of material drawn largely from *Somme le Roi*.[24] This French text, composed by a Dominican in 1280 from a variety of sources, was meant specifically for the laity (albeit initially offered to Philip III) as an aid to examination of the conscience, and itself circulated in England.[25] While the allegorical structure (of man as a stagnant pit) is unique, to *Jacob's Well*, and the treatise only survives in one manuscript, it is the product of a much broader tradition of pastoral manuals.

PENITENTIAL DISCOURSE, WOMEN, AND SEXUAL SIN

Pastoral texts aimed to educate the clergy and, directly or indirectly, the laity (for example, through preaching and the practice of confession). They were often explicitly designed as aids to confession and structured around the sins or the commandments. As such, they have their origins in the interconciliar period of 1179–1215 and represent an approach to penance and confession which had been gaining ground since the Gregorian reform movement of the late eleventh century, one which emphasized that the priest should consider the status of the sinner (for example, wife, husband, labourer, merchant), the circumstances of each sin, and, as the penitent must be contrite, the interior disposition of the penitent.[26] After the Fourth Lateran Council of 1215, which gave papal and conciliar authority to the requirement of annual confession for all men and women over the age of discretion, confession (which first required contrition) was added to the sacramental definition of

laypeople in the 15th and 16th centuries, also took *Speculum Vitae* as its source: *Myrour*, ed. Nelson, pp. 9, 25.

[24] On the rearrangement, see W. A. Pantin, *The English Church in the Fourteenth Century* (Cambridge: Cambridge University Press, 1955), pp. 227–8; Raymo, 'Works', p. 2261. Of the other translations of *Somme le Roi* into Middle English, *Ayenbite* only exists in one manuscript, and the *Book of Vices and Virtues* is extant in three. But at least eight other translations of *Somme le Roi* into Middle English, partial or complete, survive. For example at the request of a London mercer, William Caxton translated it again and this was printed as the *Ryal Book c.* 1485–8, and reprinted in 1507 by Wynkyn de Worde and Richard Pynson. *Somme le Roi* also had redactions. For example Caxton also translated the *Doctrinal of Sapience*, a prose text largely based on *Somme le Roi*. See Raymo, 'Works', pp. 2258–63; Newhauser, *Treatise on Vices and Virtues*, p. 142.

[25] See Newhauser, *Treatise on Vices and Virtues*, p. 141; *Book of Vices*, ed. Francis, pp. xi, xxi–xxvii.

[26] See Boyle, 'Fourth Lateran Council', pp. 33–4.

penance, which also included satisfaction and absolution. This new emphasis on sacramental penance was widely disseminated through preaching, particularly by the mendicant orders, as well as by an increase in related literature to educate the priest or his parishioners, such as confessors' manuals, collections of sermons and sermon *exempla*, and general manuals of pastoral care, in Latin or the vernacular.[27] While the focus in this chapter is on the classifying systems used in some pastoral manuals, such texts should be understood in the wider context of preaching and the conduct of confession. *Jacob's Well*, for example, has been viewed as 'standing at the junction of sermon and treatise'.[28] Its theme is that, while the sinful body of man is a stagnant pit, one's conscience can be cleansed through the sacrament of penance.[29] Carruthers argues that it was perhaps designed to be preached from Ash Wednesday to the Vigil of Pentecost, as Lent fits with the text's theme of penance, with Easter representing regeneration.[30]

A penitential discourse had an interest in categorizing sin according to various criteria so that an appropriate penance could be assigned. As Rita Copeland puts it, 'sin is mostly a tissue of petty affairs, and so the techniques for probing the conscience, extracting confession and imposing appropriate penance are designed to be responsive to the least minutiae'.[31] Thus confessors needed to take into account the 'who' and 'with whom', as well as the 'what', 'why', and so on. There has been some debate about whether the Church's increasing emphasis on confession and the cure of souls should be viewed as a benevolent Church looking after the well-being of its flock, or more as an elaborate surveillance mechanism.[32] Some have argued that the act of confession was not

---

[27] See K. L. Jansen, 'Mary Magdalen and the Mendicants: The Preaching of Penance in the Late Middle Ages', *Journal of Medieval History*, 21 (1995), pp. 3–17; K. L. Jansen, *The Making of the Magdalen: Preaching and Popular Devotion in the Later Middle Ages* (Princeton, NJ: Princeton University Press, 2000), pp. 199–202; N. Bériou, 'Autour de Latran IV (1215): La naissance de la confession moderne et sa diffusion', in Groupe de la Bussière (eds.), *Pratiques de la confession: Des pères du desert à Vatican II* (Paris: CERF, 1983), pp. 73–93; R. Rusconi, 'De la prédication à la confession: transmission et contrôle de modèles de comportement au XIIIᵉ siècle', in *Faire Croire: Modalités de la diffusion et de la réception des messages religieux du XIIᵉ au XVᵉ siècle* (Rome: Ecole Française de Rome, 1981), 67–85; Boyle, 'Fourth Lateran Council'.

[28] Carruthers, 'Know Thyself', p. 219. [29] See n. 11 above.

[30] Carruthers, 'Liturgical Setting', pp. 14–24.

[31] Woods and Copeland, 'Classroom and Confession', p. 402.

[32] For the original debate see T. N. Tentler, 'The Summa for Confessors as an Instrument of Social Control', in C. Trinkaus and H. A. Oberman (eds.), *The Pursuit of Holiness in Late Medieval and Renaissance Religion* (Leiden: Brill, 1974), pp. 103–26;

actually an effective mechanism for policing society, given that most people only confessed once a year, yet the literature about confession and penance (the manuals and the didactic texts) itself produced and sustained 'an elaborate system of power', even if it was not always enforced in practice.[33] For example, the conceptual apparatus that grew up around confession was in part about making the laity adopt a particular way of thinking about their actions.[34] Michel Foucault emphasized the foundational importance of confession for the discourse of sex.[35] While medievalists, with some justification, have criticized his work for neglecting other elements of confessional discourse than the sexual, it is in the context of sexual sin that women are specifically discussed in pastoral manuals.[36] Jacqueline Murray found, in an analysis of fifteen Latin confessors' manuals from the first half of the thirteenth century, that these texts construct women as 'primarily, even exclusively, sexual'.[37] Explicit references to women occur almost exclusively in

L. E. Boyle, 'The Summa for Confessors as a Genre and its Religious Intent', in ibid., pp. 126–30; T. N. Tentler, 'Response and Retraction', in ibid., pp. 131–7; commented upon in Payer, 'Confession and the Study of Sex', p. 15. See also J. Bossy, 'The Social History of Confession in the Age of the Reformation', *Transactions of the Royal Historical Society*, 5th ser., 25 (1975), 21–38; H. Martin, 'Confession et contrôle social à la fin du moyen âge', in Groupe de la Bussière (eds.), *Pratiques*, pp. 117–36; K. Lochrie, *Covert Operations: The Medieval Uses of Secrecy* (Philadelphia, PA: University of Pennsylvania Press, 1999), pp. 12–42; D. Elliott, *Proving Woman: Female Spirituality and Inquisitorial Culture in the Later Middle Ages* (Princeton, NJ: Princeton University Press, 2004), pp. 9–43.

[33] Arnold, *Belief and Unbelief*, p. 181; Woods and Copeland, 'Classroom and Confession', p. 400. See also Tentler, 'The Summa for Confessors', esp. pp. 122–6.

[34] See R. Rusconi, '*Ordinate confiteri*: La confessione dei peccati nelle «summae de casibus» e nei manuali per i confessori (metà XII–inizi XIV secolo)', in *L'Aveu: Antiquité et moyen-âge*, Actes de la table ronde organisée par l'Ecole Française de Rome avec le concours du CNRS et de l'Université de Trieste, Rome 28–30 Mars 1984 (Rome: Ecole Française de Rome, 1986), pp. 297–313; J. H. Arnold, *Inquisition and Power: Catharism and the Confessing Subject in Medieval Languedoc* (Philadelphia, PA: University of Pennsylvania Press, 2001), pp. 91–3.

[35] M. Foucault, *The History of Sexuality, Volume 1: An Introduction*, trans. R. Hurley (Harmondsworth: Penguin Books, 1990), pp. 18–21, 58–63.

[36] See Lochrie, *Covert Operations*, pp. 12–42; P. J. Payer, 'Foucault on Penance and the Shaping of Sexuality', *Studies in Religion*, 14 (1985), 313–20. For the place of sex in this discourse, see also Tentler, *Sin and Confession*, pp. 165–6, 223–4.

[37] J. Murray, 'Gendered Souls in Sexed Bodies: The Male Construction of Female Sexuality in Some Medieval Confessors' Manuals', in P. Biller and A. J. Minnis (eds.), *Handling Sin: Confession in the Middle Ages* (Woodbridge: York Medieval Press, 1998), pp. 79–93 (p. 83). See also J. Murray, 'The Absent Penitent: The Cure of Women's Souls and Confessors' Manuals in Thirteenth-Century England', in L. Smith and J. H. M. Taylor (eds.), *Women, the Book, and the Godly: Selected Proceedings of the St Hilda's Conference, 1993, vol. 1* (Cambridge: D. S. Brewer, 1995), pp. 13–25.

discussions of the sin of lechery, the sacrament of marriage, or the sixth and ninth commandments, which relate respectively to adultery and not coveting a neighbour's possessions (including his wife).

There was no unitary discourse concerning sexual sin, even if we confine our search to ecclesiastical texts. In terms of types of lechery, as set out in pastoral manuals, there was no agreement as to the number of degrees or their ordering. However, Payer has identified a traditional core of six types of behaviour, which 'was relatively stable with modifications made by individual authors'.[38] The core consists of simple fornication (*fornicacio*), adultery (*adulterium*), incest (*incestus*), vice against nature (*sodomia*), violation of virgins (*stuprum*), and rape-abduction (*raptus*), but frequent additions include sacrilege and prostitution. To give an example, the thirteenth-century Anglo-Norman *Manuel des péchés*, and its fourteenth-century Middle English adaptation, Robert Mannyng of Brunne's *Handlyng Synne*, have seven types: sacrilege has been added, as has prostitution, but the latter replaces sodomy as the most sinful.[39] In the texts derived from *Somme le Roi* the degrees are generally defined by the status of the people involved.[40] Indeed, it was this emphasis on the classification of individuals rather than acts that led to the selection of a text from this tradition, *Jacob's Well*, as a case study. Both approaches, naming acts and naming status groups, can be linked to a penitential discourse that had an interest in categorizing sin according to various criteria so that an appropriate penance could be assigned. Further, although the method of classification is different, the groups named in the *Somme*-tradition do generally correlate with Payer's core of types of behaviour. This point can be illustrated with reference to *Fasciculus Morum*. The intention here is not to elide all differences, but to indicate that the ideas that lay behind the classification of persons in the *Somme*-derived texts were shared more widely.

Fasciculus Morum is an extended treatise on the seven deadly sins, written in Latin as an aid to preaching.[41] Of Payer's traditional core

---

[38] Payer, 'Confession and the Study of Sex', p. 12.

[39] *Robert of Brunne's* Handlyng Synne, ed. F. J. Furnivall, 2 parts, EETS, o.s. 119, 123 (London: Kegan Paul, Trench, Trübner & Co., 1901–3), pp. 235–8; it has the text of *Manuel des péchés* in parallel. On these texts, and other Middle English variants, see Raymo, 'Works', pp. 2255–8.

[40] See *Dan Michel's* Ayenbite, ed. Morris and Gradon, i, pp. 48–9; *Book of Vices*, ed. Francis, pp. 44–6; *Myrour*, ed. Nelson, pp. 165–7; Smeltz, '*Speculum Vitae*', pp. 440–9.

[41] See S. Wenzel, *Verses in Sermons:* Fasciculus Morum *and its Middle English Poems* (Cambridge, MA: Mediaeval Academy of America, 1978), pp. 9–59.

of six types of behaviour, *Fasciculus Morum* has five (the missing one being *raptus*).[42] While the discussions of lechery in the *Somme*-derived texts, with their fourteen degrees, look very different, the overarching order is the same. The branches in the *Somme*-derived texts are more specific than those in *Fasciculus Morum*, but they can still be mapped onto them (as illustrated in Table 2.1). Branch fourteen equates with *Fasciculus Morum*'s fifth branch, *sodomia*. In *Fasciculus Morum incestus* is said to include lechery involving clerics and the religious, as well as between persons related by blood or spiritual kinship, and so it encompasses branches seven to thirteen in the *Somme*-derived texts. *Fasciculus Morum*'s *adulterium* includes adultery between a married and a single person, between two married persons, and lechery between a husband and his own wife, and so it equates with branches five and six in the *Somme*-derived texts. *Fasciculus Morum*'s second branch, *stuprum*, maps onto the fourth branch in the other tradition. And *Fasciculus Morum*'s first branch of *fornicacio* encompasses branches one to three in the *Somme*-derived texts.

The first four degrees in the *Somme*-derived texts are explored further below, but it is worth briefly explaining my reading of *Fasciculus Morum*'s first branch, as this is the one that is key to Karras's argument: 'we must understand that while fornication is any forbidden sexual intercourse, it particularly refers to intercourse with widows, prostitutes, or concubines. But the term "prostitute" must be applied only to those women who give themselves to anyone and will refuse none, and that for monetary gain.'[43] It is of this passage that Karras has commented, 'there is no place for a singlewoman who is no longer a virgin. The only category for her is either concubine, a term that indicates the domestic partner of a priest, or *meretrix*, which would conflate her with the commercial prostitute'.[44] While it is true that there is no other category for the single woman in this text, *Fasciculus Morum* does not actually rule out the existence of unmarried women who are not widows, concubines,

[42] *Fasciculus Morum: A Fourteenth-Century Preacher's Handbook*, ed. and trans. S. Wenzel (University Park, PA: Pennsylvania State University Press, 1989), pp. 666–89. Wenzel argues that the text follows the model of *Summa de vitiis et virtutibus* by the 13th century Dominican William Peraldus: Wenzel, *Verses in Sermons*, p. 10.

[43] 'sciendum quod licet fornicacio sit illicitus cohitus, <speci>aliter tamen intelligitur in usu viduarum aut meretricium vel concubinarum. Set hoc nomine meretricum non debent mulieres appellari nisi ille tantum que se universaliter omnibus exponunt, et hoc propter lucrum, nec aliquem abnegare volunt': *Fasciculus Morum*, ed. Wenzel, pp. 668–9 (the translation is Wenzel's).

[44] Karras, 'Sex and the Singlewoman', p. 129.

Table 2.1: The branches of lechery in two different traditions

Fasciculus Morum	*Somme le Roi and derivative texts*
1. *fornicacio*	Between
	1. a man and a woman not bound by a vow
	2. a single man and a common woman
	3. a single man and a vowed widow
2. *stuprum*	Between
	4. a single man and a virgin
3. *adulterium*	Between
	5. a single man and a married woman (if both married, double the sin)
	6. a man and his own wife
4. *incestus*	Between
	7. spiritual kin (ties created at baptism)
	8. a man and his blood kin
	9. a man and his wife's kin
	10. a woman and a man in holy orders
	11. a secular man and a woman of religion
	12. a man of religion and a woman of religion
	13. a woman and a prelate
5. *sodomia*	14. sodomy or 'sin against kind'

Sources: *Fasciculus Morum*, ed. Wenzel, pp. 666–89; *Book for a Simple and Devout Woman*, ed. Diekstra, p. 400; *Dan Michel's* Ayenbite, ed. Morris and rev. Gradon, i, pp. 48–9; *Book of Vices*, ed. Francis, pp. 44–6; *Myrour*, ed. Nelson, pp. 165–7; Smeltz, 'Speculum Vitae', pp. 440–9; *Jacob's Well*, ed. Brandeis, pp. 160–2.

or prostitutes, but states that this type of lechery 'particularly' (<*speci*> *aliter*) concerns widows, concubines, or prostitutes. Other unmarried women who do not fall into these categories are not excluded but rather do not merit the same attention. Furthermore, the quotation makes clear that the term *meretrix* refers to the commercial prostitute only and thus should not be applied to other sexually-active women. *Fasciculus Morum* presents fornication, defined as 'any forbidden sexual intercourse', as a residual category that includes any sexual activity not covered by the other four branches of lechery. This analysis modifies Karras's argument in that it suggests that while *Fasciculus Morum* did not have a classificatory category for never-married, sexually-active women, it perhaps did have a conceptual space. Nevertheless, a text that defines the first degree of lechery in relation to the category 'single woman', such as *Jacob's Well*, draws attention to the group of women who fall into that category, even if it is the lowest degree of active lechery.

Texts in the *Somme*-tradition largely classify active lechery according to the status of the participants. While the focus is on sexual sin, a concern to be all-encompassing and set out a schema which would apply to anyone confessing to the sin of lechery means that the division of active lechery into fourteen degrees can be read as an interpretive scheme. The classification of society, and specifically of women, is a by-product of the classification of the sin but it is not an insignificant one. The categories 'maid' and 'widow' acquired strong associations with virginity and chastity, largely through their use in a religious discourse of chastity.[45] In this tradition of discussing sexual sin, the category 'single woman' acquires an association with prior sexual activity through its use in relation to a definition of simple fornication.

FOURTEEN DEGREES OF ACTIVE LECHERY

In the first level of *Jacob's Well*, the single man and single woman are described in the same way: 'þe firste fote depthe is betwen syngle man & syngle womman, þat are noȝt bounde be þe lawe to þe bonde of maryage, ne to ordre, ne to relygioun'.[46] This is a negative definition; the single man and woman are those who are *not* legally bound to another, either to a husband or wife or to God and the Church ('noȝt . . . ne . . . ne'). The primary concern of the writer is bonds of marriage or vows, and 'singledom' is a categorization that emerges from that concern. The definition functions as an explanation of why their act of lechery only merits the first degree of sin. It specifically excludes the married (the fifth level), and those in holy orders (the tenth), and other religious (levels eleven to thirteen). Its positioning as the first level, though, also means that, following the logic of the text, it excludes any who fall into a deeper level. It is this factor that means the single woman of the first level is not just the female equivalent of the single man of the first level. In *Jacob's Well* the category 'syngle man' is used for the first five levels and it is the woman who changes the degree by her status, as single woman, common woman, widow, maiden, and wife.[47] Although the

---

[45] See Ch. 1, 'Clean maids' above.

[46] *Jacob's Well*, ed. Brandeis, p. 160, ll. 8–10.

[47] Although it is *explicitly* the woman's status that increases the sin in the lower degrees, the language used generally does suggest an act *between* two people, rather than something that is done by the man to the woman, in contrast to some other pastoral

'wyif' of the fifth degree is self-evidently a married woman (the text refers to breaking the faith of marriage), one needs to understand to whom levels two to four refer in order to comprehend fully who is the single woman in this text.

The contention is that in *Jacob's Well* 'mayden' and 'wydewe' are not the life-stage categories of young, unmarried woman and woman who has lost her husband, but rather denote the more specific attributes of virginity and vowed chastity. The concern for chaste states creates the category of 'syngle womman' by default; commercial prostitutes, as in *Fasciculus Morum*, are also separated out, with the term 'comoun womman' referring to she 'þat leuyth by here body'.[48] The 'syngle womman' of the first degree is a residual category for unmarried women who are not virgins, commercial prostitutes, or vowed to chastity. She is not a whore, then, but she has been sexually active prior to the act of lechery that was to be classified according to this schema. This argument can be supported with reference to other *Somme*-derived texts. As illustrated above, all the *Somme*-derived texts set out fourteen degrees of lechery in a particular order. The texts, though, were translated, copied, or adapted from various sources and some explain the degrees in different ways or, where they were working from French rather than Middle English sources, translate categories differently. *Speculum Vitae* and the *Myrour*, for example, use very similar categories in the first four degrees but might elaborate on them differently, whereas *Ayenbite* describes the fourth branch as 'wiþ sengle wifman'.[49] Such differences are explored below as they not only illustrate that categories do not have

---

manuals; e.g. in *Jacob's Well*'s discussion of the fourth level it is said that 'more is þe synne to him *or to here* þat brekyth' the state of maidenhood. Its sixth level begins by defining it as 'whanne a man delyth with his wyif', but then has a caution to those who 'vse þi wyif *or þin husbonde* as þi lemman', solely for lust. Some of the other *Somme*-derived texts allow for further gender reversals; e.g. the third degree of *Ayenbite* is said to be 'of man single mi wodewe. oþer ayeward', a translation of *Somme le Roi*'s 'ou la reverse'. In Caxton's *Ryal Book* this is spelt out as 'of the man single with a wydowe or the reverse. That is a widower with a single woman'. Similarly, in the *Myrour* it is said that the fifth degree is 'bytwene a single man & another mannes wyf or bytwene a [wedded] man and anoþer sengil woman'. See *Jacob's Well*, ed. Brandeis, p. 161, ll. 19, 27–8 (my italics); *Dan Michel's* Ayenbite, ed. Morris and Gradon, i, p. 48; *Book for a Simple and Devout Woman*, ed. Diekstra, p. 395; W. Caxton, *The book was compiled [and] made atte requeste of kynge Phelyp of Fraunce* (Westminster: William Caxton, 1485; STC (2nd edn.) 21429), ch. 48, EEBO <http://gateway.proquest.com/openurl?ctx_ver=Z39.88–2003&res_id=xri:eebo &rft_id=xri:eebo:image:9643:38> (16 July 2005); *Myrour*, ed. Nelson, p. 165, ll. 18–19. Cf. Murray, 'Absent Penitent', pp. 20–1.

48 *Jacob's Well*, ed. Brandeis, p. 160, l. 13.
49 *Dan Michel's* Ayenbite, ed. Morris and Gradon, i, p. 48.

fixed meanings, but also how they acquire meaning, and how they can accrue particular associations which make them more likely to be used in some contexts rather than in others.

Jacob's Well's third level of lechery does not refer to all widows but only includes widows who have taken a vow of chastity: 'þe iij. fote depthe of þis wose in dede of leccherye is betwen' syngle [man] and wydewe, þat is vowyd chast'.[50] As the fourteen levels aim to encompass every person who might commit the sin of lechery, it follows from this that the 'syngle womman' of the first level includes those widows not included in the third level, that is, the (vast majority of) widows who have not taken vows to live chaste. The descriptions in *Speculum Vitae* and the *Myrour* do not vary much from that in *Jacob's Well*, whereas the *Book of Vices* sets out the third branch as 'a man vnbounde wi a woman bounde bi a vow'.[51] In all these texts it is the woman's vow which renders the couple's act of lechery the third degree, rather than the first. While this reading is less immediately apparent in *Ayenbite*, which sets out the third branch as 'of man sengle mid wodewe',[52] the first branch of *Ayenbite* specifically excludes those who are *vowed* to widowhood: 'habbeþ nenne bend [bond]. ne of wodewehod'.[53] Other widows, then, could also be encompassed in *Ayenbite's* first branch.

The 'maiden' in *Jacob's Well's* fourth level of lechery similarly does not refer to all young, unmarried women, but specifically to virgins. This is indicated by the explanation of why lechery between a single man and a 'mayden' is the fourth degree: because 'for to þe state of maydenhod clene folowyth most mede, ʒif it be kept, and þe more

---

[50] *Jacob's Well*, ed. Brandeis, p. 160, ll. 17–18. Cf. the argument that in the early middle ages *vidua* usually denoted vowesses only, rather than all widows: Jussen, 'On Church Organisation', p. 32; Crick, 'Men, Women and Widows', pp. 34–6.

[51] Smeltz, 'Speculum Vitae', p. 442, ll. 9576–8; *Myrour*, ed. Nelson, p. 165, ll. 12–13; *Book of Vices*, ed. Francis, p. 44, ll. 30–1.

[52] *Dan Michel's* Ayenbite, ed. Morris and Gradon, i, p. 48. The differences between the texts might have stemmed from different sources, or differing readings and translations of *Somme le Roi*. According to Diekstra, the third branch in *Somme le Roi* is of 'd'omme deslié a fame veve' and she cites this as the source for the third branch of lechery in a *Book for a Simple and Devout Woman* (*c.* 1400), which describes it as 'wiþ wodewes': *Book for a Simple and Devout Woman*, ed. Diekstra, pp. 395 and 215, l. 4573. As u's and v's were often interchangeable, though, it also makes sense as *fame veue* (a vowed woman).

[53] *Dan Michel's* Ayenbite, ed. Morris and Gradon, i, p. 48. 'Bend' is the Old English word which becomes the Middle English 'bond' meaning 'a (binding) promise': *MED*, bond (n.) 3(a).

is þe synne to him or to here þat brekyth it'.[54] The woman is in 'the state of clean maidenhood'. The reference to 'mede' is perhaps an allusion to the hundredfold reward such a woman was held to receive if she retained her virginity until death, as compared with the sixtyfold reward for the chaste widowed, and the thirtyfold reward for the chaste married.[55] What is important in this context, though, is the sin: the loss of virginity. *Speculum Vitae* and the *Myrour* also use the adjective 'clene' in association with the term 'maide' or 'mayden' in their fourth degrees.[56] *Somme le Roi*, the *Book of Vices*, and *Ayenbite* are less explicit as to who is included in the fourth degree and why. *Somme le Roi* sets it out simply as 'est a pucele', and the *Book of Vices* as 'wiþ a mayde', whereas *Ayenbite* describes the fourth degree as 'wiþ sengle wifman'.[57] The latter example might appear to be a radical departure from the other Middle English texts, which use the category 'single woman' in the first degree only (with the exception of the *Book of Vices* which does not use the category), but it actually serves to support the argument that the meanings of categories are relatively fluid, with meaning often supplied by context. One reads loss of virginity into all these descriptions of the fourth degree from the context, that this act of lechery is more sinful than that with a vowed widow, the third degree.

All the *Somme*-derived texts are in broad agreement as to what and whom are included in each degree of lechery: the fifth degree refers to adultery; the fourth to loss of virginity; the third to breaking of a vow of chastity; the second to sex with a common woman, and the first to sex between two unmarried people who had made no other vows of chastity. What differs between the texts is what categories they use, if any, in each of these degrees. While *Ayenbite* contains some inaccuracies in its translation of *Somme le Roi*, perhaps due to an imperfect source, it is usually viewed as an overly literal translation.[58] It therefore seems telling that *Somme le Roi*'s *pucele* becomes 'sengle wifman' in *Ayenbite*, whereas in *Speculum Vitae*, for example, it becomes 'a mayden clene'. By using 'sengle wifman' in the fourth branch, *Ayenbite* gives it the meaning of a virginal maiden. Indeed, there is no reason why the category could not

---

[54] *Jacob's Well*, ed. Brandeis, p. 160, ll. 20–2.

[55] See Ch. 1, 'Clean maids' above.

[56] Smeltz, '*Speculum Vitae*', p. 442, l. 9581; *Myrour*, ed. Nelson, p. 165, l. 15.

[57] *Book for a Simple and Devout Woman*, ed. Diekstra, p. 395; *Book of Vices*, ed. Francis, p. 44, l. 31; *Dan Michel's* Ayenbite, ed. Morris and Gradon, i, p. 48.

[58] See Raymo, 'Works', p. 2259. Nelson argues that *Ayenbite* contains fewer inaccuracies than the *Book of Vices: Myrour*, ed. Nelson, p. 16.

ST CHARLES COMMUNITY COLLEGE LIBRARY
WITHDRAWN

have this meaning, in the same way that *pucelle* and 'maid' have the dual meanings of young, unmarried woman and virgin.[59] It is rather that 'maid' more typically has that association and *Ayenbite* is thus departing from convention.

The use of 'sengle wifman' in *Ayenbite* (*c.* 1340) is one of the earliest written examples of the Middle English term.[60] Its use in the first degree of lechery in *Speculum Vitae* (*c.* 1349–84) was not much later in date, though; similarly, the *Lay Folks' Catechism* (1357) uses the variant 'aynlepi woman' in its discussion of fornication.[61] The association of the category 'single woman' with simple fornication, though, predates the vernacular texts. Although *Somme le Roi* did not use any categories in its discussion of the first level, earlier Latin texts did. Payer traces to the twelfth century an interest in naming and defining the sin of heterosexual intercourse between two unmarried lay people, with the penitential of Bartholomew of Exeter being one of the earliest to use the expression 'De simplici fornicatione'.[62] The definitions of simple fornication in some Latin texts, for example in a *summa* attributed to Alexander of Hales (1245), bear comparison with the later vernacular discussions. Hales's *summa* sets out that fornication is between 'solutus et soluta', and goes on to explain that this refers to sexual intercourse between a man and a woman free from ties of marriage, consanguinity, affinity, order, religion, or vows of continence; *solutus* and *soluta* have the potential meaning of 'free' as well as 'single'.[63] Again the primary concern of the writer is with bonds of marriage, kinship or vows, but categorization emerges from that concern. The use of the terms 'single man' and 'single woman' in the mid fourteenth century was presumably

---

[59] On the terms *pucelle* and 'maiden', see Taylor (ed.), *Joan of Arc*, pp. 47–8; Stoertz, 'Young Women', p. 24.

[60] Although this usage is not in the *MED*: single (adj.) 2.

[61] *The Lay Folks' Catechism*, ed. T. F. Simmons and H. E. Nolloth, EETS, o.s. 118 (London: K. Paul, Trench, Trübner & Co., 1901), p. 94, l. 547; for this adjective, see *MED*, on-lepi (adj.) (d). It is a term that merits further discussion, but is beyond the scope of this book. See e.g. G. C. Homans, *English Villagers of the Thirteenth Century* (New York, NY: Norton, 1941), pp. 136–7.

[62] Payer, 'Confession and the Study of Sex', pp. 6, 13. See A. Morey, *Bartholomew of Exeter, Bishop and Canonist: A Study in the Twelfth Century* (Cambridge: Cambridge University Press, 1937), p. 237.

[63] 'Est autem fornicatio luxuria, qua solutus solutam naturali usu cognoscit; et intelligitur solutus et soluta a vinculo coniugii, et consanguinitatis, et affinitatis, ordinis, religionis, vel voti continentiae': quoted in Payer, 'Confession and the Study of Sex', p. 23 n. 58, and see the discussion in ibid., p. 13 for other examples. See also Thomas de Chobham, *Thomae de Chobham summa confessorum*, ed. F. Broomfield (Louvain: Béatrice Nauwelaerts, [1968]), p. 341.

more to do with an increase in texts in Middle English, than to any demographic developments.[64] The earlier Anglo-Norman *Manuel des péchés*, for example, uses the term *femme hors d'espusage* in its discussion of the sin of simple fornication.[65]

Although one has to be wary of assuming that a category that arises in one context would have the same meaning in another context, categorization in vernacular texts, which were intended for broader dissemination than the Latin *summae*, in a language that was in common currency, is more likely to have had an effect on day-to-day language uses than categorization in the earlier Latin texts. That effect has to be demonstrated, though, rather than assumed. There is some evidence, for example, that categorizing sex between a single man and a single woman as the lowest degree of lechery had some impact, at the very least on the authors of such manuals who proclaimed that it increased the lay argument that such an act was not a deadly sin.[66] This also signals that the intentions of a text might differ from its effects.

The use of the category 'single woman' in the discussions of lechery can also be compared with its use in the discussions of chastity in the *Somme*-derived texts. Most of these texts set out seven branches of chastity, defined by the person's state of chastity, and so the divisions can also be read as an interpretive scheme. In the discussions of chastity the category is used to denote a different group of women to its general use in the first degree of active lechery (as we have already seen from *Ayenbite*, the meaning of the term 'single woman' could shift). Whereas the 'single woman' of the first degree of lechery might be a widow, the 'single woman' in the discussions of chastity is never

---

[64] Cf. R. M. Karras, 'Two Models, Two Standards: Moral Teaching and Sexual Mores', in B. A. Hanawalt and D. Wallace (eds.), *Bodies and Disciplines: Intersections of Literature and History in Fifteenth-Century England* (Minneapolis, MN: University of Minnesota Press, 1996), p. 133, which attempts to link concern for the sexual activity of unmarried women with demographic patterns.

[65] See *Robert of Brunne's* Handlyng Synne, ed. Furnivall, p. 235, l. 5863. Furnivall was using as a base manuscript Harley 4957 which is dated *c.* 1300–25: see E. J. Arnould, *Le Manual des péchés: etude de literature religieuse anglo-normande (XIIIᵐᵉ siècle)* (Paris: Librairie E. Droz, 1940), pp. 365–7.

[66] Payer again traces this contention back to Bartholomew's penitential. Karras, though, argues that the debate about the sinfulness of fornication in the early 15th-century treatise *Dives and Pauper*, between a worldly layman and a friar, suggests that such questioning was now more widespread and 'that there was an articulated lay point of view against the church's teaching'. See Payer, 'Confession and the Study of Sex', p. 13; Karras, 'Two Models', p. 127. See also J. F. Dedek, 'Premarital Sex: The Theological Argument from Peter Lombard to Durand', *Theological Studies*, 41 (1980), 643–67.

married only. The similarity, though, is that it again refers to a group of women who have been sexually active prior to this classification. The discussions of chastity also strive to be all-encompassing and as will be shown those who have sinned are an important group in a penitential discourse.

SEVEN STATES OF CHASTITY

Jacob's Well's discussion of lechery's opposing virtue, chastity, differs both from its treatment of lechery and from the discussions of chastity by other texts in the *Somme*-tradition in significant ways. In *Jacob's Well*, the chastity of married persons is discussed first with the next chapter relating to the widowed and then virgins (of both sexes). The following chapter discusses virgins and the continence of those in holy orders, before a fourth chapter discusses the virtue of chastity generally.[67] However, in other *Somme*-derived texts, namely *Ayenbite*, the *Book of Vices*, *Speculum Vitae*, and the *Myrour*, chastity is discussed in a more schematic way, akin to their treatments of lechery and again *Speculum Vitae* and the *Myrour* use the category 'single woman'.[68] In all these texts chastity is first divided into seven degrees, which relate to how one might avoid lechery, such as by avoiding evil company. Then, it is divided into seven branches, which are the 'states' of men and women that live in chastity:

1. virgins until marriage
2. the never married who are not virgins
3. the married
4. the widowed
5. life-long virgins
6. clerks in holy orders
7. men (and sometimes women) of religion.[69]

[67] See the headings for chapters 56–9 in *Jacob's Well*, ed. Brandeis, p. xv. I am indebted to Professor P. H. Barnum for sending me her unpublished transcription of MS Salisbury Cathedral 103, fos. 114v–123r.

[68] *Myrour*, ed. Nelson, p. 184, ll. 22–3. In *Speculum Vitae* the term used is 'woman anelopy': Smeltz, '*Speculum Vitae*', p. 507, l. 11311; see n. 61 above.

[69] See *Dan Michel's* Ayenbite, ed. Morris and Gradon, i, pp. 202–45; *Book of Vices*, ed. Francis, pp. 223–72; Smeltz, '*Speculum Vitae*', pp. 506–87; *Myrour*, ed. Nelson, pp. 167–204.

The category 'single woman' is used in the descriptions of the second branch in *Speculum Vitae* and the *Myrour*. Its meaning appears more straightforward than it did in the discussions of lechery. For example, the *Myrour*'s description of the second branch makes explicit whom it encompasses: 'Þe secounde estate is of hem þat haueþ be corupt & defouled wiþ þe syne of leccherie & loste her maydenhode, as sengil man or sengil woman þat neuer was wedded, ne neuer so bounde to chastite þat þei ne may be wedded, and haueþ in herte forþinkyng for her synne, & beþ schryuen & haueþ done her penaunce, & kepeþ hem forward in clennesse & chastite'.[70] The 'sengil woman' is a never-married woman who is not a virgin, has not taken a vow of chastity, but has repented of her lechery and been shriven. The discussions of chastity, therefore, offer a conceptual space for never-married women who have been sexually active, and thus they revise Karras's thesis further.

The group marked out by the category 'single woman' in the discussions of chastity in *Speculum Vitae* and the *Myrour* differs to that marked out by the category in the discussions of lechery in the same texts, in that this group are never married only. In order to deduce why such a group is marked out, and given its own branch along with men of the same status, the second branch must therefore be considered in relation to the other six. One of the key ways in which the discussions of chastity differ from those of lechery is that in each branch (with the exception of the seventh branch in *Speculum Vitae* and the *Myrour*) men and women are discussed together as of the same 'state'.[71] There was a long tradition of discussing the states of chastity as applying equally to both men and women.[72] Indeed, the traditional hierarchical ordering of chastity as virgins-widows-spouses is perhaps in evidence here. The discussions do not make explicit whether the branches of chastity should be read as an ordering in terms of merit from lowest

[70] *Myrour*, ed. Nelson, p. 184, ll. 21–6. Although *Speculum Vitae* is the text with the greatest circulation, quotations are from the *Myrour* in general because it lends itself to more concise quotations and is available in a critical edition.

[71] That these texts limit the seventh branch to religious men, suggests that the fifth branch includes religious women (although the *Book of Vices* does include them in the seventh, and *Ayenbite* does not exclude them). This separation of virginity from the religious, who might instead be seen as continent, was also adopted in *Jacob's Well*. See *Myrour*, ed. Nelson, p. 184, l. 15, p. 199, ll. 10–11; Smeltz, '*Speculum Vitae*', p. 506, l. 11, 196; *Book of Vices*, ed. Francis, p. 264, l. 3; *Dan Michel's* Ayenbite, ed. Morris and Gradon, i, p. 238; MS Salisbury Cathedral 103, fos. 119v–122v.

[72] See Ch. 1, 'Clean maids' above.

to highest, in the way that the discussions of lechery did in terms of sinfulness, yet there are indications that the ordering has at least some hierarchical elements.

According to the *Myrour*, the sixth and seventh branches relate to the holy orders, with the seventh referring to 'þe holynesse & perfeccioun' of the state and thus 'þe fouler is her [their] synne' if their vow of chastity was broken.[73] The fifth branch pertains to life-long virginity and contains discussion of the threefold hierarchy of salvation: 'For þei þat lyueþ in clene mariage schal haue þere [fruyte þritty-fold], and þei þat kepeþ clene wydowhode schal haue þere fruyt sixty-fold; but þei þat kepeþ clene maydenhode schall haue fruyte an hondred-fold.'[74] The hundredfold reward evidently relates to those virgins in the fifth branch, those who intended to 'kepeþ' their virginity; the fourth branch does refer to those who intend to live in chaste widowhood; and the third branch concerns the chaste married. However, the first to fourth branches can be seen as subdivisions of the married, with a life-stage ordering, as the fourth branch also discusses widows who might remarry and the first and second branches pertain to those who might marry in the future. The 'widow' differs from its vowed counterpart in the discussions of lechery in that it also refers to any person who had lost a spouse (including males). The discussion of the second branch, as we have seen, also notes that such men and women could marry, as they had not taken a vow of perpetual chastity. And the first branch of chastity concerns those who intended to remain virgins until marriage: 'The firste estate is of maydenes þat kepeþ hem clene and þenkiþ do so forto þei be weddid . . . But ȝit þei beth free of hemself to be wedded lefulliche'.[75]

One might compare the ordering of the first three branches with that of the degrees of virginity in the late thirteenth-century pastoral manual *La Compileison*, in which it was stated that the virgin who intended to marry had a lower degree before God than the chaste married woman as 'she does not know whom she wishes to have and the woman who is married does not seek anyone other than him to whom she is joined'.[76] While the *Myrour* has little to say about the first branch, *Ayenbite* and the *Book of Vices* go on to discuss this

---

[73] *Myrour to Lewde Men*, ed. Nelson, p. 199, ll. 2–7.   [74] Ibid., p. 195, ll. 34–7.
[75] *Myrour*, ed. Nelson, p. 184, ll. 16–20. The language of 'maidenhood' was sometimes applied to males: see Salih, *Versions of Virginity*, p. 16.
[76] Wogan-Browne, *Saints' Lives and Women's Literary Culture*, p. 45; discussed in Ch. 1, 'Clean maids' above.

virginity as pertaining to children;[77] perhaps there is also a parallel here with Albertus Magnus's first type of virginity, the innate virginity of infants before the age of reason, which had 'bodily fairness' but was not worthy of praise.[78] The *Book of Vices*, for example, warns that such children should be taught well and kept away from bad company who might teach them things, such as 'folie handelynges and felynges', that lead to lechery, even lechery 'a ӡens kynde' (that is, the fourteenth degree of lechery).[79] In these discussions, then, there is a fear that virginity might not be preserved until marriage. The *Myrour*, in its discussion of the fifth branch, quotes Jerome as having written that 'maydenhode of body is medeles & noght worth when þe herte is corrupte wiþynne wiþ foule þoghtes & vnclene desires'.[80] In the description of the fifth branch in the *Book of Vices*, Jerome is also credited with the assertion that 'virginite of þe body is nouӡt worþ to haue, who-so haþ wille to be maryed'.[81] Rather than putting a premium on virginity per se, as in the discussions of lechery, the emphasis here is on resolve. These statements perhaps allow for the second branch to be seen as higher than the first. In the second branch, although the men and women had experienced sex, they had also subsequently taken a decision to be chaste, at least until marriage.[82]

Whether the second branch is higher than the first or not, it clearly has an important function in a discourse which wants to stress repentance and redemption. The never-married man or woman who confessed to an act of lechery could be rehabilitated in this branch in the discussions of chastity. In the discussions of the second branch, reference is made to contrition ('haue in herte forþinkyng for her synne'), confession ('beþ schryuen'), and penance. While *Jacob's Well* does not discuss such a group in its treatment of chastity, it does include a number of *exempla* with a similar message, which lend support to the argument that the

---

[77] *Dan Michel's* Ayenbite, ed. Morris and Gradon, i, p. 220; *Book of Vices*, ed. Francis, pp. 243–4.

[78] Payer, *Bridling of Desire*, p. 162; discussed in Ch. 1, 'Clean maids' above.

[79] *Book of Vices*, ed. Francis, p. 244, ll. 5–6, 8.

[80] *Myrour*, ed. Nelson, p. 192, ll. 2–4.

[81] *Book of Vices*, ed. Francis, p. 255, ll. 32–3; cf. *Myrour*, ed. Nelson, p. 193, ll. 14–19.

[82] Cf. the Middle English treatise *Of Maydenhede* (*c.* 1450), which claims that those who intended to be virgins for ever will receive the hundredfold reward even if raped, as long as they 'sufferen aӡeynes her wille'. As Evans comments on this, '[b]odily intactness is less important than the will to remain chaste': Evans, 'Virginities', p. 27.

sexually-active single woman could have a useful place in a penitential discourse.

Jacob's Well discusses contrition, confession, and satisfaction immediately after the seventh sin of lechery (these, together with absolution, make up the sacramental definition of penance).[83] In the section on contrition all three *exempla* concern acts of lechery, such as the story of an incestuous daughter who murdered her father and became a prostitute. She died of a broken heart after a sermon moved her to sorrow for her sins, and a tree arose from her grave bearing the message that she had been forgiven her sins.[84] Similarly, in the brief discussion of contrition, confession, and satisfaction, which is included in *Jacob's Well* before consideration of the sins, one of the two *exempla* concerns an incestuous mother.[85] This miracle of the Virgin Mary tells the story of a gentle woman in Rome who was made pregnant by her son, and then killed the newborn child. She was contrite, undertook deeds of penance, and made restitution of her wrongs, but had not been shriven of her sin, that is, she had not confessed. A fiend, disguised as a clerk, publicly accused her of incest and murder. At this point, the woman went to a priest, 'wyth full sorwe of herte & wepyng', and confessed. The priest gave her a penance of reciting a Pater Noster and various Ave Marias, which she undertook, with the result that the fiend on next seeing her exclaimed, 'It is noȝt þis woman þat I haue accusyd; þis woman is holy, and marie kepith here'. The fiend vanished and the woman was regarded with 'hyȝ worschype' and was now 'clene' of her previous sins.[86] The message of such stories was that any sinner could redeem herself or himself from the category of sinner through contrition, confession, and satisfaction, but the text predominantly chose to use examples of those who had sinned sexually to make this point.[87] The 'single woman' in the other *Somme*-derived discussions of chastity, then, was a key group in such a context.

---

[83] *Jacob's Well*, ed. Brandeis, pp. 168–99; satisfaction is described as doing penance, paying one's debts, making amends for any harm done, and undertaking never to turn to sin again. Restitution is also elaborated on: ibid., pp. 199–216.

[84] Ibid., pp. 172–3. Wogan-Browne comments how the stories of repentant harlots made 'viable þe spirituality of the honorary virgin', while allowing a measure of restored virginity to women who have had to postpone celibacy': Wogan-Browne, *Saints' Lives and Women's Literary Culture*, p. 137.

[85] *Jacob's Well*, ed. Brandeis, pp. 64–8.   [86] Ibid., pp. 66–7.

[87] Copeland comments on how stories also 'offer the penitent a certain relief from the pervasive control of the penitential system itself': Woods and Copeland, 'Classroom and Confession', p. 396.

A penitential discourse classifies sin according to various criteria so that an appropriate penance can be assigned, one of these being according to the status of the confessant and the status of any other person also affected by the sin. It therefore has an interest in being all-encompassing. These sinners, once they had confessed and been penitent, ideally needed a place in a schema setting out how virtuous different types of people were, what their reward in heaven might be and, more importantly, what the consequences were of the loss of virtue, in this case chastity. The 'single woman' thus performed a different function in discussions of chastity to those of lechery, albeit still an important one, and actually denoted a slightly different group of women. This chapter has focussed on a tradition of discussing sexual sin that distinguished between the sexually-active, unmarried woman and the commercial prostitute, with the category 'single woman' being used to denote the former group in *Jacob's Well, Speculum Vitae*, and the *Myrour*. In *Speculum Vitae* and the *Myrour* the category 'single woman' is used again in the discussions of chastity. Here she is not equated with the whore, but the 'single woman' does take on some of the functions that the repentant prostitute fulfils in other religious texts. The 'single woman' thus emerges *differently* as a category depending upon the context and purpose of a particular discourse. It is not easily reducible to a pre-given category, but is an emergent identity within these texts. *Ayenbite*'s discussion of lechery reinforces this point by using the term 'sengle wifman' as a translation of *Somme le Roi*'s *pucele* in the fourth degree of lechery, which usually refers to the loss of virginity in this tradition. For one author, it seems that 'single woman' could have the associations of virginity that are normally linked with the maiden as a young, unmarried woman.

3

The Single Woman in Fiscal Discourse

It is generally held that the catalyst for the Peasants' Revolt of 1381 was the arrival of a royal commission in Brentwood, Essex to assess evasion of the poll tax granted in 1380, the third such levy since 1377.[1] These taxes, levied to help pay for England's war with France, shifted the basis of taxation from property to the individual. Yet, less well known is the story told in the chronicle of Henry Knighton, an Augustinian canon in Leicester, of how some commissioners attempted to extract the tax:

When one of them came to a village to inquire into the tax, he would assemble the men and women before him, and horrible to relate, would shamelessly raise the young girls' [*puellulas*] skirts, to discover whether they were corrupted by intercourse with men, and thus he would compel their friends and parents to pay the tax for them, for many would rather choose to pay than to see their daughters shamefully mistreated. Those and other such actions of the investigators greatly provoked the people.[2]

While this story might well be apocryphal, it can still be usefully examined, as Paul Strohm has argued for chronicles and other texts, 'if not within a sense of what did happen, at least within a sense of what might have happened, of what could be imagined, of what commonly held interpretive structures permitted a late fourteenth-century audience to believe'.[3] This discussion of how tax records conceptualized society, especially unmarried, female taxpayers, begins

---

[1] See e.g. A. Dunn, *The Great Rising of 1381* (Stroud: Tempus, 2002), p. 73; P. J. P. Goldberg, *Medieval England: A Social History, 1250–1550* (London: Arnold, 2004), pp. 174, 180–1, 183–5. See further H. Eiden, 'Joint Action against "Bad" Lordship: The Peasants' Revolt in Essex and Norfolk', *History*, 83 (1998), 11–16.

[2] *Knighton's Chronicle 1337–1396*, ed. G. H. Martin (Oxford: Clarendon Press, 1995), pp. 208–9. This passage was included in R. B. Dobson (ed.), *The Peasants' Revolt of 1381* (London: Macmillan, 1970), p. 135, and now in Goldberg, *Medieval England*, p. 185.

[3] P. Strohm, *Hochon's Arrow: The Social Imagination of Fourteenth-Century Texts* (Princeton, NJ: Princeton University Press, 1992), p. 3; for a similar approach to chronicle evidence, see W. M. Ormrod, ' "In Bed With Joan of Kent": The King's

with Knighton's vignette because it can be used to exemplify that the classification of individuals by taxation assessors was not a neutral exercise, that different interests were at work in the process, and that how an assessor classified a person could make a material difference.

Knighton's intention was presumably to portray the commissioners, specifically John Legge, one of the king's serjeants-at-arms, and three unnamed men who worked with him, as corrupt and abusive. With the use of the diminutive of the term *puella*, Knighton suggests that the girls were indeed young, and therefore under the taxable age of fifteen in 1380–1, but the threat of such shameful treatment was used to make their elders pay for them regardless. Elsewhere he alleges that Legge offered the king money in order to secure the commission of investigating the tax collectors in Kent, Norfolk, and other counties.[4] The implication is that this was a lucrative task. Even if we are sceptical about Knighton's account, the commissioners had a job to do: to collect the money that the Exchequer had calculated was outstanding. There might also have been financial penalties for failing to do the job; a number of the original commissions had been fined in February 1381 for making false returns.[5]

For the taxpayers themselves there were also material consequences: if deemed liable, they had to pay this tax and the amount varied according to their means, as determined by the assessors. In Knighton's account, the commissioners investigating evasion focused on the young and female and it is possible to deduce a different logic from their behaviour to that suggested by the chronicler. There are low proportions of unmarried, female taxpayers in the surviving returns but the third tax should have created some new taxpayers from such a group; in 1379 the age criterion was set at sixteen and over, but in 1381 it was from age fifteen and so those who were aged thirteen to fifteen in 1379

Mother and the Peasants' Revolt', in J. Wogan-Browne *et al.* (eds.), *Medieval Women: Texts and Contexts in Late Medieval Britain* (Turnhout: Brepols, 2000), pp. 277–92.

[4] *Knighton's Chronicle*, ed. Martin, pp. 206–9.

[5] C. C. Fenwick (ed.), *The Poll Taxes of 1377, 1379 and 1381*, Records of Social and Economic History, new ser., 3 vols. (Oxford: Oxford University Press for the British Academy, 1998–2006), i, p. xvii. The *Anonimalle Chronicle* suggests that the original collectors had not levied the rich, to their own 'great profit and advantage': Dobson (ed.), *Peasants' Revolt*, pp. 123–4 (p. 123); *The Anonimalle Chronicle, 1333 to 1381*, ed. V. H. Galbraith (Manchester: Manchester University Press, 1927), p. 134. Akin to Knighton, this Chronicle attributes the outbreak of the revolt in Essex to the corrupt activities of poll tax commissioners. On John Legge in particular, see Dobson (ed.), *Peasants' Revolt*, p. 126; *Anonimalle Chronicle*, ed. Galbraith, p. 136.

would now have been liable.[6] Some unmarried women would have been genuinely exempt on the grounds of poverty, particularly in smaller vills where paid employment was agricultural, seasonal, and mostly for men.[7] The low proportion of unmarried women in the returns might have been noticed and treated with suspicion at the time by the reassessment commissions. One purpose of the apparent 'virginity test' could have been to ascertain if the young girls who had not yet been taxed were over the age of fifteen and so potentially liable.[8] This is not to suggest that the commissioners were intimately examining the girls to surmise their ages, but rather to hypothesize that there might have been some logic behind commissioners calling such girls before them to deduce how old they might have been. It was not uncommon in the late medieval period, as there was no official system for recording births until the sixteenth century, for age to be inferred from physical appearance.[9] It was probably more difficult for sub-collectors to be sure if a young female was of age than a young male, as the latter had to join a tithing group at age twelve.[10]

A third set of interests must also be considered: those of the local community. In Knighton's account, the commissioners gathered the men and women of the village to watch the examination and some felt shamed into paying the tax for the girls. Some local men actually had a more formal role in the process of tax assessment and collection. Usually it was the constable and two other men from every taxation area who were called upon to provide the original commissions with information about individuals, from which the lists of taxpayers were drawn up, and

[6] Fenwick (ed.), *Poll Taxes*, i, p. xxiii. On the under-enumeration of unmarried women in the 1381 returns in particular, see Poos, *Rural Society*, pp. 152, 188, 297.

[7] Fenwick (ed.), *Poll Taxes*, i, pp. xxiii–iv. Goldberg argues that the low numbers might also reflect greater migration of women than men from rural districts into towns: P. J. P. Goldberg, 'Urban Identity and the Poll Taxes of 1377, 1379, and 1381', *Economic History Review*, new ser., 43 (1990), p. 197.

[8] Federico, who discusses this passage, argues that the commissioners were searching for married women but this does not explain the logic of the examination as all women, married or single, were liable for the tax count, as they had been in 1377: S. Federico, 'The Imaginary Society: Women in 1381', *Journal of British Studies*, 40 (2001), pp. 178–9. My initial thoughts on the Knighton passage were formed before publication of Federico's essay: C. Beattie, 'Meanings of Singleness: The Single Woman in Late Medieval England', D.Phil. thesis (York, 2001), p. 83 n. 116.

[9] See Phillips, *Medieval Maidens*, pp. 24–30. For an e.g., see P. J. P. Goldberg (ed.), *Women in England c.1275–1525* (Manchester: Manchester University Press, 1995), pp. 62, 61. See also S. S. Walker, 'Proof of Age of Feudal Heirs in Medieval England', *Mediaeval Studies*, 35 (1973), p. 307 n. 3.

[10] Poos, *Rural Society*, p. 297. On the tithing system see ibid., pp. 91–2.

to carry out the door-to-door collection of the tax.[11] When suspicions were first raised in early 1381 about the honesty of the collection, sheriffs and escheators were ordered to draw up their own lists of who was liable and to report separately to the Exchequer.[12] Like the commissioners, local officials had to answer to the Crown but, as Carolyn Fenwick points out, it is likely that they helped their neighbours by ignoring those on the borderline of exemption. Her logic is that the 'possibility of potential taxpayers evading or paying less than they should was virtually impossible without the connivance of the local taxers, who had been selected because they knew the number and financial circumstances of their fellow villagers'.[13] Also, as the terms of the 1380–1 tax meant that a taxation area was required to find an average of 1s. per taxpayer, but with the rich paying more than the poor, it was in the interests of everyone in the area to keep the number of taxpayers down.[14]

All of this suggests a two-way relationship between 'real' events and circumstances and the classification of taxpayers in the surviving returns; the first influenced the second, which in turn had an impact beyond the texts created. This chapter argues that nominative tax returns should not only be understood as pragmatic documents, which were created in response to a fiscal demand, but also as value-laden texts, which are revealing of how certain groups conceptualized society and the people within it.[15] It demonstrates this with particular reference to the unmarried, female taxpayer in 1379, by analysing how the category 'single woman' is used in relation to other categories, such as 'widow', 'daughter', or an occupational status.[16] In 1379 the tax was to be levied largely according to a person's 'estate and degree', with the pertinent criteria set out by the Exchequer in a schedule.[17] It is in the returns for this year that marital statuses are most frequently given (because

---

[11] Fenwick (ed.), *Poll Taxes*, i, pp. xix–xx. She also found that many commissioners lived in the areas for which they were responsible: ibid., p. xxvi.

[12] Ibid., pp. xvi–xvii.   [13] Ibid., p. xxvi.

[14] See C. Given-Wilson *et al.* (eds.), *The Parliament Rolls of Medieval England, 1275–1504*, 16 vols. (London: Boydell Press, 2005), vi, pp. 191–2.

[15] Cf. Joan Scott's comment, in relation to statistical reports from mid-nineteenth-century France, that 'we have plucked out the numbers without questioning the categories into which they are arranged, . . . rarely feeling the need to situate the authors of these texts within particular discursive contexts': J. W. Scott, 'A Statistical Representation of Work: *La Statistique de l'Industrie à Paris, 1847–1848*', in J. W. Scott, *Gender and the Politics of History* (New York, NY: Columbia University Press, 1988), pp. 114–15.

[16] The subsidies of 1524–5 are discussed in Ch. 5 below and contribute to an argument about how the use of terms changes over time.

[17] Fenwick (ed.), *Poll Taxes*, i, p. xiv.

married women were not counted as taxpayers in 1379), but there are significant variations in the use of classifications from one taxation area to another and not all the terms employed are ones necessitated by the tax's criteria, which suggest a degree of lexical choice on the part of local assessors. The 1379 return for the borough of Bishop's Lynn in Norfolk has been selected as the primary case study for a number of reasons. First, it classifies virtually all taxpayers by a category that reveals their marital status, either *con'* (*coniugatus*, married), *sol'* (*solus/a*, single), *vidua* (widow), or *puella* (maiden or girl). Second, while a few other returns use some of the same classifications, this is the only extant return to use the term *puella* and its significance in a poll tax return needs to be interrogated.[18] Third, many of the taxpayers in this return are also described by another status, either an occupational designation or a relational one (for example, his/her servant or son or daughter) and this dual classification sheds further light on the relationship between categories. The findings are compared with some other 1379 returns that, through their use of particular terminology, or dual classification, or of two related categories, also enable consideration of the value-laden, choices that assessors made in their classification of unmarried, female taxpayers.

This study maintains that categories can accrue associations through their use in influential cultural discourses with the result that, in other contexts, these associations might (consciously or not) influence the lexical choice of the classifier.[19] It is therefore important that we consider what categories were offered to assessors within a narrower fiscal discourse, in order that we can more readily ascertain the points at which other discourses, which categorize women in other ways, had an effect.

THE SCHEDULE FOR THE 1379 TAX AND THE CLASSIFICATION PROCESS

As Knighton's story illustrated, various groups had a stake in the taxation process. The texts that we can isolate as having had a particular

---

[18] I am grateful to Carolyn Fenwick, who has edited all the poll tax returns, for confirmation on this point (personal communication, July 1998).

[19] See the Introduction and Ch. 1 above, but on the relationship between intent and meaning see also Justice, 'Inquisition', pp. 297–300.

effect on the 1379 returns relate to two of these groups: the Crown and the Exchequer's schedule for the 1379 tax, and local assessors and the 1377 poll tax listings (which appear to have been made use of in 1379). Richard II's third parliament of 24 April to 27 May 1379 granted 'another subsidy to be taken from the goods of certain persons throughout the kingdom', probably in the closing days of the parliament.[20] The King's Exchequer devised the graduated tax, submitted its conditions to parliament for approval, and this schedule is included verbatim (in Anglo-Norman) in the parliamentary rolls. The tax was to be levied on every man and unmarried woman over the age of sixteen, except for genuine paupers. Presumably what led one chronicler to call it 'a subsidy so wonderful [*mervaillous*] that no one had ever seen or heard of the like'[21] was that, rather than being a flat rate tax, it was to be levied according to a person's 'estate and degree and . . . property, lands, rents, possessions, goods and chattels'.[22] The schedule thus maps out the pertinent social and economic distinctions. While the schedule should have had some influence on every 1379 return, the local dimension brought in the potential for varying use of classifications. In 1379 those who drew up the return, the commissioners and other local men, appear to have made use of documents from the 1377 tax collection. The requirements for the first poll tax were different from those set out in the 1379 schedule and any returns drawn up for the former were created for collection purposes, rather than required by the Exchequer, both factors which might have affected the information included.

The schedule offered a variety of categories to assessors. One of the features of the 1379 tax schedule that has attracted modern attention is that it does not simply start with those who should pay the highest amount and proceed down to those who should pay the lowest. The hierarchy of charges is divided into five groups: the first contains the assessments for the nobility; the second, those for the knights hospitaller; the third, the assessments for those who worked in the legal system; the fourth is largely concerned with how much substantial urban burgesses and citizens should pay; and the fifth deals with the assessments of

---

[20] Given-Wilson *et al.* (eds.), *Parliament Rolls*, vi, pp. 114–16; all quotations, in Anglo-Norman and in translation, are from this edition.

[21] Dobson (ed.), *Peasants' Revolt*, p. 106; *Anonimalle Chronicle*, ed. Galbraith, p. 127.

[22] The quotation is from a text naming the collectors in the county of Leicestershire: M. Bateson *et al.* (eds.), *Records of the Borough of Leicester*, 7 vols. ([S.I.], 1899–1974), ii, pp. 186–91 (p. 190); I owe the reference to Fenwick (ed.), *Poll Taxes*, i, p. xiv.

anyone not yet discussed. For example, the first grouping runs from the dukes of Lancaster and Brittany, who were to be assessed at 10 marks each, down to every squire not in possession of lands, rents, or chattels, who was in service or had borne arms, who were to be assessed at 3s. 4d. The second grouping starts with the chief prior of the Hospital of St John, who was to pay 'as much as a baron' (40s.), and continues down to 'all the other brothers of the said order', who were to pay 'as much as a squire without possessions' (3s. 4d.). The fourth grouping begins with the mayor of London who was to pay 'as much as an earl' (£4). The schedule has therefore been discussed as an attempt 'to reschematize the ordering of their changing society', with the focus on how men who offered skilled and specialized services (such as lawyers, merchants, and civic officials) were fitted into a social framework previously based on military service and land tenure.[23]

If one reads the schedule as a schematization of society, as an interpretive scheme, its conception of women's place is fairly conventional; while the schedule might include a range of occupations and social positions for men, for a woman it was marital status and the social status of the man to whom she was married that mattered. Women are explicitly mentioned in the first and fifth groupings only. In the first, the above-named dukes are followed by earls, then by 'every widowed countess in England, as much as the earls' (£4). Next are the barons and bannerets, followed by 'every widowed baroness, as much as a baron, and a banneress as much as a banneret' (40s.). Then gentlemen and squires who ought to be, according to statute, knights, are followed by 'every widowed lady [*veove dame*], wife [*femme*] of a gentleman or a squire', all to be assessed at 20s. Squires of lesser estate and every 'widowed wife' [*femme veove*] of such a squire or of a sufficient merchant were to pay a tax of 6s. 8d. Widows of the landless squires who end this grouping are not mentioned, although landless squires were to be assessed at 40d.[24] In this section of the schedule, then, men are classified by their social and economic status, women by their marital status as well as by the

---

[23] Keen, *English Society*, pp. 8–9; Strohm, *Social Chaucer*, pp. 1–2, 5, 7–8, 190 n. 16. As discussed in the Introduction above, it is not so much that such groups were new in 1379 but rather that they are not included in other interpretive schemes such as that of knights, priests, and peasants.

[24] 'Sufficient merchants' were, according to the fourth grouping, to be assessed at 13s. 4d. If their widows were to be assessed at 6s. 8d., this was perhaps a recognition that the wealth of such men—presumably being based more on trade than land—was less likely to remain at the same value after their deaths unless their widows also became 'sufficient merchants'.

social and economic status of their former husbands. The logic was presumably that, at these high levels, wealth was based on land or goods that a widow inherited from her late husband. The unmarried woman in this section, predominantly the tax-paying noblewoman, is specifically the tax-paying, noble widow. There is no discussion of, for example, the unmarried daughters of the nobility, although it is unlikely that all such females would have been married by age sixteen. Presumably, though, they would not have any independent wealth if their fathers were still alive and so could be taxed at the minimum rate.[25]

The second and third groupings deal exclusively with men, the knights hospitaller and legal practitioners. The fourth, while it does not explicitly refer to female taxpayers, is also of relevance in that some of the occupational categories could apply to unmarried women, for example, sufficient merchants (13s. 4d.) or, more likely, 'lesser merchants and artificers who have profit from the land, according to the extent of their estate' (6s. 8d., 3s. 4d., 2s., 12d., or 6d.).[26] It is presumably in part because of such criteria that occupational designations are included in the 1379 returns. When women are explicitly mentioned in the fifth grouping, marital status is again the main reason. The schedule, having run through all the statuses that might affect assessment, states the following:

every married man [*homme mariee*], for himself and his wife [*pur lui et sa femme*], if they do not belong to the estates named above and are over the age of 16, except genuine beggars 4d.
And every single man and woman [*homme et femme soles*] of such estate and over the said age 4d.

Women are thus only explicitly discussed in the schedule again, after the widow of a squire or of a sufficient merchant (in the first grouping), at the level applicable to the vast majority of taxpayers, those who

---

[25] See e.g. the return for South Acre and Newton (South Greenhoe Hundred, Norfolk), where a squire ['armiger'] is assessed at 40d. but his daughter at 4d.: Fenwick (ed.), *Poll Taxes*, ii, p. 147. On aristocratic daughters, marriage, and inheritance see S. J. Payling, 'Social Mobility, Demographic Change, and Landed Society in Late Medieval England', *Economic History Review*, new ser., 45 (1992), 51–73; C. Given-Wilson, *The English Nobility in the Late Middle Ages: The Fourteenth-Century Political Community* (London: Routledge & Kegan Paul, 1987), ch. 6; Fleming, *Family and Household*, pp. 21–2; Phillips, *Medieval Maidens*, pp. 36–42.

[26] See n. 24 above for a discussion of sufficient merchants and their widows. I discuss some examples below of women, with occupational designations in the surviving returns, assessed at 6d. or over.

were expected to contribute 4d. each.[27] The married man is separated out here from the single to make clear that his payment would also cover his wife ('sa femme'), as this was a change from the previous poll tax. The female taxpayer here is the unmarried woman, the *femme sole*. At this level in the schedule, whether someone was never married or widowed was not considered important. While the legal construct *femme sole* is not being deliberately invoked here, the term *femme sole* is inflected with those associations of legal and economic responsibility; it is because the single woman is a 'woman not under coverture' that she is included in the 1379 tax when married women are not.[28] Indeed, the 1379 tax schedule extends common law's conception of the married woman's coverture, in which the husband is held responsible for his wife's debts, to the point that the husband's single payment of 4d. is sufficient to cover his wife too (whereas in 1377 every individual, including married women, warranted a payment to the Crown of 4d.).[29]

Once the tax had been devised and approved, the next important stages were the assessment of the populace (the classification stage), and the actual collection of the tax. On the day that Richard II's third parliament was dissolved, writs were sent to county sheriffs appointing two commissions for each county and for those boroughs which were taxed separately: one to assess the tax and one to collect it. It was, of course, unfeasible for the small number of men appointed to a commission to assess every potential taxpayer in their area and then collect the tax from them.[30] Although a commission would be appointed for a county or borough, such administrative units were divided into smaller ones (such as hundreds or wards). These in turn might be made up of a number of taxation areas, such as a vill or parish.[31] The commissions were to summon the mayor and bailiff and two men from every city and borough and two men and the constable from every other taxation area. These local men were to provide the commissions with information about individuals;[32] they would also have been liable for

---

[27] Fenwick calculates that over 86% of taxpayers on the extant rolls for 1379 paid the minimum rate: Fenwick (ed.), *Poll Taxes*, i, p. xxv.

[28] See Ch. 5, '*Femmes soles*' above.

[29] On the 1377 tax, see Fenwick (ed.), *Poll Taxes*, i, p. xiv.   [30] Ibid., pp. xiv, xix.

[31] Ibid., pp. xxxvii–ix. On these administrative units, see Pollock and Maitland, *History of English Law*, i, pp. 534–5, 556–7, 560–4, 634–5, or H. M. Jewell, *English Local Administration in the Middle Ages* (Newton Abbot: David & Charles, 1972), pp. 47–61.

[32] Fenwick (ed.), *Poll Taxes*, i, p. xix.

the tax and some of the returns mark them out as tax assessors.[33] From the information provided, nominative lists of taxpayers were drawn up on indentured rolls. One half of the rolls was used by the collection commissions (and local men would have been involved in the actual door-to-door collection of the tax) and the other half was returned to the Exchequer for examination.[34]

Fenwick comments that many of the 1379 detailed rolls are organized so that taxpayers assessed at the same rates, or with the same occupational or marital status, are grouped together: 'These returns are clearly not the result of house-to-house assessments nor the random naming of inhabitants by local collectors, but are a tidy reorganization of other listings'.[35] This does suggest the influence of the schedule on many of the returns. For example, the returns for Sussex's Rape of Lewes begin by listing anyone of social rank or their widows (the schedule's first grouping), any lawyers (third grouping; the second grouping was not relevant here), or artificers (fourth grouping), then the married, and then the single (both from the fifth grouping).[36] Such reorganization must have relied on earlier drafts, though, and would have been facilitated by the existence of listings drawn up to aid collection in 1377. Apart from married women, exactly the same people were liable for the tax in 1379 as in 1377, as the minimum age criterion had been raised by two years, and therefore checking with a collection list from the first poll tax would have made good sense. The Commons seems to have thought earlier listings had been used in 1379 as, when the third tax was announced in 1380, they proclaimed that this time new rolls should be drawn up.[37] The categories used in the 1377 listings, then, would have been at hand for the assessors in 1379.

While nominative listings for the 1377 tax have survived amongst the Exchequer records for only a few areas, this is a reflection of the fact that the Exchequer did not require the submission of listings, rather than because such documents were not usually drawn up. The information contained in the surviving documents largely fits with the aim of aiding collection. For example, clearly some of the 1377 listings are ordered topographically (those for Hull and Derby are divided up

---

[33] See e.g. the returns for Tunstead Hundred (Norfolk): Fenwick (ed.), *Poll Taxes*, ii, pp. 159–70.

[34] Fenwick (ed.), *Poll Taxes*, i, pp. xix–xx.   [35] Ibid., p. xxxiv.

[36] Ibid., ii, pp. 608–15, 619–24. The returns for most of the Streat hundred are organized differently: ibid., pp. 615–19.

[37] Ibid., i, p. xxxiv.

by street names).[38] They also seem to be further ordered by household: in the return for Hull, for example, one William Baxter is said to pay for himself, his wife, their daughter, and a female servant.[39] It seems probable that a householder was viewed as responsible for handing over the tax for those under his or her roof, just as the tax collection process had been devolved from the Exchequer, to commissions, to local assessors.[40] The result of collection from a single individual is that, while there was no need to assign a status to justify a tax assessment in 1377 because all were to pay 4d., the returns often describe people relationally as, for example, his wife, servant, son, or daughter. While comparatively fewer of the 1379 returns seem to be organized by household than those of 1377, use of earlier listings might account for some of the relational descriptions that persist. Indeed, it might help explain the references to wives in some of the 1379 returns, even though they did not warrant assessment.[41]

The categories provided by the 1379 tax schedule, then, include those which denote social status at the level of the nobility, occupational categories for those below the nobility but who should pay more than the minimum rate, and those of marital status ('married' to signal the payment was to stand for a wife too, 'single' for both men and women at the minimum rate to denote the opposite, and, at the top end of the social structure, 'widow' to associate a woman with the status of her former husband). The 1377 poll tax listings offer further categories such as 'daughter' and 'servant' to signal the taxed person's relationship to the household head who was responsible for handing over the tax. The relational description 'his wife' also indicates marital status with the single marked out by default (the 1377 listings do not use the category 'widow').[42] The 1379 return for Bishop's Lynn uses some of these

[38] See Fenwick (ed.), *Poll Taxes*, iii, pp. 188–94; ibid., i, p. 97. For York, see the argument in C. Beattie, 'A Room of One's Own? The Legal Evidence for the Residential Arrangements of Women Without Husbands in Late Fourteenth- and Early Fifteenth-Century York', in N. J. Menuge (ed.), *Medieval Women and the Law* (Woodbridge: Boydell Press, 2000), p. 46.

[39] TNA: PRO, E 179/206/45d r.1 [Hullstrete]: 'Willelmus Baxter pro se uxore sua Alicia filia eorumdem et Isolda de Langwath' famula 16d'.

[40] See Beattie, 'A Room of One's Own?', p. 45; Fenwick (ed.), *Poll Taxes*, i, pp. xix–xx.

[41] See e.g. Fenwick (ed.), *Poll Taxes*, pp. xxxiv, 4–8, 150–2, 442–4, 514–88.

[42] I have not found a single example of the category 'widow' being used as a classification in the 1377 returns, although there are a couple of women with the byname *vidua* in the return of the Coquetdale ward, Northumberland, and a woman in York's return is described as the former wife of Henry Tailor: Fenwick (ed.), *Poll Taxes*, ii, pp. 266 (Beatrix vidua), 268 (Margareta vidua); J. I. Leggett, 'The 1377 Poll Tax Returns

categories in related ways: occupational statuses which sometimes justify the rate of assessment, relational descriptions which suggest household ordering, and the division of men into the single and the married (*solus* and *coniugtatus*), although both were equally liable for the tax.[43] For the unmarried woman, though, the terms *vidua* and *puella* are used in addition to *sola*. While 'widow' is a category used in the schedule, although not for women assessed at under 6s. 8d., the category 'maiden' has no obvious place in a fiscal discourse.

THE BISHOP'S LYNN POLL TAX RETURN OF 1379

The surviving return for Bishop's Lynn exists in partial form in two membranes, with script on both sides in two columns.[44] The names of taxpayers are listed one after another in columns. At the start of each entry the amount of tax paid is given, then the name, and then the statuses (the majority of taxpayers are classified in two different ways and in these cases it is the occupational or relational status that is given first), as follows: '6d Johannes Grym ballivus coniugatus / 4d Rogerus Gaoler s'[erviens] eius sol'[us]'.[45] The occupational designations often justify the rate of assessment. For example, the designation *lab'* (*laborarius*, labourer) is used for those assessed at the minimum rate, whereas *art'* (*artifex*, artisan) justifies an assessment of 6d., as in the schedule. Other terms relate to more specific crafts such as 'bowyer', assessed from 6d. upwards, or categories used in the schedule such as 'hosteller' and *merc'* (*mercator*, merchant), variously assessed. The relational descriptions, 'his/her servant' (*s' eius*) or 'son' or 'daughter' ('his/her' referring to the person listed above) suggest that this return is organized by household, perhaps derived from a 1377 listing. The second status given is one which signifies marital status: *coniugatus* (applied to men only as married women were not assessed in 1379),

---

for the City of York', *Yorkshire Archaeological Journal*, 43 (1971), p. 135. See also Poos, *Rural Society*, p. 295.

[43] It is not a division that is made in every 1379 return.

[44] TNA: PRO, EXT 6/99, membranes 156.1 and 156.2. The first membrane is torn away from about half way down the left side, is badly faded, and a large number of entries are now illegible; the left hand side of the second is torn away and there is only one column on its dorse, which ends with the total sum levied. See the description in Fenwick (ed.), *Poll Taxes*, ii, p. 74.

[45] Fenwick (ed.), *Poll Taxes*, ii, p. 180.

solus/a, *vidua*, or *puella* (the latter two applied only to females). When a number of taxpayers share the same designations they are bracketed together so that the scribe had to write the designations only once.[46]

A study of how this return uses the term *sola* in relation to other categories casts light on what the assessors in Bishop's Lynn, in the context of a tax assessment, selected as the key constituents of social and economic identity. The return's use of dual classification for many taxpayers means that we must consider how different statuses intersect as well as compete. The term *sola* can be compared with how the masculine form *solus* is used. It can also be considered in relation to the terms *vidua* and *puella*, which are also applied to unmarried, female taxpayers. A key part of such comparisons, though, must be how all these categories relate to other forms of classification, such as occupational or relational designations. To facilitate this argument, the classification of male and female taxpayers has been set out in tabular form (tables 3.1 and 3.2).[47] In line with the subject of enquiry, the terms that denote marital status are prioritized here, rather than the first designation in the return which was usually an occupational or relational status; the value of this exercise lies more in indicating trends rather than in the precise numbers, as not all of the return for Bishop's Lynn has survived.[48]

Of the 515 readable entries for male taxpayers, only twenty (3.9 per cent) do not use the terms *solus* or *coniugatus* (see Table 3.1). We have seen that the categories of single or married are ones that were introduced at the end of the schedule for the 1379 tax. Although both a married and an unmarried man might warrant a minimum payment of 4d., there are a number of possible reasons why a return might signal a male taxpayer's marital status. First, this information was readily available to the assessors if they were working from a listing from 1377,

---

[46] It has been argued that the brackets denote households but this is clearly not the case: D. M. Owen (ed.), *The Making of King's Lynn: A Documentary Survey*, Records of Social and Economic History, new ser., 9 (London: Oxford University Press for the British Academy, 1984), p. 221. For an example from the Bishop's Lynn return, see p. 80 below. For another example of the bracketing together of people with the same designation see the return for Lewes (Streat Hundred, Rape of Lewes, Sussex) in Fenwick (ed.), *Poll Taxes*, ii, pp. 619–20.

[47] The tables were calculated from checking the 1984 edition with the original: TNA: PRO, EXT 6/99/156.1–2; Owen (ed.), *Making of King's Lynn*, pp. 221–32. There is now an edition in Fenwick (ed.), *Poll Taxes*, ii, pp. 180–5; differences from this edition have been rechecked with the original and, where directly relevant, are noted below.

[48] Those entries that were damaged to the extent that they could not be divided into male and *solus*, *coniugatus*, or no marital status, or female and *sola*, *vidua*, *puella*, or no marital status (about 20% of all extant entries) have not been included.

Table 3.1: The correlation of categories describing males in the 1379 Bishop's Lynn poll tax return

Status	*solus*	*coniugatus*	no marital status	TOTAL
servant	97	0	7	104
occupation	20	369	8	397
son	3	0	0	3
no other status	3	1	5	9
damaged entry	0	2	0	2
TOTAL	123	372	20	515

Source: TNA: PRO, EXT 6/99/156.

when married women were liable for the tax. Second, such information might have been of use to the Exchequer in that it readily shows where some of the taxpayers from 1377 had gone; Fenwick believes that the shortfall in revenue raised from the second poll tax was in part due to the Exchequer under-calculating the effect of excluding married women from the tax.[49] Third, perhaps the wife's economic status was a factor when the assessors decided on the amount a married man was to pay. The schedule states that the 4d. payment was for 'every married man, for himself and his wife, if *they* do not belong [*qi ne sont mye*] to the estates named above'.[50]

As *solus* operates as one half of a binary pairing with *coniugatus* in this return, it denotes any male taxpayer who was not married. There is no attempt to distinguish between never-married and widowed men. Many of the 123 men classified as *solus* would have been never married in that 100 (81 per cent) are described in relation to a householder as servants (implying co-residence) or, less frequently, as sons, both designations that connote youth.[51] Fenwick counts as 'probable' widowers (and widows) those of unknown marital status

[49] Fenwick (ed.), *Poll Taxes*, i, p. xxv.
[50] Given-Wilson *et al.* (eds.), *Parliament Rolls*, vi, p. 116 (my italics). For example in the 1379 return for Shropham Hundred, Norfolk, wives are not usually listed but when they are, the women are given an occupational designation and the tax assessment seems to reflect this: Fenwick (ed.), *Poll Taxes*, ii, pp. 130–2. Fenwick comments that 'an individual charged at non-schedule rates was usually paying for both his own and his wife's trade': Fenwick (ed.), *Poll Taxes*, i, p. xxiv.
[51] On the age and not-married status of resident servants see Goldberg, *Women, Work, and Life Cycle*, pp. 168–72; Poos, *Rural Society*, pp. 188–95.

who resided with children or who headed households comprising two or more people.[52] There are only three men who fit these criteria in that they are listed as heads of households that included servants or apprentices. For example, Roger de Byntr' is described as *solus* and a *mercator* (merchant), assessed at 3s. 4d., and listed above three male servants and two female servants.[53] Philip Wyht' is another single merchant assessed at 3s. 4d., with a male apprentice,[54] and Adam Fullere is classified as an artisan and single, above his male servant who is also described as a labourer.[55] In contrast, twenty-nine women are marked out as widows. The significant point is not in terms of numbers (it is probable that there were more widows than widowers), but that the category 'widower' was not considered relevant in a tax return but that of 'widow' evidently was.[56]

While all female taxpayers in 1379 were unmarried, due to the criteria for the tax, not all women in the Bishop's Lynn return are classified as *sola*. Some females are labelled *puella*, which suggests youth and the never-married state, and some are classified as *vidua*, which denotes their widowed state. Thus one needs to explore why some never-married and widowed women are more specifically labelled and why some are not, and the clues can be found in the other categories used to describe such taxpayers (see Table 3.2). Some 125 of the 183 readable entries (68.3 per cent) also identify the female taxpayer in relation to the work that she did, either as a servant or by a more specific occupational designation (this compares with 97.3 per cent of male taxpayers). Of these, 114 use the category *sola*. More significantly, none of the females classified as *puella* or *vidua* is identified in such a way. As it is unlikely that no maiden or widow in Bishop's Lynn worked, some prioritization of statuses was

[52] C. C. Fenwick, 'The English Poll Taxes of 1377, 1379, and 1381: A Critical Examination of the Returns', Ph.D. thesis (London, 1983), esp. pp. 156, 179, 184; see also Kowaleski, 'Singlewomen', pp. 71–2 n. 39.

[53] TNA: PRO, EXT 6/99/156.1 c. 2; Owen (ed.), *Making of King's Lynn*, p. 223; Fenwick (ed.), *Poll Taxes*, ii, p. 181.

[54] TNA: PRO, EXT 6/99/156.2d c.1; Owen (ed.), *Making of King's Lynn*, p. 231; Fenwick (ed.), *Poll Taxes*, ii, p. 185, incorrectly has Philip at 6d. and his apprentice at 3s. 4d.

[55] TNA: PRO, EXT 6/99/156.2 c. 2; Owen (ed.), *Making of King's Lynn*, p. 229; Fenwick (ed.), *Poll Taxes*, ii, p. 184.

[56] There are examples of the term *viduarius* from 1257 and 1356 and of *wydyarius* from *c.* 1280 but it was rarely used in this period: R. E. Latham, *Revised Medieval Latin Word-List from British and Irish Sources* (London: Oxford University Press for the British Academy, 1965), p. 512. This issue will be returned to in the discussion of later tax returns in Ch. 5 below.

Table 3.2: The correlation of categories describing females in the 1379 Bishop's Lynn poll tax return

Status	*sola*	*puella*	*vidua*	no marital status	TOTAL
servant	102	0	0	10	112
occupation	12	0	0	1	13
daughter	5	6	0	0	11
mother	0	0	1	0	1
no other status	15	0	28	0	43
damaged entry	2	1	0	0	3
TOTAL	136	7	29	11	183

Source: TNA: PRO, EXT 6/99/156.

evidently operating here. The contention is that *sola* could function as an umbrella category for both the never married and the widowed, as *solus* did, but for daughters still living at home the category of 'maiden' was largely selected instead, and for widowed women the term *vidua* usually, although perhaps not always, was chosen as the key status. In the classification of these female taxpayers, the categories 'maiden' and 'widow' preclude an occupational designation. In contrast, for those females identified in relation to work that they did, the more general marital status of *sola* was considered adequate. Such choices on the part of the assessors signal the value-laden nature of the returns.

Of the twenty-nine females described as *vidua*, only one has another category assigned (the relational one of 'mother'), in contrast with those described as *puella*, all of whom are described relationally as 'daughter' (with the exception of one entry which was too damaged to be read), and those described as *sola*, of whom only 10.9 per cent do not have another designation. This suggests that the Bishop's Lynn assessors saw *vidua* as a key category that could stand alone in a tax return, but it still needs to be asked why it was used and what it signified. We have seen that the schedule employed the category 'widow' down to the level of the widows of squires of lesser estate and of sufficient merchants (assessed at 6s. 8d.). One of the women classified as *vidua* in the Bishop's Lynn return was indeed assessed at 6s. 8d., but (according to the surviving return) only two of the others classified in this way paid above the minimum rate, each assessed at 12d., whereas sixteen paid the minimum of 4d. (nine of the relevant entries are damaged so that the tax levied cannot be determined).[57] Thus the category of 'widow' was not functioning in exactly the same way here as it did in the schedule.

If one looks for other female taxpayers who paid more than the minimum rate in the return there are only four others, one of whom is described as *sola*, one has no status, and two are damaged entries. All fit Fenwick's criteria for 'probable' widows, that is, those of unknown marital status who resided with children or who headed households comprising two or more people.[58] While the taxpayers in the two damaged entries might have been classified as widows in the original return (they paid 3s. 4d. and 12d. respectively),[59] in the other two cases it could be argued that an occupational designation was prioritized. Matilda de Ramesseye, assessed at 12d., is described as *brac'* (*braciatrix*, brewster), with no marital status, and listed above her three servants, two female and one male.[60] Johanna de Fakenham, assessed at 6d., is described as *venditrix cervisie* (beer seller) and *sola*, and listed above her two female servants.[61] Both occupational designations are used to account for the women having to pay over the minimum rate and they are the only occupational terms which function in this way for women in the Bishop's Lynn return; the other eleven female taxpayers classified by occupation are either described as *lab'* or 'spynner', and all were charged the minimum rate of assessment.

The woman known as Isabella Wydewe and described as *sola* could well have been a widow, in that bynames seem to function in this way elsewhere.[62] Perhaps additional classification as a widow was

[57] For Alice de Swanton', *vidua*, assessed at 6s. 8d., see TNA: PRO, EXT 6/99/156.1 c. 2; Owen (ed.), *Making of King's Lynn*, p. 225; Fenwick (ed.), *Poll Taxes*, ii, p. 183. For Margaret de Coventr', *vidua*, at 12d., see EXT 6/99/156.1d c.1; Owen (ed.), *Making of King's Lynn*, p. 227; Fenwick (ed.), *Poll Taxes*, ii, p. 182, incorrectly has the amount as 4d. For Helena Lomb, *vidua*, at 12d., see EXT 6/99/156.2d c.1; Owen (ed.), *Making of King's Lynn*, p. 232; Fenwick (ed.), *Poll Taxes*, ii, p. 185.

[58] This is not to say that I think these women were definitely widows, but that the *possibility* that they were merits consideration here.

[59] For Johanna atte Wythe at 3s. 4d., see TNA: PRO, EXT 6/99/156.2d c.1; Owen (ed.), *Making of King's Lynn*, p. 231; Fenwick (ed.), *Poll Taxes*, ii, p. 185. For Beatrix [de B?] at 12d., see EXT 6/99/156.1 c. 2; *Making of King's Lynn*, ed. Owen, p. 226; Fenwick (ed.), *Poll Taxes*, ii, p. 183, incorrectly has the amount as 6d.

[60] TNA: PRO, EXT 6/99/156.2d c.1; Owen (ed.), *Making of King's Lynn*, p. 232; Fenwick (ed.), *Poll Taxes*, ii, p. 185.

[61] TNA: PRO, EXT 6/99/156.2 c. 2; Owen (ed.), *Making of King's Lynn*, p. 228; Fenwick (ed.), *Poll Taxes*, ii, p. 184.

[62] See e.g. n. 42 above. There is an Anabilla Wydow in the return for the Barkston Ash Wapentake, West Riding, Yorkshire: Fenwick (ed.), *Poll Taxes*, iii, p. 374. See also D. Postles, *The Surnames of Devon* (Oxford: Leopard's Head Press, 1995), p. 244.

considered unnecessary in this case, just as occupational designations were sometimes not given when someone's actual occupation was signalled by their byname.[63] The evidence of the Bishop's Lynn return suggests not so much that widows were excluded from the term *sola*, but that in general widowed women were specifically marked out as *vidua* (with the possible exceptions of when they practiced an occupation pertinent to their assessed taxation rate). The category 'widow' was one provided to the assessors by the 1379 schedule, but only to signal a particular rate of assessment. There was no imperative for the classifiers to distinguish between never-married and widowed taxpayers, and the assessors in 1377 had not felt the need to use the category 'widow'. However, in a return when marital status was generally denoted, the assessors chose to be more specific about women's marital status as 'single' taxpayers, than men's. Once the category 'widow' was introduced to signal a higher rate of assessment in certain cases, perhaps it was then available for application to other women known to be widows, even if it did not affect their assessment. It is at such points that we need to recognize the influence of other discourses on the compilation of the return than just the fiscal one, discourses in which the category of 'widow' has cultural significance that extends beyond its economic implications.[64]

The use of the term *puella* in the Bishop's Lynn tax return is one that requires even more explanation, since it is not a category that occurs in the schedule and the term does not occur in any other poll tax listing. While none of the females classified as *puella* is also described as a servant or by a more specific occupational designation, they are all also described as daughters (with the exception of a damaged entry which might well have used both categories) in relation to a parent who is listed above, which suggests that they were probably still living at home. There are five more females in the return who are also described as daughters of parents listed above but they are designated *sol'*. The correlation between use of the term *puella* and the description of someone as a daughter is nevertheless significant. First, the five daughters described as *sol'* were part of just two households, with the term *sol'* only written twice, and with

[63] Goldberg, *Women, Work, and Life Cycle*, p. 43; N. Bartlett (ed.), *The Lay Poll Tax Returns for the City of York in 1381* (London: A. Brown & Son, 1953), p. 1 n. 2.
[64] This issue is discussed further in relation to the Derby return below.

just two entries between the two households.[65] Second, no female who had left the parental home is described as *puella*. To take one illustrative example from the return, within one bracket labelled as *art' coniugati*, seven people are listed of whom two were clearly not married artisans:[66]

6d Adam de Tiryngton'
4d Matilda serviens eius sol'
6d Johannes de Tyrington'
4d Marg' filia eius puella
6d Ricardus Hattere
6d Willelmus Wyth'

Adam de Tiryngton's servant, Matilda, is described as *sol'* and John de Tyrington's daughter is described as *puella*. Both are assessed at the minimum rate, rather than at the artificer's minimum rate of 6d. A choice has therefore been made to describe one of these females as *puella* and the other as *sola*. Indeed, it is the difference between the daughters, who are on the whole described as *puellae*, and the servants, who are overwhelmingly described as *sol'*, which seems to be the significant one to the assessors (rather than that between the *puellae* and the *sol'* daughters). In order to determine what this distinction was one needs to consider how the term *puella* was used in other contexts and which of these associations might have influenced its use, consciously or not, in the Bishop's Lynn return (and also which meanings perhaps inflect the term once it had been used).

Puella had a range of meanings in other contexts: it could be used to denote a virgin, a young girl, or a maidservant, all meanings which cluster around the Middle English term 'maiden'.[67] It seems unlikely that in the Bishop's Lynn return it denoted a 'maidservant', given its use at the point in an entry where a marital status was usually given (also this return only refers to servants in a relational way (his/her servant)

[65] TNA: PRO, EXT 6/99/156.1d c.1; Owen (ed.), *Making of King's Lynn*, p. 225; Fenwick (ed.), *Poll Taxes*, ii, p. 182, actually has the fifth child as male (but I do not think the reading as Ric[ardus] is correct).

[66] TNA: PRO, EXT 6/99/156.1 c. 2; Owen (ed.), *Making of King's Lynn*, p. 223 (although the bracket here mistakenly includes an 8th person); Fenwick (ed.), *Poll Taxes*, ii, p. 181.

[67] See e.g. Latham, *Revised Medieval Latin Word-List*, p. 381: *puellaritas*, maidenhood pre-1300; *puellitas*, girlhood 1461. It is used in the *Legenda aurea* (*c.* 1260–75) to suggest youth as well as virginity, and in a manuscript of the York Mystery Plays (*c.* 1463–77) to refer to a servant: see Phillips, *Medieval Maidens*, p. 47; R. Beadle (ed.), *The York Plays* (London: Edward Arnold, 1982), pp. 119–20.

rather than as an occupational status). Those few returns which use the Middle English 'maiden' do so where other taxpayers are identified by occupation. For example, in the return for the vill of Langsett, Stayncrosse Wapentake (West Riding, Yorkshire), Johanna Hattirslay is classified as 'mayden' and seems to be in the employ of John de Swyndene junior and his wife; other female taxpayers listed near Joan in the return are classified as *ancilla*.[68] It is also unlikely that *puella* is being used in the Bishop's Lynn return to mark out a young cohort. Everyone assessed in 1379 had to be over the age of sixteen and presumably some of the 112 servants were not significantly older than that.[69] The pertinent issue is not whether there was an *actual* difference between *puellae* daughters and *sol'* servants, but rather why the assessors *suggest* a distinction with the introduction of the term *puella*. For example, the term may have been used to suggest youth or immaturity, in the sense that those females who had stayed in the parental home were perhaps not seen as having progressed as far along the path to social adulthood as those who had gone into service.[70] Similarly, if it did suggest virginity and social respectability, this could only have been a distinction in the minds of assessors between those who had stayed in the parental home and those who had left.

Given the context in which the term is used, a tax return, one might expect an economic dimension at least to inflect the term *puella*, even if this was not the only grounds for the term's selection. As we have seen, the category 'widow' functioned in the schedule, and at times in the return, to denote that the woman was assessed according to the status of her deceased husband. The term *puella*, with its connotations

---

[68] Fenwick (ed.), *Poll Taxes*, iii, p. 347. See also ibid. i, pp. 580 (Marg' lady mayden), 582 (Emma the Prest maiden). In other returns 'mayden' seems to be part of the byname for a female servant, as 'man' is for a male servant, although not all the older editions make this clear, e.g. E. Lloyd (ed.), 'Poll Tax Returns for the East Riding 4 Ric. II', *Yorkshire Archaeological Journal*, 20 (1909), p. 347; 'Rolls of the Collectors in the West-Riding of the Lay-Subsidy (Poll Tax) 2 Richard II', *Yorkshire Archaeological Journal*, 5, 6, 7 (1879–84), 6, p. 38, cf. p. 39. I am grateful to Drs Carolyn Fenwick and Dave Postles for discussion on this matter.

[69] Female servants in late medieval Yorkshire were found (from consistory court depositions) to be mostly between the ages of 12 and 24: Goldberg, *Women, Work, and Life Cycle*, pp. 168–72. These figures have been used as suggestive of England as a whole: Smith, 'Geographical Diversity', p. 39.

[70] Cf. P. J. P. Goldberg, 'Migration, Youth and Gender in Later Medieval England', in P. J. P. Goldberg and F. Riddy (eds.), *Youth in the Middle Ages* (Woodbridge: York Medieval Press, 2004), pp. 85–99, which argues that social adulthood was achieved through marriage and householding.

of youth, perhaps signals financial dependence.[71] The parents of the daughters labelled *puellae* do not appear to be particularly wealthy: two are described as married labourers; two as married artisans (assessed at 6d. and 12d. respectively); and a widow headed the household with two daughters. None of them is recorded as having servants and perhaps the young women had been retained in preference to employing servants;[72] it has been argued that this happened with children, especially daughters, particularly in rural areas and by widows.[73] In contrast, of the three households in the Bishop's Lynn return that contained a dependent son (in the sense that he was not classified by an occupation), three also employed servants.[74] It could, of course, be questioned whether servants were necessarily financially independent; some of the 1377 listings suggest that employers paid the tax, initially at least, for resident servants, and it seems many servants worked for bed and board rather than regular wages.[75] Again, though, the point is that the compilers of the Bishop's Lynn return evidently saw some distinction between the two groups.[76] *Puella*, then, was not used for every young, never-married woman in Bishop's Lynn, but to differentiate a group of female taxpayers, from the larger group described as *sola*, because they were still residing at home. For these daughters, any work that they did within the parental home was not recorded.

The category *sola* was thus potentially able to encompass all never-married and widowed women in the way that *solus* did for men in this return, but for widows *vidua* predominantly acted as a priority category, and for daughters *puella* was generally a priority category (although an

---

[71] Cf. Dillard's finding that in Leonese and Castilian *fueros extensos* (charters guaranteeing certain privileges to townspeople) the term *filia* or *fija emparentada* (parented girl) denoted economic dependence on one or both parents: H. Dillard, *Daughters of the Reconquest: Women in Castilian Town Society, 1100–1300* (Cambridge: Cambridge University Press, 1984), p. 18.

[72] TNA, PRO, EXT 6/99/156.1 c. 2 (two usages), 156.1d c.1 (two usages), 156.2d c.1; Owen (ed.), *Making of King's Lynn*, pp. 222, 223, 224, 227, 232; Fenwick (ed.), *Poll Taxes*, ii, pp. 181, 182, 185.

[73] Goldberg, 'Urban Identity', p. 212; Goldberg, *Women, Work, and Life Cycle*, pp. 100–1, 165–8; Goldberg, 'Migration, Youth and Gender', p. 95, n. 43.

[74] TNA, PRO, EXT 6/99/156.1 c. 2, 156.1d c.1 (two); Owen (ed.), *Making of King's Lynn*, pp. 224, 226, 227; Fenwick (ed.), *Poll Taxes*, ii, p. 182.

[75] See e.g. Goldberg, *Women, Work, and Life Cycle*, pp. 185–6, 358; Goldberg, 'What Was a Servant?', in A. Curry and E. Matthew (eds.), *Concepts and Patterns of Service in the Later Middle Ages* (Woodbridge: Boydell Press, 2000), pp. 7, 15–17; Beattie, 'Single Women, Work and Family', pp. 186–9; Mate, *Daughters*, p. 46.

[76] We shall see below that there was a different perception of daughters in the Howdenshire returns.

unusual choice of term for a tax return). For those females labelled *vidua* or *puella*, a marital designation took precedence over an occupational one, but for many of the women labelled *sola* the opposite prioritization was operating. That is, for those female taxpayers described as servants or by a more specific occupational designation (the majority in this return) their work identity was the defining aspect and the one that justified their tax assessment, just as it was for most of the male taxpayers. This is how the assessors in Bishop's Lynn classified the unmarried, female taxpayer. Other assessors made different choices, as we shall now see.

WIDOWS, DAUGHTERS, AND WORK

The returns for Salisbury, Derby, and Howdenshire in 1379 have been selected because they demonstrate some of the different ways that marital status, and the categories 'widow' and 'daughter' in particular, could function in relation to occupational status in the classification of the unmarried, female taxpayer. The Salisbury return is also one of the few other returns that uses both the terms *sola* and *vidua*, and the largest of those that do, which enables consideration of how the two terms relate in this return. The returns for the boroughs of Salisbury and Derby tend to have only one classification per taxpayer, which means that the assessors had selected in each case whether it should be, for example, a marital or an occupational status. While marital status was prioritized for the female taxpayer in the Salisbury return, the Derby return generally classifies female taxpayers by occupation, particularly as spinners. It uses the term *vidua*, but not *sola*, and it sometimes adds qualifying adjectives to the term, such as *paupercula* (poor little) and *vetula* (old), which clearly signal the value-laden nature of the classification process and the return. The Derby return thus allows for consideration of the relationship between the category 'widow' and an occupational status. The third return is that for Howdenshire (East Riding, Yorkshire). This bears comparison with the return for Bishop's Lynn in that many taxpayers have two designations, that is, a relational one and an occupational status. Most taxpayers, though, are not explicitly classified by marital status. This return is used to consider how a different set of assessors classified daughters who were still resident in the parental home.

The 1379 return for the borough of Salisbury classifies some females as *sola* and some as *vidua*. While a couple of listings for small vills also use both terms,[77] the Salisbury return contains nearly two thousand names and so it is possible to suggest patterns in the use of such categories, as can be seen from the tables setting out the classification of female and male taxpayers below (Tables 3.3 and 3.4).[78] As with the return for Bishop's Lynn, names are listed one after another in columns. After the name is given, there is generally a status (either occupational, relational, or marital), and then the amount of tax to be paid. The majority of female taxpayers in this return are described in a relational way, as the servant or daughter or sister or companion of another taxpayer (see Table 3.3); such descriptions suggest that the return is organized by household. Occupational designations for women (beyond identification as a servant) are rare, with only one woman identified as a labourer and one as an artisan (*labor'; art'*).[79] The second most common form of designation is a marital one, either *sola* or *vidua*. In contrast, the majority of male taxpayers in the Salisbury return are identified by an occupational designation (64.3 per cent),

Table 3.3: The classification of females in the 1379 Salisbury poll tax return

Status	No.	%
servant of	287	65
daughter of	12	3
sister of	2	1
companion of	1	0
sola	117	26
vidua	9	2
artisan	1	0
labourer	1	0
no status	9	2
damaged entry	3	1
TOTAL	443	100

Source: Fenwick (ed.), *Poll Taxes*, iii, pp. 110–19.

---

[77] See Fenwick (ed.), *Poll Taxes,* ii, pp. 583, 590.

[78] Fenwick (ed.), *Poll Taxes*, iii, pp. 110–19; I am indebted to Dr Carolyn Fenwick for letting me see her edition in advance of its publication. I have examined the documents that make up this edition: TNA: PRO, E 179/239/193/20, EXT 6/99/44, EXT 6/99/90, and EXT 6/99/162.

[79] Fenwick (ed.), *Poll Taxes,* iii, pp. 115 (Alicia Immere art' 12d.), 117 (Alicia Goldyng labor' 4d.).

then by a relational status (31.7 per cent, again mainly as servants), with only two out of 1,412 readable entries using a marital status (see Table 3.4).[80] Thus, in the Salisbury return, for females marital status was often prioritized over an occupational one, with the converse being true for the male taxpayer, whereas in the return for Bishop's Lynn this was only the case for some females (those described as *vidua* or *puella*). A closer study of the women classified as *sola* and *vidua* in the Salisbury return suggests that the assessors here were making different choices about how to classify the unmarried, female taxpayer.

While 117 females are described as *sola* in the Salisbury return, only nine are classified as *vidua*. An examination of those described by the former term suggests that they do include some widows. For example, all five women listed with children over the taxation age of sixteen, and presumably still resident at home, are labelled *sola*, although it is unlikely that none of these women was widowed.[81] If we use Fenwick's criteria for 'probable' widows (those of unknown marital status who resided with children or who headed households comprising two or more people), a further ten women can be identified, nine of whom

Table 3.4: The classification of males in the 1379 Salisbury poll tax return

Status	No.	%
servant of	442	31.3
son of	5	0.4
solus/a (sic)	2	0.4
artisan	490	34.7
labourer	379	26.8
merchant	28	2.0
hosteller	5	0.4
miscellaneous	5	0.4
no status	13	0.9
damaged entry	43	3.0
TOTAL	1412	100.0

Source: Fenwick (ed.), *Poll Taxes*, iii, pp. 110–19.

[80] Ibid., pp. 111 (Johannes Hanek solus 4d.), 116 (Johannes Goldsmyth' sola [sic] 4d.).

[81] Ibid., pp. 111 (Ferstina Fisshere), 112 (Editha Shupestre), 113 (Johanna Doder), 114 (Cecilia Volumes), 117 (Sibilla Cartere); all the children are daughters.

are classified by the term *sola*. For example, of the women listed as having servants, nine are described as *sola*, three as *vidua*, and one has no status.[82] If *sola* in this return could include both the never married and the widowed, it therefore needs to be asked why the term *vidua* was used for nine female taxpayers.

For some of the women classified as *vidua*, it is possible that the term was used to justify a particular rate of assessment. Four of the nine uses of the term in this return are for women assessed above the minimum rate of 4d.: one at 40d., two at 2s., and one at 6d.[83] This seems significant given that only one of the 117 women described as *sola* was assessed above the minimum rate.[84] It seems that the way that 'widow' functioned in the schedule has been adopted but for those paying less than 40d., although more than the minimum; 2s. and 6d. are amounts that were applicable for lesser merchants and artificers. The women in question might well have been assessed according to the status of a former husband. However, as occupational designations are so rarely used for female taxpayers in the Salisbury return, unlike in that for Bishop's Lynn, it is possible that these women were being assessed according to their own occupations. But why were five women who were assessed at the minimum rate also described as widows? This also occurs in the Bishop's Lynn return but there most widows were labelled as such, which is not the case in the Salisbury return. Such inconsistencies within a return cannot be fully explained, although they do emphasize that assessors were making choices about how to classify taxpayers. It might simply be that, having used the category 'widow' for some widows paying at higher rates, this term was then applied to some other women known to be widows (assessed at the minimum rate), although by no means all. In this return, *sola* is the default marital status for women, whether never-married or widowed.

[82] For the women classified as *sola* with servants see ibid., pp. 111 (Dionisia Shuppestre: 2 female servants), 112 (Agnes Doudyng: 3 male and 2 female servants), 114 (Juliana Coukes, Editha Spencer, Editha Bourscoube, and Editha Tappestre: 1 female servant each), 115 (Margareta Smartes: 2 male servants), 116 (Editha Burgeis: 2 female servants; Johanna Hockestre: 1 female servant). See ibid., p. 118 for Elena Bemynstre, no status given but 1 female servant.

[83] Ibid., pp. 114 (Alicia Ruteshale 2s.), 115 (Editha Abbot 6d.), 116 (Agnes Bottenham 40d.), 118 (Agnes Brewere 2s.). For the other women labelled *vidua* see ibid., pp. 111 (Agnes Latener), 114 (Agnes Houtle), 115 (Alicia Duryngton), 116 (Agnes Sobbury), 118 (Isabella Cole).

[84] Ibid., p. 111: 'Matilles Nyweman sola 12d.'.

The 1379 return for Derby differs from the Salisbury return in that it generally prioritizes occupational status over marital status (see tables 3.5 and 3.6).[85] The return again seems to be ordered by household as relational descriptions are used, such as 'his/her son', or 'daughter', or 'servant', and the occupational and marital statuses appear to have been added at a later stage than the names and amounts. The category 'widow' is only used for six women, all assessed at the minimum rate.[86] Of the eight women who evidently had children over the age of sixteen residing with them, none is identified as a widow, although it is unlikely that none of the eight had been married: seven are identified by an occupation and one has no classification (although her daughter is described as a 'spinner').[87] Similarly, of the three women listed with resident servants, one is one of the two women described as *vetula vidua* but the other two have occupational designations.[88] It seems, then, that not all widows are designated as such in this return so the first questions to be explored are why six women are classified in this way and why qualifying adjectives such as *vetula* and *paupercula* are used in four of these cases.

Martha Carlin's argument regarding use of the category 'widow' in the 1381 return for Southwark is pertinent here, despite the tax criteria being different in that year. The Southwark return, like that for Derby, classifies most unmarried female taxpayers by an occupational designation or as servants.[89] Only four women are described as widows out of 1,060 names. Carlin argues that '[t]he four women designated as "widow" seem to have been the most well-to-do group of women householders in Southwark . . . This suggests that the term "widow" as used by the Southwark assessors meant something like "widow who

---

[85] TNA: PRO, EXT 6/99/22; Fenwick (ed.), *Poll Taxes*, i, pp. 97–100.

[86] See Fenwick (ed.), *Poll Taxes*, i, pp. 98 (Margeria de Bynynton' *vidua paupercula*; Joan, mother of Nicholas Cotyler, *vidua paupercula*; Fenwick transcribes *paupercula* as two words), 99 (Isabella de Brasynton *vetula vidua*; Fenwick incorrectly has the assessment at 12d. rather than 4d.), 100 (damaged entry, *vidua vetula*).

[87] Ibid., pp. 97 (Margareta de Basynton', no status given), 98 (Agn' Bernard, spinn': 1 daughter; Emma Lokesmyth' spinn': 1 son; Matill' Canon' spinner': 1 son), 99 (Johanna de Hasulden' spinn': 1 daughter; Margareta Prentys spynn': 1 daughter; Agn' Naill' *filatrice* [spinner]: 1 daughter; Elena s'[erviens Henrici de Coton']: 1 daughter).

[88] See n. 91 below and also Fenwick (ed.), *Poll Taxes*, i, p. 98 (Cecilia Lord, spinn': 1 female servant).

[89] TNA: PRO, E 179/184/30; Fenwick (ed.), *Poll Taxes*, ii, pp. 558–64. See Figure 1.1 in C. Beattie, 'The Problem of Women's Work Identities in Post Black Death England', in J. Bothwell *et al.* (eds.), *The Problem of Labour in Fourteenth-Century England* (Woodbridge: York Medieval Press, 2000), p. 5.

doesn't need to work", and was an indicator of high economic status.'[90] The Derby return differs in that all six women classified as widows only paid the minimum rate. Indeed, in this return only one woman paid above the minimum rate: Agnes Walker, dyer, with the occupation accounting for her assessment at 2s.[91] Yet, given the emphasis placed on occupational designations in the Derby return, it could be that all usages of the category 'widow' denoted a woman who no longer worked, whether due to old age or poverty. But it must still be asked why the specific formulation 'poor little widow' (*paupercula vidua* and *vidua paupercula*) was used.

In other returns for 1379 *pauper* seems to be used to justify assessing someone at the bottom rate for their status. For example, in the return for two vills in Andover Hundred (Hampshire) there is a man classified as *pauper mercator* and assessed at 6d., a *pauper firmar'* (*firmarius*, farmer) at 12d., a couple of *pauper artif'* at 6d., and a *pauper labor'* at 4d.[92] All of these rates are the lowest ones set for the relevant category in the schedule. In the return for the vill of Sileby, Goscote Hundred (Leicestershire) three men listed under the heading *mercator'* are classified as *pauper* and assessed at 8d., in contrast to two other merchants who are assessed at 2s.[93] According to the schedule, lesser merchants should be assessed at 6s. 8d., 3s. 4d., 2s., 12d., or 6d., according to the extent of their estates.[94] The term *pauper* was possibly used here to justify the non-schedule rate. The description of two women as a 'poor little widow' in the Derby return, then, was perhaps used to justify the minimum rate for women who might have been expected, perhaps because of a former husband's status, to be assessed at a higher one. One of the women was apparently living in her son's household as she is listed below a Nicholas Cotyler, who was assessed at 6d., and described additionally as *matre eius*.[95] The diminutive form *paupercula* requires further explanation, though. The specific formulation of *vidua paupercula* can be found in the Vulgate Bible, in Luke's story about the widow's mite; it was

[90] M. Carlin, *Medieval Southwark* (London: Hambledon Press, 1996), pp. 175–6 (and p. 137 for the total).

[91] Fenwick (ed.), *Poll Taxes*, i, p. 99 (Agn' Walker dyst'). Two female servants are listed beneath her entry but earlier in the return one John Betamy is also described as a servant of Agnes Walker: ibid.

[92] Ibid., p. 323; the artisans are further described by a specific trade (butcher and tailor). See also Fenwick (ed.), *Poll Taxes*, ii, p. 330.

[93] Fenwick (ed.), *Poll Taxes*, i, p. 565. See also ibid., p. 521.

[94] See Given-Wilson, *et al.* (eds.), *Parliament Rolls*, vi, p. 116.

[95] Fenwick (ed.), *Poll Taxes*, i, p. 98.

translated in a Wycliffite Bible (*c.* 1384) as 'litel pore widowe'.[96] Its use in the Derby return suggests the influence of a particular way of thinking about widows that did not pertain to *all* unmarried women.[97] The assessors evidently did not think 'poor little woman' but 'poor little *widow*'. According to the Old Testament, widows should be pitied and seen as deserving of charity, along with strangers, orphans, and the poor. As Thurston has pointed out, such ideas stemmed from a particular historical context. The Hebrew law code, for example, made no provisions for a widow's rights of inheritance.[98] However, these Biblical ideas about widows continued to be upheld into the later medieval period, partly through canon law, and this way of thinking about widows seems to have found its way into the Derby return.[99]

Most female taxpayers in the Derby return, like their male equivalents, are classified by an occupational designation, regardless of whether they were never married or widowed. Where the sexes do differ is in the variety of occupational designations used to describe them. Male taxpayers are classified by a vast array of designations (see Table 3.5), not all of which are necessary to justify an assessment as some of the men with a trade designation are assessed at the minimum rate; some of the designations actually replicate the man's byname.[100] Of the sixty-four women described by an occupational status, two are classified as dyers, five as labourers, but fifty-seven are described as spinners, either by a Middle English or a Latin term (see Table 3.6). Was it likely that all those women were chiefly engaged in spinning, or was this some form of shorthand to justify the minimum rate in a return that generally assigns most taxpayers an occupational designation? There are indications that some of the women so classified had other occupations, if we take the evidence of bynames.[101] There is, for example, a Margareta le Mustarder (mustard-maker), an Emma Lokesmyth (locksmith), an Alicia Pulter

[96] Vulgate Bible, Luke 21:2. The Wycliffite Bible is one used by the *MED*: see litel (adj) 5(e). In Mark's version of the story the phrase is *vidua pauper*: Mark 12: 42.

[97] Cf. the 'poor widow' discussed p. 30 above.

[98] Thurston, *Widows*, esp. pp. 13–14.

[99] See Brundage, 'Widows as Disadvantaged Persons'. See also Hanawalt, 'Widow's Mite', p. 21.

[100] See e.g. 'Henrico Barbour barbit[onsor]': Fenwick (ed.), *Poll Taxes*, i, p. 98. There is a tendency towards using the more general categories of 'labourer' and 'artisan' at the beginning and end of the return, though: ibid., pp. 97–9.

[101] Goldberg evidently used byname evidence for his analysis of women's occupations from poll tax returns. Compare his assessment of women's occupations as revealed by the return for Bishop's Lynn with Table 3.2 above: Goldberg, *Women, Work, and Life Cycle*, pp. 94–6.

Table 3.5: The classification of males in the 1379 Derby poll tax return

Categories	No.
labourer	185
servant	62
artisan	17
son	11
brewer	10
cobbler	10
butcher	6
merchant	6
barker	5
shearman	5
ironmonger	4
miller	3
baker	3
painter	3
cultivator	3
fisherman	3
thresher	2
swineherd	2
glazer	2
roper	2
saddler	2
harrower	1
smith	1
clerk	1
cutler	1
fletcher	1
barber	1
doctor	1
master scholar	1
dyer	1
draper	1
carter	1
walker	1
potter	1
gentleman	1
glover	1
minstrel	1
weaver	1
watchman	1
plumber	1
no status	1
TOTAL	**366**

Source: Fenwick (ed.), *Poll Taxes*, i, pp. 97–100.

Table 3.6: The classification of females
in the 1379 Derby poll tax return

Status	No.	%
Occupational:	64	43
spinner	*57*	*39*
labourer	*5*	*3*
dyer	*2*	*1*
servant	59	40
daughter	16	11
widow	6	4
mother	1	1
no status	1	1
TOTAL	147	100

Source: Fenwick (ed.), *Poll Taxes*, i, pp. 97–100.

(poulterer), an Agnes Naill' (nail-maker), and an Agnes Chaloner (weaver of chalouns, a figured woollen material). A similar range of occupations has been noted for women in other late fourteenth-century towns.[102] Perhaps women had less clearly identifiable occupational statuses than men: the 1363 Artificers' Act ruled that men should keep to one trade, but did not try to apply this to women.[103] It is possible that women who made mustard or nails might have supplemented their livelihoods by spinning. Yet, the lack of variety in the occupational designations for women does suggest that, while the Derby assessors generally used an occupational rather than a marital status for female as well as male taxpayers, there was less interest in the form of the work that women undertook, hence the default classification as a spinner.

The 1379 return for Howdenshire enables further consideration of the significance of occupational statuses to a person's fiscal identity in that some of those assessed have both a relational status, such as 'his wife', 'son', or 'daughter', and an occupational one.[104] It is, therefore,

---

[102] See e.g. Goldberg, *Women, Work, and Life Cycle*, ch. 3 (esp. pp. 86–104); Carlin, *Medieval Southwark*, pp. 174–5.

[103] Luders (ed.), *Statutes of the Realm*, i, pp. 379–80; H. Swanson, *Medieval Artisans: An Urban Class in Late Medieval England* (Oxford: Basil Blackwell, 1989), pp. 4–5; cf. Goldberg, *Women, Work, and Life Cycle*, p. 99.

[104] 'Assessment Roll of the Poll-Tax for Howdenshire, Etc., in the Second Year of the Reign of King Richard II (1379)', *Yorkshire Archaeological Journal*, 9 (1886), 129–62; see now Fenwick (ed.), *Poll Taxes*, iii, pp. 194–209.

one of a small number of returns that not only refers to the existence of a wife but also gives her an occupational status.[105] The interest of the Howdenshire return here, though, lies in its treatment of daughters residing in the parental home, as compared with that in the Bishop's Lynn return. In the Howdenshire return, resident sons and daughters, those described as 'his/her son' or 'daughter' in relation to a parent listed above and without a spouse, frequently have another category denoting an occupation (102 of the 117 daughters and ninety-four of the 116 sons). The majority of them are described as servants (eighty-one of the females, seventy-three of the males), then as labourers (fifteen and nineteen respectively), all assessed at the minimum rate. When other occupational designations are used the assessment increases to 6d.: the daughters are labelled as weavers (four) or brewsters (two), and the sons as a carpenter (one) and a poulterer (one).[106] These occupations evidently indicated that the person should pay at the rate for an artificer. For those assessed at the minimum rate, though, the additional designation also makes evident the economic contribution of sons and daughters within their households.[107] While the Bishop's Lynn return did not classify resident daughters in relation to work, and generally assigned them a different marital designation than that for females who lived outside the parental home as servants, this return makes no such distinction, to the extent that resident daughters are classified as servants. It thus reinforces the earlier arguments that assessors make choices about how to classify taxpayers and that they might be influenced by ideas from outside the immediate context of taxation in their classification of female taxpayers.

The schedule for the 1379 tax categorized the majority of female taxpayers as *femmes soles*, with the category of 'widow' relevant for the better-off only to associate a woman with the status of her former husband. The 1377 poll tax listings indicate wives (in a relational way), but other female taxpayers are not divided into never-married or widowed. In the 1379 returns there was also no need to distinguish between the never-married and widowed, unless the widow was to be assessed according to her former husband's status (and this is generally the case in the Salisbury return, which uses *sola* for both the never-married and the widowed). Yet some returns (including

105 This supports the earlier contention that a wife's occupation might be taken into account in the married man's assessment: see p. 75 above.

106 'Assessment Roll of the Poll-Tax for Howdenshire', pp. 132, 133, 141, 144, 146, 153, 156, 159.

107 See also Goldberg, *Women, Work, and Life Cycle*, pp. 166–7.

that of Bishop's Lynn) do use the category 'widow' more generally, when there does not appear to be a fiscal logic for such classifications. The Bishop's Lynn return goes further still and also marks out a particular group of never-married females, the resident daughter, with its use of the term *puella*. Although this usage in a poll tax return is unique to this listing, other 1379 returns demonstrate that assessors made choices between marital and occupational statuses when classifying the unmarried, female taxpayer. A particularly telling intersection is that between work identity and widowhood or daughterhood. In the Bishop's Lynn return, widows and resident daughters are generally marked out in preference to an occupational designation, whereas in the Derby return the converse is true (with 'spinner' as the default category), to the extent that the category 'widow' appears to denote a woman who did not work, albeit with associations from outside a fiscal discourse with its use of the formulation *vidua paupercula*.

THINKING WITH SINGLE WOMEN

To my knowledge, the only other text to use *puella* in relation to the poll tax (albeit the investigation into evasion of the third poll tax) is Knighton's Chronicle. A consideration of its use in Knighton's account enables further reflection on what it might connote in such a context and about how unmarried, female taxpayers might be conceptualized. Knighton used the story about tax assessors threatening to examine young girls to see if they had been sexually active to make a point about the corruption of the royal officials. But, that the story of the 'virginity test' was selected to exemplify the commissioners' corruption from, in Knighton's words, 'other such actions', does reveal a particular way of thinking about women. As this episode is used to stand for corrupt practices more generally, it can also be said that women—and, indeed, their bodies—are used symbolically in Knighton's account.

The use of women as signs, having diverse meanings assigned to them, has been discussed for a variety of historical contexts, following Lévi-Strauss's assertion that women are good for 'thinking with'.[108]

---

[108] See e.g. C. Lévi-Strauss, *Structural Anthropology*, trans. C. Jacobson and B. G. Schoepf (London: Allen Lane, 1968), pp. 61–2; Brown, *Body and Society*, pp. 153–4; J. L. Nelson, 'Women and the Word in the Earlier Middle Ages', in W. J. Sheils and

Sylvia Federico has suggested how this might function in two different ways in Knighton's account: to suggest a violation of a community's rights and to stigmatize the same community by implying that the young girls might have had sex.[109] Both readings are plausible when we accept that Knighton, while critical of the royal commissioners, was unlikely to have been sympathetic to those rebelling in 1381.[110] The first reading fits with the argument that it is women's social subordination to men, in theory at least, which allowed them to function as symbols of the marginalized more generally.[111] The second stems from a tradition in which not only was a woman's honour bound up with her chastity, but so too was that of her kin.[112] There was also a tradition in clerically authored lyrics, for example, of portraying rural maidens as sexually active.[113] The effect of Knighton's account is to draw our attention to the sexuality of the *puellulae*: we can either assume the girls were virgins or follow the commissioners in Knighton's portrayal and suspect that they had been sexually active. We can also see how the reputation of the girls had an effect on the community. It is in such a context that it perhaps makes sense for the local assessors in Bishop's Lynn to classify some people's daughters as *puellae*. In Knighton's account, though, the depiction of the female is not just in terms of her violated body. Her relationship to others in the community is stressed: she is someone's daughter. Further, she is financially dependent: 'friends and parents' pay the tax in order to avert the examinations. Again there are similarities with the *puellae* of the Bishop's Lynn return.

D. Wood (eds.), *Women in the Church: Papers Read at the 1989 Summer Meeting and the 1990 Winter Meeting of the Ecclesiastical History Society*, Studies in Church History, 27 (Oxford: Basil Blackwell, 1990), pp. 58–9; S. Lambert, 'Crusading or Spinning', in S. B. Edgington and S. Lambert (eds.), *Gendering the Crusades* (Cardiff: University of Wales Press, 2001), pp. 1–15.

[109] Federico, 'Imaginary Society', pp. 178–9; she discusses other accounts of the revolt in similar ways, pp. 174–80.

[110] See S. Justice, *Writing and Rebellion: England in 1381* (Berkeley and Los Angeles, CA: University of California Press, 1994).

[111] On the use of women and the feminine in this way, see Federico, 'Imaginary Society', p. 177; Scott, *Gender and the Politics of History*, pp. 47–8; N. Z. Davis, *Society and Culture in Early Modern France* (Cambridge: Polity Press, 1987), p. 127. For a useful discussion of whether gender subordination operated in practice in late medieval England, see Rigby, *English Society*, pp. 243–83.

[112] See e.g. Phillips, *Medieval Maidens*, pp. 146–53. See also the Lancaster guild return, discussed below: p. 111.

[113] See e.g. N. Cartlidge, '"Alas, I go with chylde": Representations of Extra-marital Pregnancy in the Middle English Lyric', *English Studies*, 5 (1998), pp. 403–5.

While historians are now attuned to the many different ways of reading a chronicle, this chapter has suggested that a poll tax return can also be subjected to a similar reading. The returns offer different and conflicting representations of the unmarried, female taxpayer, and not all of these are ones necessitated by the tax criteria. The compilers of the returns were, like Knighton, products of a particular society and would have been influenced by a range of discourses. Tax returns can therefore offer another way into how contemporaries conceptualized their society and the people within it.

4

The Single Woman in Guild Texts

The ordinances of the fraternity of St Christopher in Norwich set out a prayer, which was to be said at all of its meetings, for all estates of society:

we shul preyen deuotely for ye state of holy chirche, and for ye pees of ye londe; for ye pope of Rome and his Cardinals; . . . for alle Erchebisshopes and bisshopes, and specialy for oure bisshope of Norwiche; for all parsones and prestes, and alle orders of holy chirche. . . for oure lorde ye kyng, for oure lady ye qwen, Duckes, Erles, Barouns, and Bachelers of ye londe, . . . for alle knyghtes, squyers, cite3enis and Burgeys, fraunkeleyns, and alle trewe tyliers and men of craft, wydoues, maydenes, wyfes, and for alle ye communalte and cristen peple, . . . for alle trewe shipmen, and trewe pilgrymes, . . . for alle ye men y^t bene in fals beleue, . . . for oure faders soules, and moders, bretheren and sisteren, and for all ye bretheren and sisteren of yis gilde, and for all cristen soules: amen.[1]

The prayer uses an ordering that would not look out of place in estates literature.[2] It is conventional in its vision of society and in some ways it is reminiscent of the model of society contained in the schedule for the 1379 poll tax.[3] The first estate, the clergy, is discussed first, followed by the laity, from the king downwards. Strohm comments that it contains an element of anachronism in its high ranking of the knights-bachelor among the lords.[4] Urban groups are integrated into this hierarchy but, with the exception of the queen, women are discussed after most of the status and occupational groups as widows, maidens, and wives. Thus we have here a model of society that classified men generally by

[1] Smith (ed.), *English Gilds*, pp. 22–3.
[2] On this genre see R. Mohl, *The Three Estates in Medieval and Renaissance Literature* (New York, NY: Columbia University Press, 1933); J. Mann, *Chaucer and Medieval Estates Satire: The Literature of Social Classes and the* General Prologue *to the* Canterbury Tales (Cambridge: Cambridge University Press, 1973).
[3] See Ch. 3, 'The schedule for the 1379 tax', above.
[4] Strohm, *Social Chaucer*, p. 191 n. 20.

their social or occupational status, but women by their stage in the life-cycle. This prayer was included in the fraternity's return of 1388–9, a return demanded by the Cambridge Parliament of 1388. However, guild texts rarely attempted to conceptualize society in general; their classifications normally relate to guild members. The fraternity or guild, a voluntary association of people bound together by an oath, was not typically an all-inclusive association: there was usually an enrolment fee plus an annual subscription, and some guilds selected their own membership through various other entrance criteria.[5] This prayer, with its attention to social hierarchies, only refers to the guild member in the language of equal brotherhood, as a brother or a sister.[6] Yet guilds and their texts, with their mixture of religious and economic concerns, provide an opportunity to discuss how different concerns might affect the classification of women, albeit the women who were eligible to join.

While distinctions between 'craft' and 'religious' guilds can be over-drawn,[7] this chapter is largely concerned with fraternities that did not limit membership to a particular craft, as the latter were less open to women.[8] Guilds generally served a number of functions: the mainte-nance of lights before images, usually of the guild's patron saint, in the form of a great torch or candles; a decent burial for a deceased

---

[5] See further G. Rosser, 'Communities of Parish and Guild in the Late Middle Ages', in S. J. Wright (ed.), *Parish, Church and People: Local Studies in Lay Religion 1350–1750* (London: Hutchinson, 1998), pp. 29–55; B. A. Hanawalt and B. R. McRee, 'The Guilds of *homo prudens* in Late Medieval England', *Continuity and Change*, 7 (1992), 163–79; E. Duffy, *The Stripping of the Altars: Traditional Religion in England c. 1400–c. 1580* (New Haven, CT: Yale University Press, 1992), pp. 141–54.

[6] The tension between espousing equality and observing hierarchies was a feature of guild life. See further G. Rosser, 'Going to the Fraternity Feast: Commensality and Social Relations in Late Medieval England', *Journal of British Studies*, 33 (1994), 430–46.

[7] See V. R. Bainbridge, *Gilds in the Medieval Countryside: Social and Religious Change in Cambridgeshire c.1350–1558* (Woodbridge: Boydell Press, 1996), pp. 1–5; C. M. Barron, 'The Parish Fraternities of Medieval London', in C. M. Barron and C. Harper-Bill (eds.), *The Church in Pre-Reformation Society: Essays in Honour of F.R.H. Du Boulay* (Woodbridge: Boydell Press, 1985), p. 14.

[8] See M. Kowaleski and J. M. Bennett, 'Crafts, Gilds, and Women in the Middle Ages: Fifty Years After Marian K. Dale', in J. M. Bennett *et al.* (eds.), *Sisters and Workers in the Middle Ages* (Chicago, IL: University of Chicago Press, 1989), pp. 11–25; G. Rosser, 'Crafts, Guilds and the Negotiation of Work in the Medieval Town', *Past and Present*, 154 (1997), 3–31, esp. p. 22; H. Swanson, 'The Illusion of Economic Structure: Craft Guilds in Later Medieval English Towns', *Past and Present*, 121 (1988), 29–48, esp. pp. 39–40; P. J. P. Goldberg, 'Craft Guilds, The Corpus Christi Play and Civic Government', in S. Rees Jones (ed.), *The Government of Medieval York: Essays in Commemoration of the 1396 Royal Charter* (York: Borthwick Institute of Historical Research, 1997), pp. 141–63, esp. pp. 147–8.

member (if not paid for, then at least attended by the entire company); posthumous intercession on his or her behalf, and the promotion of mutual charity and sociability, often at a communal feast associated with a saint's day.[9] While all these functions had a religious dimension, they also provided economic, social, and political benefits to guild members. Gervase Rosser's work on guilds in urban society has emphasized how guilds offered members a means of gaining 'social credit', establishing themselves as persons of good repute, which was crucial for securing economic credit. For recent immigrants and women in general this was undoubtedly an important function of guilds. In return members had to commit to active involvement (turning up at funerals, meetings, and feasts, and praying if the guild could not afford its own priest), pay regular dues and often an entrance fee, and agree to a certain code of behaviour.[10] Some fraternities might encompass the entire parish community, as well as select outsiders, whereas others were more elite groupings. Thus these were influential groups within society, albeit ones that functioned locally. This chapter also briefly considers 'maidens' lights' and 'wives' stores', sub-parochial groupings according to age and marital status, which are often referred to as 'guilds' in the scholarly literature.

The intersection of moral and economic concerns is a recurring theme in this study; the dominant view of marriage saw it as the proper place for sex and the male control of property, with the result that the category 'single woman' sometimes emerges from concerns about sexual morality, but sometimes signals legal and economic independence. This chapter first considers what prompts the use of the category 'single woman' in some guild returns of 1388–9. It can be found in five of the extant returns, seven if one counts 'single sister' as an equivalent.[11] In the five that use 'single woman' and one of those that uses 'single

---

[9] See n. 5 above for references.

[10] G. Rosser, 'Workers' Associations in English Medieval Towns', in P. Lambrechts and J-P. Sosson (eds.), *Les Métiers au moyen âge: aspects économiques et sociaux* (Louvain-la-Neuve: Institut d'Études Médiévales de l'Université Catholique de Louvain, 1994), pp. 285–91; Rosser, 'Crafts, Guilds and the Negotiation of Work', pp. 9–11. On women and 'personal credit', see also McIntosh, *Working Women*, pp. 9–13. On guilds' codes of conduct see B. R. McRee, 'Religious Gilds and Regulation of Behavior in Late Medieval Towns', in J. Rosenthal and C. Richmond (eds.), *People, Politics and Community in the Later Middle Ages* (Gloucester: Alan Sutton, 1987), pp. 108–22; Rosser, 'Communities of Parish and Guild', pp. 36–7.

[11] This is based on an examination of all the returns in TNA: PRO, C 47/38–46, in conjunction with the 471 summaries in H. F. Westlake, *The Parish Gilds of Mediæval England* (London: Society for Promoting Christian Knowledge, 1919), pp. 137–238,

sister' the terminology appears in ordinances concerned with payments; the seventh example occurs in relation to who had the right to attend guild meetings. The contention is that in these returns the categories 'single woman' and 'single sister', in Middle English and Latin, generally carry with them connotations of the legal construct *femme sole*, that is, a woman who was not under coverture and thus was legally and economically independent.[12] Yet, as with *femme sole*, other associations are also evoked by the categories; for example, that of the woman alone. The chapter then turns to guild registers and account books, which record the entry and transactions of individual members. While there are variants of the Middle English 'sengle woman' in an early sixteenth-century guild account book, the focus here is on a text, the Register of the Guild of the Holy Cross, the Blessed Mary, and St John the Baptist of Stratford-upon-Avon, that continues to use the categories 'maiden' and 'widow' for unmarried women but introduces the vernacular term 'sengilman' for unmarried (probably never-married) men in the fifteenth century. As with the poll tax returns, this suggests that the classification of individuals entailed value-laden choices and one must consider the potentially different moral associations of categories such as 'single woman', 'single man', and 'maiden'.

SINGLE SISTERS AND THE GUILD RETURNS OF 1388–9

Guild ordinances that divide their members into different categories can be read as interpretive schemes, albeit ones that are concerned with a particular subset of society. Such ordinances have largely been preserved in the guild returns of 1388–9. The texts that use the category 'single woman' or 'single sister' are all based on pre-existing guild material, which was then incorporated into the returns. There is a need, then, to consider first why the texts were written, both originally and in 1388–9.

The returns were made in response to a writ issued by the Cambridge Parliament of 1388, which asked about a guild's foundation, organization, and government (including information about oaths, meetings,

---

and the transcriptions and summaries in Smith (ed.), *English Gilds*. Some returns, though, have been found in the Bodleian Library; e.g. see C. M. Barron and L. Wright, 'The London Middle English Guild Certificates of 1388–9', *Nottingham Medieval Studies*, 39 (1995), pp. 109, 119.

[12] See Ch. 1, '*Femmes soles*' above.

ordinances), and the value of all its lands and chattels.[13] A second writ ordered masters, wardens, and surveyors of misteries or crafts to bring their royal charters or letters patent to Chancery for inspection, which reveals that the main focus of the enquiry was on informal guilds (often referred to as religious guilds).[14] The writs were initiated by a Commons petition, cited in the Westminster Chronicle, which asked that all guilds and fraternities be abolished with the exception of those acquired in mortmain by royal licence, those ordained to the honour of Holy Church and the increase of divine service, and chantries of ancient foundation.[15] One motive was clearly financial: the petition asks that the goods and lands of the suppressed guilds be spent on the war in France. Another seems to be about law and order: the petition states that those guilds which could continue should be 'without livery, confederacy, maintenance, or riots in hindrance of the law', and it follows on from a request that liveries generally should be abolished because of the disorder they cause.[16] It has been suggested that the Commons were fearful of collective activities after the Peasants' Revolt in particular.[17] Yet this petition never became law and nothing was done with the information that the Cambridge Parliament requested.[18] While the guild returns, unlike the poll tax ones, were therefore not directly linked to a state collection of revenue, their creation can be viewed as part of a bureaucratic exercise for a State that had an interest in knowing who owned what and for what purposes. In this case it was not individuals who had their details recorded, but groupings of individuals.

So who produced the returns: bureaucrats or the guilds themselves? Jan Gerchow has demonstrated that a large number of returns were produced in the royal Chancery at Westminster and that, of those not produced in Chancery, a considerable number were produced by local

[13] The writ is translated in Smith (ed.), *English Gilds*, pp. 127–9.

[14] Translated in ibid., p. 130. The writs are discussed in Barron and Wright, 'London Middle English Guild Certificates', pp. 108–9.

[15] L. C. Hector and B. F. Harvey (eds.), *The Westminster Chronicle 1381–1394* (Oxford: Clarendon Press, 1982), pp. 356–69.

[16] Ibid., pp. 356–7.

[17] J. A. Tuck, 'The Cambridge Parliament, 1388', *English Historical Review*, 84 (1969), 225–43; J. A. Tuck, 'Nobles, Commons and the Great Revolt of 1381', in R. H. Hilton and T. H. Aston (eds.), *The English Rising of 1381* (Cambridge: Cambridge University Press, 1984), pp. 208–10; Barron, 'Parish Fraternities', p. 20; D. J. F. Crouch, *Piety, Fraternity and Power: Religious Gilds in Late Medieval Yorkshire 1389–1547* (Woodbridge: York Medieval Press, 2000), pp. 14, 16.

[18] Tuck, 'Cambridge Parliament', p. 237.

scribes or chanceries, rather than by the guilds themselves.[19] Yet this does not mean that such returns do not reveal guild values. Gerchow divides the returns into what he calls the 'redaction-type' and the 'insert-type'. Redaction-type returns were composed from the responses that guild officials gave to questions but their responses were reformulated and thus strongly influenced by chancery scribes.[20] Insert-type returns quote pre-existing documents word for word and just add a preface and conclusion (or, to use diplomatic nomenclature, protocol and eschatocol), and thus can lay claim to being guild texts; all the returns discussed below are of this type.

The information relayed by the guild officials was doubtless affected by that requested in the writ, namely details of its foundation, organization, government, and possessions. It was probably also affected by what the guild officials thought lay behind the inquiry. Although the writs did not set out the reasons for the inquiry, the returns suggest that guilds were careful to present themselves in certain ways.[21] For example, some were concerned to allay any suspicions that they encouraged dissent against either the State or the Church, at a time when the memory of the Peasants' Revolt was still fresh and the fear of Lollardy was growing.[22] The prayer quoted at the start of the chapter, with its inclusion of the ecclesiastical and lay hierarchies and its concern for the peace of the land and false believers, certainly fulfills this function for the fraternity of St Christopher in Norwich.[23] Further, the insert-type return would have been affected by the nature of the written texts that the guild possessed, such as their ordinances. Ordinances, by their very nature, are prescriptive. They state what members should and should not do. Thus they tend either to the normative (what applied to most members in most situations), or the atypical (if a member was to do X then he would be expelled, suggesting that X was something that rarely

---

[19] J. Gerchow, 'Gilds and Fourteenth-Century Bureaucracy: The Case of 1388–9', *Nottingham Medieval Studies*, 40 (1996), p. 113.

[20] Ibid., p. 128.

[21] Gerchow comments on how first the writs and then the responses helped create artificial distinctions between 'religious' and 'craft' guilds: ibid., pp. 134–5.

[22] C. Sanok, 'Performing Feminine Sanctity in Late Medieval England: Parish Guilds, Saints' Plays, and the *Second Nun's Tale*', *Journal of Medieval and Early Modern Studies*, 32 (2002), pp. 276–7, 282. See further M. E. Aston, 'Lollardy and Sedition, 1381–1431', *Past and Present*, 17 (1960), 1–44.

[23] Tuck argues that guilds in the eastern counties, where the 1381 rebellion began, were particularly concerned to show that their activities were legitimate: Tuck, 'Cambridge Parliament', p. 237.

happened or, as Ben McRee has suggested, something that a member could not be allowed to be caught doing).[24]

The reasons why the texts were written, both originally and in 1388–9, results in texts that portray guilds according to what guilds thought a guild should be and what they thought would reassure parliament.[25] One therefore needs to consider the extent to which the representation of guild members in a return relates to the social reality of the guild's membership. The language of the returns has been analysed previously by those interested in the sexual composition of guilds. Barbara Hanawalt and Ben McRee counted which returns made a reference to guild sisters in order to ascertain which allowed female membership and found such references in 79.4 per cent of the over 500 surviving guild returns.[26] Caroline Barron has used references to 'sisters' in the returns for the London parish guilds to argue that their membership was 'markedly feminine'.[27] Virginia Bainbridge, in her study of the Cambridgeshire guild returns, has taken this type of analysis a stage further:

When the 1389 statutes are analysed closely the occurrence of the term *soror* shows that some areas of gild life were open to women and others were not . . . In all the urban statutes of 1389 the term *soror* is confined to the passages detailing funerals, commemorative rites and prayers for the dead . . . In the statutes from rural fraternities the term *soror* is used more widely, which suggests that women may have played a broader role in rural guild life.[28]

Although the approach taken here is also to look for the incidence of certain terms and where they occur, it is important that we do not assume that the returns can always be taken at face value. For example, just because a return explicitly states that a single woman could join if she paid a certain amount does not mean that single women were a core group within that guild. Perhaps the purpose of the statement was to set a high entrance fee so that single women would be deterred from joining.[29] Such statements therefore need to be understood in the

[24] McRee, 'Religious Gilds and Regulation of Behavior', esp. pp. 115–16. For the statutes of craft guilds as normative or idealistic, see Rosser, 'Crafts, Guilds and the Negotiation of Work', p. 5.

[25] See also Bainbridge, *Gilds in the Medieval Countryside*, pp. 25–7.

[26] Hanawalt and McRee, 'Guilds of *homo prudens*', pp. 166, 177 n. 7.

[27] Barron, 'Parish Fraternities', p. 30.

[28] Bainbridge, *Gilds in the Medieval Countryside*, pp. 46–7.

[29] On membership dues restricting membership see Rosser, 'Communities of Parish and Guild', p. 36; Hanawalt and McRee, 'Guilds of *homo prudens*', p. 167; B. R. McRee,

context of the return as a whole. The intention here is to analyse how guilds conceptualize their membership.

The category 'single woman' is found in five of the extant returns, seven if one counts 'single sister' as an equivalent. All of these returns relate to urban guilds, which were probably more likely to recruit single women as members (scholars have found a higher concentration of women in towns, perhaps because of increased opportunities for work).[30] In two of these, the returns for the London guilds of St Katherine and SS Fabian and Sebastian, both in the church of St Botolph Aldersgate, it is the Middle English 'sengle womman' that is used.[31] In the other returns Latin is used. In the returns for the Kingston-upon-Hull guilds of St Mary (in the church of St Mary) and St John the Baptist (church of Holy Trinity) the formulation is 'mulier sola sine viro'.[32] In those for the Cambridge guilds of Holy Trinity (church of St Mary) and St Katherine (church of St Andrew) the expressions are 'mulier non maritata' and 'soror sine viro' respectively.[33] In all six returns the categories appear in ordinances concerned with payments; in the returns for Cambridge's St Katherine's guild and Kingston-upon-Hull's St Mary's guild it is also used elsewhere in the returns. The seventh example is in the return for Lancaster's guild of the Holy Trinity and St Leonard, which uses the formulation 'consorores non habentes viros' in relation to who had the right to attend guild meetings.[34] It is therefore the matter of payment that generally produces the category 'single woman' in these guild returns. In contrast, the category 'single man' is only used in two of these returns; the typical guild entrant is usually conceptualized as the married man or couple and, as will be seen, this emphasis on marriage also has an effect on the use of the category 'single woman'.

There are ten extant returns for London guilds, all written in Middle English.[35] Of these, eight refer to sisters, the exceptions being

'Religious Gilds and Civil Order: The Case of Norwich in the Late Middle Ages', *Speculum*, 67 (1992), p. 80.

[30] See Goldberg, *Women, Work, and Life Cycle*, esp. pp. 290–1, 297–8, 342–3, 356, 369–70; Kowaleski, 'Singlewomen', pp. 46–51.

[31] TNA: PRO, C 47/41/198; C 47/41/196. Only guilds in London and Norwich make their returns in Middle English: see Barron and Wright, 'London Middle English Guild Certificates', p. 110.

[32] C 47/46/451; C 47/46/450.

[33] C 47/38/6; C 47/38/11.   [34] C 47/39/69.

[35] They are all edited in Barron and Wright, 'London Middle English Guild Certificates', pp. 119–45 (quotations will be from this edition).

the return for the fraternity of St Nicholas (church of St Stephen's, Coleman Street), and that for the fraternity of the Annunciation and Assumption, Craft of Pouchmakers (church of St Mary Bedlam without Bishopsgate and St Paul's), although the latter makes some funeral provision for the wife of a brother.[36] Two returns, those for the guilds of St Katherine and SS Fabian and Sebastian, both in the church of St Botolph Aldersgate, use the term 'sengle womman' in their sections dealing with how much members had to pay to the guild. The Latin protocol for the St Katherine's return makes it clear that the guild had pre-existing written material, presumably from which the return was copied with the addition of this brief explanatory preface.[37] Similarities with the return of their neighbouring guild, St Fabian's, suggest that the two guilds may have consulted each other when drawing up their ordinances.[38] The two passages concerning membership dues are very similar in layout, although there are some differences, for example in subscription rates (3d. per person to join St Katherine's guild; 4d. to join that of St Fabian), and in phrasing, which will be discussed below.

Whereas the return for the guild of St Anne's Chantry (church of St Lawrence, old Jewry) simply states 'that eueri man & woman of this companye paie eueri yeer by terme of his lyf foure tymes a yeer iijd for his quartrages',[39] the corresponding ordinance in the St Katherine's return divides up its members, despite them all meriting the same quarterly charge:

that what man is take in to be brother schal paie to the almesse at his entre as the maystres & he mowe acorde & eueri quarter for to meyntene the liyt & the almesse of the brotherhede iij. d'. And yif he haue a wyf & zhe wil be a suster than schal he paie six pans for hem bothe in the quarter that is ij. s'. in the yeer & yif a sengle womman come in to the brotherhede paie as a brother doth.[40]

The ordinance starts with the male entrant, the archetypal guild member. His marital status is not specified initially but it is then noted that,

---

[36] See ibid., p. 141. On fraternities in London see further Barron, 'Parish Fraternities'.

[37] Barron and Wright, 'London Middle English Guild Certificates', p. 136; discussed in ibid., p. 112.

[38] Although written in the same hand, the similarities were probably not down to the scribe as the same hand can be seen in the returns for St Anne's Chantry guild (St Lawrence, Old Jewry) and the Annunciation and Assumption guild of the Craft of Pouchmakers (St Paul), which have very different sections dealing with entry: ibid., pp. 119, 122, 140 (the St Anne's guild return will be discussed below).

[39] Ibid., p. 122.   [40] Ibid., p. 136.

if he was married, his wife could also join if she wanted. Then the 'sengle womman' is discussed, although her entry seems less typical: '*yif* a sengle womman come in to the brotherhede' (my italics). She should pay the same as the man, that is an entrance fee (amount unspecified) and 3d. a quarter. The wife incurred the quarterly rate but not a joining fee. It was also expected that her husband would pay for both of them ('than schal he paie . . . for hem bothe'). The ordinance thus makes use of a single/married binary division for women, with the key difference being how much was to be paid and by whom: the 'sengle womman' was liable for all her payments, but the married woman's dues were to be paid by her husband, and her entry fee was covered by his. The binary here equates with that of the legal concepts *femme sole* and *femme coverte*.

The corresponding ordinance for the St Fabian's guild is very similar in layout to the St Katherine's one but there are differences in the phrasing, some of which are significant:

that eueri man schal paie atte ffurste comynge in to the brotherhede half a mark & iiijd. eueri quarter to meyntene the liyt of the brotherhede & the almesse & yif the man wil haue his wyf a suster than schal that paiement stonde for hem bothe & zhe to paie in the quarter othere iiijd. that is two schillinges in the yeer for hem bothe And yif a sengle womman come in to the bretherhede zhe schal paie no lasse than a brother doth.[41]

The male entrant is again discussed first but it is then assumed that he has a wife, although (according to this ordinance) it is up to him whether she joins: '*yif* the man wil haue his wyf a suster' (my italics). His entrance fee of half a mark was to stand for them both. The statement that 'zhe to paie in the quarter othere iiijd' presumably means that the wife only needed to pay 4d. in alternate quarters (8d. in a year), which with the husband's 16d. would total 2s. per annum.[42] Thus the wife warranted a reduced quarterly payment in this guild. Although the statement initially seems to suggest that the wife would pay ('zhe to paie'), the adding together of the husband and wife's fees perhaps indicates that the man was again expected to pay. The 'sengle womman' is then discussed. Here it is said that 'zhe schal paie no lasse than a brother doth', presumably because the married woman had warranted

---

[41] Ibid., p. 138.

[42] *MED*, other (adj.) 1a. (a) Second of two; cf. ibid., 7. (a) Additional, further. If the clause meant that the wife warranted 'another' four pence payment a quarter, the joint payment would be 2s. 8d.

a reduced rate.[43] In this ordinance it is not just that the husband was liable for his wife's dues but also that he could pay a reduced rate for her.

In these London guilds the single woman is not set an elevated rate; the annual rates of 1s. 4d. and 1s. respectively are quite typical amounts, although they might deter the unskilled worker on a daily wage of around 3d.[44] Yet both guilds made it cheaper for the wife of a brother to join (no entrance fee), particularly the guild of St Fabian's with its reduced subscription rate. Four of the five other examples of the category 'single woman' or 'single sister' in a guild return not only appear in sections setting out how much the single woman should pay to join, but in sections that state she had to pay the same as a married couple. The married couple in these returns, those for guilds in Cambridge and Kingston-upon-Hull, are thus treated as though one person (reminiscent of St Paul's dicta that a husband and wife become one flesh).[45] They therefore surpass the common law conception of a married woman's coverture, in which the husband is held responsible for his wife's debts, in that they allow a single payment to cover both husband and wife.[46]

There are eight extant guild returns for the town of Cambridge, all written in Latin, of which six make reference to women as guild sisters (the other two refer to women only as the wives of brothers).[47] That the returns for the great Cambridge guilds use the expression *uxor fratris* more frequently than *soror*, and limit use of the term *soror* to certain ordinances, led Bainbridge to conclude that '[t]hese organisations may have been rather like the gentlemen's or working men's clubs which still exist today: male clannish affairs with ladies in attendance only on high

[43] Elsewhere some single women paid a lower fee. See 'Maidens and single men' below; Hanawalt and McRee, 'Guilds of *homo prudens*', p. 166.

[44] The majority of the London guilds that made a return had an annual rate of 1s. and Hanawalt and McRee calculated a national average to be 1s. 4d.: Barron and Wright, 'London Middle English Guild Certificates', p. 116; Hanawalt and McRee, 'Guilds of *homo prudens*', p. 167. For the argument that women earned less than men in the late fourteenth century, see Bardsley, 'Women's Work'; Bennett, 'Medieval Women, Modern Women', pp. 160–2.

[45] Ephesians 5: 31: see Kerr, 'Husband and Wife', p. 212.

[46] Cf. the 1379 tax schedule, which also does this: Ch. 3, 'The schedule for the 1379 tax' above.

[47] They are all edited in M. Bateson (ed.), *Cambridge Gild Records*, Cambridge Antiquarian Society, 8th ser., 39 (London: George Bell and Sons, 1903), and quotations will be from this edition; the returns for the guild of St Mary's (church of St Botulph) and the guild of the Purification (Great St Mary's) are the ones that refer to brothers' wives only. On the former as a wealthy guild see ibid., p. xxxiii.

days or holidays, at feasts and funerals'.[48] Yet two of these returns, those for the guilds of Holy Trinity (church of St Mary) and St Katherine (church of St Andrew), refer to the single woman or the single sister in ordinances concerned with payments, although the latter guild also refers to her elsewhere in the return.

The Holy Trinity return states that the guild wardens are returning their certificate of foundation in answer to the 1389 proclamation, then gives the text of their certificate (which includes ordinances), and ends by certifying that the guild has no lands or goods.[49] It thus equates with Gerchow's 'insert-type'; the ordinances are from a pre-existing guild text. The ordinance about membership dues sets out that any brother or sister who joined the guild should pay 14d. per annum, but the expression 'pro se et uxore sua' shifts the focus swiftly from the 'fratrem sive sororem' to the married man as the typical entrant, accompanied by his wife.[50] This is also reflected in the list of the guild's founders, who were all men and their wives.[51] However, the unmarried woman (*mulier non maritata*) is referred to specifically later on, where it is spelt out that, *if* such a woman was to join, she should pay the same 'as a brother and his wife'.[52] The single woman is defined in opposition to the norm of the married couple: she is the 'woman not married'. It is the single woman's financial independence, her legal position as *femme sole*, which produces the category 'single woman' in this text (in contrast to the absence of the category 'single man'). A man's payment covered the membership of his wife (assuming he had one, as this return did).

The return for the guild of St Katherine (church of St Andrew) also appears to be a copy of their foundation deed but it does not have a protocol or eschatocol.[53] It sets out that each brother should pay 1s. per annum, payable in quarterly instalments. Although it discusses the fine for arrears for brothers and sisters, wives excluded ('uxoribus

---

[48] Bainbridge, *Gilds in the Medieval Countryside*, p. 47. The returns make clear that guilds are not confined to residents of a particular parish; see Bateson (ed.), *Cambridge Gild Records*, p. xxix.

[49] Ibid., pp. 124–8.   [50] Ibid., p. 127.   [51] Ibid., p. 124.

[52] Ibid., p. 127: 'si aliqua mulier non maritata . . . fuerit admissa tunc in eadem forma solvat sicut frater et uxor ejus solvant prout superius declaratum est'. Bainbridge incorrectly refers to this return as belonging to Cambridge's other Holy Trinity guild, that associated with Holy Trinity church, which was one of the town's elite guilds: Bainbridge, *Gilds in the Medieval Countryside*, p. 47. That guild's return is TNA: PRO, C 47/38/10, edited in Bateson (ed.), *Cambridge Gild Records*, pp. 108–28, and discussed in Bainbridge, *Gilds in the Medieval Countryside*, pp. 36, 44, 88–9, 134.

[53] Bateson (ed.), *Cambridge Gild Records*, pp. 77–81.

fratrum istius gilde dumtaxat exceptis'), the subscription rate for the single woman is not set out until further on in the return, where it is stated that an unmarried sister (*soror sine viro*) should also pay 1s. a year.[54] This is followed by the statement that *when* she marries ('et cum pervenerit ad maritagium'), her husband could enter the guild for a fee to be arranged with the masters; the single woman is therefore also the 'to-be-married woman'.[55] But this return does refer to the single woman again, perhaps reflecting the list of founders, which names two women with trade bynames alongside nineteen men (three who are listed with their wives): the single woman was also liable for an official's fee, along with any brother and the guild's cleric, but not married women.[56] Within the return, then, the single woman is again largely discussed in relation to what she should pay. The married woman, in contrast, is again portrayed as covered by all her husband's payments, apart from a symbolic offering of half a penny on the guild's saint's day, which all members should make.[57]

The two returns for Kingston-upon-Hull, also written in Latin, have similar emphases on the single woman as economically liable and on the married couple as the guild norm, although the membership rates set out in these returns are much higher than those for the other guilds discussed. Again the returns are essentially the guild's foundation deeds (which include ordinances), with eschatocols setting out the guilds' assets, as requested by the 1388 writ.[58] In the return for the guild of St Mary (church of St Mary), the married man (*virum sponsatum*) is discussed first in relation to membership dues and was to pay 2s. 2d. per annum for himself and his wife ('pro se et uxore eius').[59] The single man and the single woman (*solus sine uxore*; *sola sine viro*) are discussed next and were to pay 2s. 2d. each per annum. If they were then to

[54] Bateson (ed.), *Cambridge Gild Records*, pp. 78, 80.

[55] Ibid., p. 80: 'et cum pervenerit ad maritagium, si maritus suus volverit ingredi hujusmodi fraternitatem, solvet'. Cf. the return for Cambridge's guild of the Annunciation (church of St Mary), which states that no *uxor* whose husband was not a guild member could be admitted: ibid., p. 67.

[56] Ibid., p. 77 (Margeria Sheremanne and Helwysia Kempster). See also Bainbridge, *Gilds in the Medieval Countryside*, p. 49. The text is dated 1385, suggesting the guild's recent creation. Bateson (ed.), *Cambridge Gild Records*, p. 81: 'Et apparitor recipiet quolibet fratre ingrediente sive sorore sine viro unum denarium et clericus similiter tantum'.

[57] Bateson (ed.), *Cambridge Gild Records*, p. 80.

[58] See Smith (ed.), *English Gilds*, pp. 155–62, esp. pp. 155, 160, 162. On the three extant returns for Kingston-upon-Hull see Crouch, *Piety, Fraternity and Power*, pp. 31, 104–5.

[59] TNA: PRO, C 47/46/451; see also the summary in Smith (ed.), *English Gilds*, p. 155.

marry, those membership dues would cover the spouse too. Similarly, if either of the married couple died then the other would continue paying the annual rate of 2s. The corresponding part of the return for the guild of St John the Baptist (church of Holy Trinity) is similar. It sets out that a married couple should pay 2s. a year for them both, but a single man or single woman would also pay the same, and there are analogous references to how this would be affected by marriage or the death of a spouse. For example, another ordinance in this return refers to what happened if a man were to marry a sister of the guild: he was to pay an entrance fee of not less than 6s. 8d. to the guild. This clearly implies that he would receive a reduced rate, in that others paid 13s. 4d.[60] In contrast, the return for the guild of St Mary considers the widowed brother who remarries, as is natural and often done ('ut est moris naturaliter'): the second wife could become a sister without any entry payment.[61] The different focus in these two guilds, on the eligible guild sister or the eligible brother, might again be a reflection of the marital status of the founding members of these guilds. The return for the guild of St John the Baptist names eight married couples and five other men as its founders, and some of the latter could have been single.[62] That of St Mary lists nine married couples, another man, and three women as its founders but notes at the end of the deed that the wife of the lone man named had since joined the guild, whereas the three women were single, as will be discussed below.[63] Nevertheless, both returns set up marriage as the norm for their members. It is also telling that the new husband had to pay to join the guild, whereas the new wife could enter without charge.

The high price of entry to these guilds, but with exemptions or reductions for spouses, suggests that these guilds sought to limit their membership to a select group and their families. Kingston-upon-Hull's Corpus Christi guild (church of Holy Trinity) allowed sons and daughters of existing guild members to enter the guild without charge, but required others to pay 3 lb. of silver, which was presumably a deterrent.[64] The two Kingston-upon-Hull returns which discuss the

[60] TNA: PRO, C 47/46/450; see the translation in J. M. Lambert, *Two Thousand Years of Gild Life* (Hull: A. Brown & Sons, 1891), pp. 112–13, or the summary in Smith (ed.), *English Gilds*, p. 162.

[61] Smith (ed.), *English Gilds*, p. 159.

[62] See Lambert, *Two Thousand Years*, p. 112.

[63] The single women are named as Johanna de Patryngton, Cecilia de Balne, and Alicia de Lecarnell: C 47/46/451. See also Smith (ed.), *English Gilds*, pp. 155, 160.

[64] TNA: PRO, C 47/46/449. See Smith (ed.), *English Gilds*, p. 161.

single woman at various points discuss her not just as a woman without a husband, but also as a woman who does not have a brother or sister within the guild ('mulier sola sine viro frater vel soror in predictam gildam'). For example, this formulation is used in the return for the guild of St John when discussing the single person's subscription fee (although the single man is just a man without a wife).[65] This perhaps suggests that an unmarried woman who was related to an existing guild member could be covered by his/her payment in the same way that a married woman was covered by her husband's payment. The purpose of the formulation in the return for the guild of St Mary is more apparent in that it is used when discussing what would happen if the single man or the single woman fell into arrears with his/her payments to the guild: their goods would be seized and, if they did not have any, the sum would be levied on whoever in the guild had stood as surety for their entrance.[66] Presumably if the single woman had a close relative in the guild then it would have been expected that s/he would help pay in such a situation.[67] In these formulations, then, *mulier sola* is not just a single woman but a woman alone. The apparently tautological 'single without a husband' (*sola sine viro*) should perhaps be read as 'alone without a husband', a less neutral formulation than 'single woman'.[68]

In the return for Kingston-upon-Hull's guild of St Mary there are two further references to single women: one in relation to loans and one regarding some of the guild's founders. The former considers the potential poverty of a member from a different perspective but again it is only concerned with men or unmarried women. It sets out that if any brother or unmarried sister ('sororem solam sine viro'), who was young and able to work, had become (through no fault of his or her own) so poor that help was needed, the guild would loan each one 10s. so that they could find some form of work that would allow them to pay back the loan and be self-sufficient again.[69] This is one of the few ordinances in which the formulation 'brother or unmarried sister' is used as opposed to the generic 'brother or sister'. A comparable ordinance in the return for the guild of Corpus Christi suggests that it was open

[65] The single man is denoted as 'homus solus sine viro [sic]': C 47/46/450.
[66] The single man is denoted as 'homus solus sine uxore': C 47/46/451.
[67] One of the female founders, Johanna de Patryngton, was perhaps related to Richard de Patryngton and his wife Isabel: ibid.
[68] Cf. *Liber Albus,* which used the formulation 'sola mulier sine viro': see Ch. 2, '*Femmes soles*' above.
[69] C 47/46/451; see also Smith (ed.), *English Gilds*, pp. 156–7.

to any brother or sister, whereas this return implicitly excludes married women.[70] The context is financial again but the focus has shifted to the guild member as worker. One can understand why the married woman is not included, as her husband would be eligible for such a payment if their household needed it. The result, though, is the conceptualization of the single woman as an independent worker.

A statement about the founders at the end of the return further reinforces the significance of coverture in these guild returns. It is recorded that all the men of the guild set their seals to the deed on behalf of themselves and their wives, as the latter are 'sub potestate viri sui', whereas the three unmarried female founders do the same because they 'are alone without husbands' ('sine viris sole sunt').[71] The wording, about wives being 'under the power of their husbands', is reminiscent of a discussion of how the law relates to persons, according to various conditions, in a thirteenth-century legal treatise known as *Bracton*: one division is whether someone was legally responsible for himself (*sui juris*) or in the *potestas* of another, and the treatise notes that 'some are under the rod, as wives etcetera'.[72] That husbands should act on behalf of their wives as well as themselves is also signalled by a statement in the return for Lancaster's guild of the Holy Trinity and St Leonard, which states that all the brothers and unmarried sisters ('consorores non habentes viros') of the guild shall meet four times a year.[73] The Lancaster return, also of the insert-type, has nothing further to say regarding the unmarried sisters of the guild.[74] Indeed, the only other point at which women are explicitly mentioned in this return is as the wives, daughters, or sisters of guild members (presumed here to be male). It is stated that 'no one shall know carnally the wife or daughter or sister of another [guild member] nor shall allow her to be known carnally by others'.[75] Not only is the female conceived of in terms of her relationship to a man, but she is also constructed as sexually passive in contrast to the male.[76]

---

[70] Smith (ed.), *English Gilds*, pp. 160–1.   [71] C 47/46/451.

[72] *Bracton*, ed. Woodbine, ii, p. 36.

[73] C 47/39/69; see also Smith (ed.), *English Gilds*, p. 164.

[74] See Gerchow, 'Gilds and Fourteenth-Century Bureaucracy', p. 126 n. 80.

[75] 'nullus eorum uxorem vel filiam vel sororem alterus cognoscat nec permittat ab alio cognosci': Westlake, *Parish Gilds*, p. 154. This is translated euphemistically as 'No one of the gild shall wrong the wife or daughter or sister of another, nor shall allow her to be wronged', in Smith (ed.), *English Gilds*, p. 163.

[76] For the argument that medieval texts present sex as something that was done by one person to another, with the active/passive distinction gendered masculine/feminine, see Karras, *Sexuality in Medieval Europe*, pp. 3–4, 23, 35. Cf. Ch. 2, n. 47 above.

To a large extent, then, it is the single woman's economic and legal independence, in contrast to the married woman's coverture, that produces the category 'single woman' in these guild returns. Of course, only some guilds draw attention to the difference, and some were perhaps prompted by their own particular circumstances: two of these guilds (St Katherine's, Cambridge and St Mary's, Kingston-upon-Hull) record unmarried female founders, which might have prompted the explicit classification of some guild members as single women.[77] Yet all the Cambridge and Kingston-upon-Hull returns that refer to the single woman seem to do so because of an emphasis placed on the married couple as the typical guild members. The unmarried member might (probably would, to adopt the guild position) bring a spouse into the guild and so their status before and after marriage needed to be addressed. In the Kingston-upon-Hull returns this also applied to the single man, but in the Cambridge return for St Katherine's it only applied to women. Indeed, of those returns that use the category 'single woman', only the two for guilds in Kingston-upon-Hull explicitly refer to the single man.

The one London return that uses the term 'sengle man', that of St Anne's Chantry (church of St Lawrence, Old Jewry), does so in relation to sexual immorality:

yif any of the company be of wikked fame of his body & take othere wyues than his owene or yif he be a sengle man & be holde a comone lechour or contecour or rebell' of his tonge he schal be warned by the wardeins iij tymes & yif he wile nat hym self amende he schal paie to the wardeins al the arrerages that he oweth to the companye & he schal be put of for euermor so that the godemen of this companye ne be nat sclaundred bi cause of hym.[78]

Although the concern of this passage is also with other forms of misbehaviour, such as brawling and insolence, the category 'single man' is produced by concern about sexual misbehaviour in particular. The ordinance begins with the married man who is not named as such; he is 'any of the company', but his status is revealed by the concern that he 'take othere wyues than his owene'. The 'single man' is thus a necessary

---

[77] As we have seen, the Cambridge guild of the Holy Trinity (church of St Mary) only had married founders and the Kingston-upon-Hull guild of St John only had married and male founders. There is no evidence regarding the founders for the London guild of St Fabian's nor Lancaster's guild of the Holy Trinity. The return for London's guild of St Katherine notes two male founders: Barron and Wright, 'London Middle English Guild Certificates', p. 136.

[78] Ibid., p. 123.

category in that the ordinance also wants to cover guild members guilty of fornication, albeit male ones only (even though the return does refer to female members).[79] Women are not discussed here apart from as the objects of the married man's attentions. This is not to say that other guild returns were not concerned with the unmarried woman's behaviour, but that such concerns do not produce the category 'single woman' in the returns.[80] In the Lancaster return, for example, when the concern was with sexual behaviour, the unmarried woman was conceptualized as someone's sister or daughter, the done-to rather than the doer. One might consider whether a different understanding and treatment of the sexualities of the single man and the single woman is also signalled by guilds, in a different context, preferring the terminology of 'maiden' to that of 'single woman', as will be discussed below.

MAIDENS AND SINGLE MEN: THE REGISTER OF THE GUILD OF THE HOLY CROSS, STRATFORD-UPON-AVON (1406–1535)

Although the returns of 1388–9 are one of our major sources for the study of English guilds, some guilds did produce and keep their own texts, such as membership registers and account books in which their members are sometimes given a personal designation. The text to be considered here is the register of the Guild of the Holy Cross, the Blessed Mary, and St John the Baptist of Stratford-upon Avon (1406–1535), along with some related material, such as the guild's account books.[81] While some men are described in the register by the Middle English term 'sengilman' from 1435–6, the category 'single woman' is not used in the period up to 1535 when the register ends. Instead the Latin terms

---

[79] See p. 104 above.

[80] See e.g. the return for Cambridge's guild of Holy Trinity (church of Holy Trinity), which states that a widow of a brother is eligible for the same poor relief as a brother or a brother's wife if she conducts herself well and does not remarry, or that for Ludlow's guild of the Palmers of St Mary (church of St Lawrence), which provided dowries for the poor 'filia bene fame': Bateson (ed.), *Cambridge Gild Records*, p. 116; TNA: PRO, C 47/46/392; see also Smith (ed.), *English Gilds*, p. 194.

[81] Shakespeare Birthplace Trust Records Office, Stratford-upon-Avon (SBTRO), MS BRT 1/1; *The Register of the Gild of the Holy Cross, the Blessed Mary and St. John the Baptist . . . of Stratford-upon-Avon*, ed. J. H. Bloom (London: Phillimore and Co., 1907); W. J. Hardy (ed.), *Stratford-on-Avon Corporation Records: The Guild Accounts* (Stratford-upon-Avon: reprinted from the Stratford-upon-Avon Herald [1886]).

for 'maiden' (*virgo* and *puella*) and 'widow' (*vidua*) are used. Chapter 5 tracks chronological changes in the use of such personal designations. It demonstrates that the term 'singlewoman' was thought an appropriate label for some women in various fifteenth- and early sixteenth-century texts, although it more generally replaced the category 'maiden' than that of 'widow'. Suffice for the moment to note that the sixteenth-century account book for the guild of St Peter in Bardwell, Suffolk, classified some of its members in the period 1512–27 by variants of the Middle English 'sengle woman' as well as, amongst others, variants of the terms 'syngle man' and 'wedowe'.[82] The contention here is that the retention of the category 'maiden', over the term 'singlewoman', in Stratford's guild register is nevertheless revealing. The Bardwell example demonstrates that not all guild records followed the same practice (although I know of no other examples), but this does not invalidate the key point, which is that the terms used to describe unmarried men and women in the Stratford register varied.[83] Such categories, particularly that of 'maiden', were perhaps retained for females because of their moral associations. It will also be demonstrated below that 'maiden' was a key category in parish collective activities, perhaps for similar reasons.

Guild registers contain a record of a guild's members and were undoubtedly important as guilds promised benefits to their members.[84] The registers vary in how they set out this information: for example, that for Coventry's guild of the Holy Trinity, St John the Baptist and St Katherine was in alphabetical order, whereas that for Luton's guild of the Holy and Undivided Trinity and the Blessed Virgin Mary was ordered by social status.[85] The latter was a lavish manuscript intended for display.[86] Stratford's register was clearly a functional record of who

[82] F. E. Warren, 'Gild of St. Peter in Bardwell', *Proceedings of the Suffolk Institute of Archaeology and Natural History*, 11 (1901), pp. 83–4. For the dating of these entries, on which Warren's edition is misleading, I am indebted to Dr Ken Farnhill (personal communication, Dec. 2000). The Latin *vidua* is also used.

[83] I am grateful to Dr Farnhill for the information that the term 'singlewoman' does not occur in the East Anglian guild account books of a similar date. On these see K. Farnhill, *Guilds and the Parish Community in Late Medieval East Anglia, c.1470–1550* (Woodbridge: York Medieval Press, 2001).

[84] See Rosser, 'Communities of Parish and Guild', p. 37. Farnhill notes that guilds also had bede rolls to record deceased members for intercessory purposes: Farnhill, *Guilds and the Parish Community*, p. 42.

[85] Farnhill, *Guilds and the Parish Community*, p. 42 n. 1.

[86] See R. Marks, 'Two Illuminated Guild Registers from Bedfordshire', in M. P. Brown and S. McKendrick (eds.), *Illuminating the Book: Makers and Interpreters. Essays*

had paid (and who owed) what to the guild and for what reason, albeit a fair copy. It begins, in English, by setting out the guild's rules for members and regarding the election of its officials. After that the register has annual headings and records, in Latin, the names and payments of its members. It is neatly written, with one hand responsible for the entries from 1406–60, another for 1460–1500, and a third for 1500–35, and these changes do affect the formulae used.[87] It seems unlikely that the entries were written up only at approximately forty-year intervals as the register also records miscellaneous debts, payments, and agreements concerning the guild, which suggests a close relationship with the guild's account books.[88] The register was perhaps written up from the account books at the end of each year, as, for example, one man who is recorded as single in the account books, is recorded alongside a wife in the register.[89] The classifications in the Stratford register can be analysed in terms of how different guild entrants were conceptualized.

The Stratford guild was actually an amalgamation of three guilds that had previously been separate and, although the majority of its members were from the town, it also recruited from a wide scattering of market villages and even from Bristol and London.[90] In the register most guild entrants are named but not given personal designations, although some occupational statuses are noted. Relational designations are sometimes given when a person joined as part of a group, such as 'his wife' or 'his son', but also to refer to another person, sometimes an existing member, in the form of 'wife of . . .' but also 'widow of . . .'. The first use of a specific category to denote marital status was of the term *virgo* (virgin or maiden), applied to two females who entered the guild in 1418–19.[91] The next was for males: *nonmaritatus*, which was used in 1428–9 and 1430–1.[92] In 1430–1 another female is classified as *virgo*, whilst *vidua*, its first occurrence as a personal designation in the register,

---

in Honour of Janet Backhouse (London: The British Library and University of Toronto Press, 1998), pp. 121–41, esp. p. 128.

[87] See *Register of the Gild of the Holy Cross*, ed. Bloom, p. x.

[88] See e.g. ibid., pp. 10, 22.

[89] The example of William Purdon is discussed below.

[90] See *Register of the Gild of the Holy Cross*, ed. Bloom, pp. v–ix, 148; Rosser, 'Communities of Parish and Guild', pp. 33–4. See further L. Fox, *The Borough Town of Stratford-upon-Avon* (Stratford-upon-Avon: Corporation of Stratford-upon-Avon, 1953), ch. 11.

[91] MS BRT 1/1, fo. 15; *Register of the Gild of the Holy Cross*, ed. Bloom, p. 32.

[92] MS BRT 1/1, fos. 32v, 37v; *Register of the Gild of the Holy Cross*, ed. Bloom, pp. 60, 67.

is applied to two women.[93] The key change comes in 1435–6 when the register, largely written in Latin, classifies three men by the term 'sengilman'.[94] The Middle English term is used again, once in 1436–7, once in 1442–3, twice in 1443–4, although then not until 1503–4.[95] For women, though, there is no vernacular shift. The term *vidua* is used again in 1437–8 but, for the never-married woman, the next specific marital status given is *puella* in 1469–70.[96] This latter term is also used regarding two deceased females in 1472–3 and 1473–4,[97] and the category 'widow' continues to be used into the sixteenth century.[98] Thus, when the choice was made to classify an entrant according to marital status, males were simply not married or single, whereas females were maidens and widows; this is the case even if we just focus on the period 1406–60 when the register is written in a single hand.

Two of the three females classified as *virgo* are discussed with reference to future marriages. In the year 1418–19 Alice Whitard and Elizabeth Sempster were each charged an entrance fee of 20s. plus 10d. to the light. Both are recorded as having paid the 10d. but only 6s. 8d. of the entrance fee, with it noted that they could pay the remaining 13s. 4d. when they married.[99] These arrangements in relation to marriage are unique in the register as a whole, which suggests that the correlation with the term *virgo*, while small, might be significant.[100] For example, when Margaret sister of Thomas Scheperd, chaplain, and Leticia daughter of John Crowenhale joined the guild in 1414–15, it was agreed that their fines of 13s. 4d. should be paid in two installments, one on entry and one at the next guild feast.[101] Two unmarried women who joined in 1424–5 only had to pay 6s. 8d. (and 10d. to the light), and Joan

[93] MS BRT 1/1, fos. 36v, 39; *Register of the Gild of the Holy Cross*, ed. Bloom, pp. 65, 66, 69.

[94] MS BRT 1/1, fos. 41, 41v; *Register of the Gild of the Holy Cross*, ed. Bloom, pp. 72–3.

[95] MS BRT 1/1, fos. 43v, 55, 57v, 58, 141v; *Register of the Gild of the Holy Cross*, ed. Bloom, pp. 76, 90, 95, 97, 199.

[96] MS BRT 1/1, fos. 44v, 92v; *Register of the Gild of the Holy Cross*, ed. Bloom, pp. 77, 144.

[97] MS BRT 1/1, fos 99, 102; *Register of the Gild of the Holy Cross*, ed. Bloom, pp. 154, 158.

[98] See e.g. MS BRT 1/1, fos 95v, 96, 135, 163v; *Register of the Gild of the Holy Cross*, ed. Bloom, pp. 148, 149, 191, 227.

[99] MS BRT 1/1, fo. 15; *Register of the Gild of the Holy Cross*, ed. Bloom, p. 32 (the amounts in this edition do not add up because the entries have been abridged).

[100] Cf. Rosser 'Going to the Fraternity Feast', p. 443.

[101] MS BRT 1/1, fos. 8, 8v; *Register of the Gild of the Holy Cross*, Bloom, p. 21.

daughter of Alice Bayly paid it immediately, whereas Agnes daughter of Thomas Whytard was given a year in which to pay.[102] (None of the above women are given a personal designation in the register although, as can be seen, all were described in relational terms.) It is noticeable that Alice Whitard and Elizabeth Sempster were actually charged more to enter the guild than these other women, although a husband entering the guild together with his wife was often charged 40s. in total, a not insubstantial amount.[103] Perhaps it was known that a marriage for Alice and for Elizabeth was imminent and this accounts for the relatively high entrance fees. Further, perhaps it was the evocation of future marriages that brought to (the scribe's) mind the term *virgo*, which could denote a young woman, a virgin, or a girl of marriageable age. As Phillips has argued regarding medieval maidens, it suggests both the pre-marital state of virginity and the desirability of the young woman.[104] While the known context of the use of the term *virgo* in 1430–1 has nothing to add to this thesis (Joan Beele was charged 7s. 6d. to enter the guild, with 10d. to the light, to be paid within the year), some of the examples regarding the terms *nonmaritatus* and 'singleman' also suggest links between use of a marital status and perceived marital eligibility.[105]

The first male classified as *nonmaritatus* is a William Tommus. It is recorded that he was charged an entry fee of 20s. plus 10d. to the light, like Alice and Elizabeth, but his was to be paid within the year. It is also noted that when he marries he should pay for his wife 6s. and 10d. to the light, so again there is a demonstrable link between the person labelled and his/her current marital status.[106] The next example of the term *nonmaritatus* is for John Felypes, 'barbor', in 1430–1. The entry just records that he was to pay his fee within two years, but he did subsequently marry as in 1436–7 Alice, wife of John Phelip, barber, joined the guild for a payment of 3s. 4d. and 10d. to the light.[107] The

---

[102] MS BRT 1/1, fos. 21, 21v; *Register of the Gild of the Holy Cross*, ed. Bloom, pp. 40, 41.

[103] Cf. Hanawalt and McRee, 'Guilds of *homo prudens*', p. 167.

[104] Phillips, *Medieval Maidens*, pp. 7, 43–51; K. M. Phillips, 'Maidenhood as the Perfect Age of Woman's Life', in K. J. Lewis, N. J. Menuge, and K. M. Phillips (eds.), *Young Medieval Women* (Stroud: Sutton Publishing, 1999), pp. 1–24. See also K. M. Phillips, 'Desiring Virgins: Maidens, Martyrs and Femininity in Late Medieval England', in Goldberg and Riddy, *Youth in the Middle Ages*, pp. 45–59.

[105] MS BRT 1/1, fo. 36v; *Register of the Gild of the Holy Cross*, ed. Bloom, p. 65.

[106] MS BRT 1/1, fo. 32v; *Register of the Gild of the Holy Cross*, ed. Bloom, p. 60.

[107] MS BRT 1/1, fos. 32v, 43v; *Register of the Gild of the Holy Cross*, ed. Bloom, pp. 67, 76. In 1446–7 his second wife, Alice, joined the guild and was charged 6s. 8d.: MS BRT 1/1, fo. 63v; *Register of the Gild of the Holy Cross*, ed. Bloom, p. 106.

entries for the three men classified as 'sengilman' in 1435–6, William Hale, John Saunndorys, and Gregory Barnard, yield little information on their own.[108] However, in the guild account books for this year, a fourth man is classified as 'sengilman', William Purdon, and it is noted that, if he married, his wife could join without paying a fine.[109] Such a marriage was possibly already mooted, as the register records the entry of William Purdon and his wife Alice in that year.[110] These examples signal that some of the men at least were being thought about in relation to a future marriage, which (as was argued for Alice and Elizabeth) perhaps prompted the use of a marital designation, albeit ones with less evident moral associations.

The references to future marriages for male entrants are not confined to those with marital status designations, though. For example, when Richard Gylberd junior was recorded as entering the guild in 1414–15, it was also noted that if he married his wife's entry would cost 13s. 4d., a lower rate than his own 20s.[111] Similarly, Thomas son of Robert Pernell, who entered the guild in the same year as William Tommus (1428–9), had to pay 13s. 4d. for himself but a future wife could enter for 6s. 8d. plus 10d. to the light.[112] Such entries are worth considering further for what they reveal about how the guild viewed its male and female members. Whereas Alice and Elizabeth could delay the balance of their fines until marriage, William, Richard, and Thomas not only had to pay off their own fines within a set amount of time, but also were expected, on marriage, to pay their wives' fines too, albeit at a reduced rate. Even if Alice and Elizabeth are exceptional examples, it is still the case that no man was allowed to delay payment until marriage and no woman was told that she would be responsible for her future husband's fine. Further, many of the female entrants (whether single or married) were allowed to join the guild at a lower rate than was typical for male entrants; in the returns discussed above a reduced rate was sometimes applied to the married woman, but not to the

---

[108] William Hale and John Saundorys were charged 10s. and 10d. to the light, to be paid within the year, whereas Gregory Barnard (from Wyche) was to pay in kind (3 quarters of salt) before Michaelmas next and 10d. to the light: MS BRT 1/1, fos. 41, 41v; *Register of the Gild of the Holy Cross*, ed. Bloom, pp. 72–3.

[109] Hardy (ed.), *Stratford-on-Avon Corporation Records*, p. 24.

[110] MS BRT 1/1, fo. 41v; *Register of the Gild of the Holy Cross*, ed. Bloom, p. 73.

[111] MS BRT 1/1, fo. 9; *Register of the Gild of the Holy Cross*, ed. Bloom, p. 21 (although he mistakenly notes that Richard had to marry within a year to get this reduction rather than that the wife's payment would be due within a year).

[112] MS BRT 1/1, fo. 32v; *Register of the Gild of the Holy Cross*, ed. Bloom, p. 61.

single woman.[113] This perhaps reflects a social reality of who could afford what, but the result of such entries is a conceptualization of guild members that is subtly different from that in the returns. The single (and the married) man is viewed as economically independent, the married woman as covered, and the single woman as somewhere between the two: expected to pay something, but either a down payment until a husband could pay off the balance or a reduced rate, like the married woman. The single woman in the register is less the *femme sole*, in the sense of the woman as legally and economically independent, and more the to-be-married woman, a representation that also appeared in some of the guild returns.[114]

So far the argument that the category 'maiden', with its associations of virginity as well as marital eligibility, was one worth retaining in the guild register has rested on a few small but significant trends. It can be further substantiated, though, by placing the text in a wider discursive context. We have seen that the category appears in a range of sources, including property deeds and tax returns.[115] But a closer parallel can be found in the fifteenth- and sixteenth-century churchwardens' accounts, which reveal the existence of various groupings (referred to, for example, as 'maidens', 'wives', and 'young men'), who maintained their own lights and made regular payments for the support of the fabric and services of the parish church.[116] Such parish groupings can be discussed for what they suggest about the different ways in which young women and young men were viewed, as well as what they suggest about how women in general were classified.

Katherine French calls such associations 'guilds', although she acknowledges that they were 'not as formal or as institutionalized as some of the older or wealthier mixed-sex guilds'.[117] Christine Peters agrees that the groups of wives, maidens, and young men were similar

---

[113] See esp. the return for the London guild of St Fabian, but also that for the London guild of St Katherine, for which the wife paid no entry fee, and the Kingston-upon-Hull guild returns, in which she was covered by her husband's payment. The guild of St John the Baptist, Kingston-upon-Hull, allowed married *men* a reduced rate if their wives were already members.

[114] For example in those for Cambridge's guild of St Katherine and Kingston-upon-Hull's guild of St John the Baptist.

[115] See Ch. 1, pp. 23–4 and Ch. 3 'The Bishop's Lynn poll tax return' above.

[116] Duffy, *Stripping of the Altars*, pp. 146–8.

[117] K. L. French, 'Maidens' Lights and Wives' Stores: Women's Parish Guilds in Late Medieval England', *Sixteenth Century Journal*, 29 (1998), 399–425 (quotation at p. 404). See also Duffy, *Stripping of the Altars*, pp. 148–51.

in function to guilds and suggests that the difference was that they were theoretically open to all in the parish, in the sense that there was no formal process of joining nor an entrance fee to pay.[118] Instead the groups raised money through fundraising activities such as holding church ales and dances.[119] According to Joanna Mattingley there was a hierarchy of associations within each parish, with the fraternities at the top and, below them, groups associated with the lights before the saints, the plough light, and the wives' groups. She argues that the lesser groups conferred limited benefits on those not wealthy enough to join a fraternity.[120] Although there are regional variations, the divisions into maidens, wives, and young men are the most common.[121] Thus the groups pertain to young, unmarried women, other women, and young men, that is, they include those who are not the core guild member, the married man.[122]

French, in her analysis of the evidence for the female associations in late medieval England, found eleven parishes with maidens' groups, and fifteen with wives' groups; she also found one reference to a midwives' group, and one reference to a group of sisters, the latter in St Neot, Cornwall, which probably meant the sisters of the *iuvenes* (young men) and so also denoted young women.[123] Peters looked for references to groupings of young men, maidens, and wives and found references to young men's groups in twenty-seven parishes, to maidens' groups in eighteen, and to wives' groups in seven (although here she excluded references to wives taking part in Hocktide activities, which perhaps accounts for her lower number).[124] The young men are variously referred to as young men ('yong men', 'yonglings', *iuvenes*), single men,

[118] C. Peters, *Patterns of Piety: Women, Gender and Religion in Late Medieval and Reformation England* (Cambridge: Cambridge University Press, 2003), p. 28.

[119] See Phillips, *Medieval Maidens*, pp. 189, 192–3; French, 'Maidens' Lights and Wives' Stores', pp. 406, 407, 412, 418.

[120] J. Mattingley, 'The Medieval Parish Guilds of Cornwall', *Journal of the Royal Institution of Cornwall*, new ser., 10 (1989), pp. 298–9; see also Bainbridge, *Gilds in the Medieval Countryside*, p. 49.

[121] See Duffy, *Stripping of the Altars*, pp. 147–8, 150; Peters, *Patterns of Piety*, pp. 25, 28–32; Mattingley, 'Medieval Parish Guilds', p. 291.

[122] Cf. Peters, *Patterns of Piety*, p. 32.

[123] French, 'Maidens' Lights and Wives' Stores', pp. 421–2; G. M. Rushforth, *A Short Guide to the Painted Windows in the Church of St. Neot, Cornwall* (London: SPCK, 1937), p. 36 (the evidence is from inscriptions in stained glass windows).

[124] Peters, *Patterns of Piety*, p. 31 n. 55; she does not cite French's 1998 essay but her book of 2001, which is less detailed on these groups. See K. L. French, *The People of the Parish: Community Life in a Late Medieval Diocese* (Philadelphia, PA: University of Pennsylvania Press, 2001). On hocking, which involved all three groups, see K. L.

bachelors, and, in one case, grooms. The young women are usually referred to as maidens ('maydens', 'virgens', *virgines*), but also in one case as daughters. As in Stratford's register, the language used to refer to young women generally has associations of virginity, as opposed to the terms for young men, which suggest youth and their unmarried status only. For example, the late fifteenth-century churchwardens' accounts for Croscombe (Somerset) refer to the 'maydens' and the 'young men', the churchwardens' records for Morebath (Devon) in 1534 refer to 'ye yong men and maydens', and a window at Dullingham (Cambridgeshire) had an inscription referring to 'the yeng men and maydens'.[125] The guild register for Luton's fraternity of the Holy and Undivided Trinity, discussed above, had a category of maidens and bachelors from 1519.[126] The labels given to such groups signal a gendered difference in how the young were viewed, a difference which meant that while the label 'single men' was thought appropriate (as in Bassingbourne, Cambridgeshire), that of 'single women' was not.[127]

The two-fold division of females into maidens and wives ('wyves', *uxores, mulieres*) is that of the never married and the ever married.[128] Peters comments that widows, like married men, perhaps did not need an association, as they were householders.[129] Yet widows were also largely excluded from the core of guilds' activities, such as office-holding and the decision-making processes.[130] It also seems unlikely that a woman would be asked to leave the wives' group when her husband died. 'Wife' as a term was sometimes used to refer to (older) women generally, and was retained as a title by some widows.[131] Indeed, the Bassingbourne accounts show that at least one widow was active in the

French, ' "To Free Them From Binding": Women in the Late Medieval English Parish', *Journal of Interdisciplinary History*, 27 (1996–7), 387–412.

[125] E. Hobhouse (ed.), *Church-Wardens' Accounts of Croscombe, Pilton, Patton, Tintinhull, Morebath, and St. Michael's, Bath*, Somerset Record Society, 4 ([London]: Somerset Record Society, 1890), p. 4 (for Croscombe); French, 'Maidens' Lights and Wives' Stores', p. 411 (for Morebath); Peters, *Patterns of Piety*, p. 30 n. 52 (for Dullingham).

[126] Marks, 'Two Illuminated Guild Registers', p. 131.

[127] For Bassingbourn see Peters, *Patterns of Piety*, p. 31.

[128] For the term ever married see Froide, 'Marital Status', p. 237.

[129] Peters, *Patterns of Piety*, p. 32.

[130] See e.g. Bainbridge, *Gilds in the Medieval Countryside*, pp. 46–7, 9; Mattingley, 'Medieval Parish Guilds', pp. 296–7; Barron, 'Parish Fraternities', p. 31.

[131] See e.g. M. Pelling, 'Finding Widowers: Men Without Women in English Towns Before 1700', in Cavallo and Warner (eds.), *Widowhood in Medieval and Early Modern Europe*, p. 41. Mattingly also makes this assumption: Mattingley, 'Medieval Parish Guilds', p. 291.

wives' group.[132] Thus the division of women into maidens and wives is one both of age and marital status.

Marriage conventionally came with age, and these are conventional groupings. Associations of maidens and wives can be found in at least thirty-six parishes (spanning sixteen counties).[133] There has been some debate about the extent to which such groups were used by those with social power to control and socialize and the extent to which they offered those outside the key power structures an important role in parish life.[134] Yet whatever position one takes on this debate, it seems that the grouping a woman could join was predetermined: if she was young and unmarried she would join a maidens' group; if she was older and had married she would join the wives' group. This classification of women was probably both influenced by social reality (the young and unmarried were perhaps more likely to socialize with each other due to shared interests and experiences, as could be said regarding the older and married), and in turn affected reality, in that it reinforced the division according to age and marital status. Further, that young unmarried women were labelled and accepted the labelling of 'maidens', whereas young men were just young men, was both a product of a society that placed a higher premium on female virginity and reinforced that view. Such factors perhaps account for Stratford's register retaining the category 'maiden' at the expense of the term 'singlewoman'.

The guild texts discussed here reveal the influence of different discourses, as they adopt the category 'single woman' in some contexts but avoid it in others. When the guild returns used the category 'single woman' in the late fourteenth century it was with the various associations of *femme sole* in mind, be it economic and legal independence, or that of the woman alone. The 'single woman' operated as one half of a binary pairing with the married woman, either in respect of coverture or simply as the not-yet married woman. The Stratford guild register also signals the relevance of marriage to guild membership but, in its labelling of named individuals, unmarried women are more specifically classified as maidens (before marriage) and widows (after marriage).

---

[132] See A. Douglas, 'Salisbury Women and the Pre-Elizabethan Parish', in Rousseau and Rosenthal (eds.), *Women, Marriage, and Family*, p. 110.

[133] These figures were derived through comparing the lists for maidens' and wives' groups in French, 'Maidens' Lights and Wives' Stores', pp. 421–2 and Peters, *Patterns of Piety*, p. 31 n. 55.

[134] See French, 'Maidens' Lights and Wives' Stores', pp. 401, 420; Phillips, *Medieval Maidens*, pp. 186–94.

Its use of Latin variants of the category 'maiden', terms inflected with associations of virginity and respectability, alongside the vernacular 'sengilman' suggests the value-laden nature of the classification process. Other classifiers made different choices, consciously or not, and the next chapter demonstrates that the term 'singlewoman' was increasingly used as a personal designation in fifteenth- and early sixteenth-century texts, generally in place of the category 'maiden'.

5

'Singlewoman' as a Personal Designation

As with interpretive schemes, personal designations can be used to impose order on society. Medieval naming practices resulted in a relatively small pool of names and an additional designation was often required to distinguish one John or Joan Smith from another, such as a social or occupational status.[1] In 1413 the Statute of Additions attempted to standardize personal designations (or 'additions') in legal writs and appeals. When justices in the king's courts discussed what additions were appropriate for women, the term 'singlewoman' was suggested for unmarried women, including widows. Yet, because the term *vidua* (or a vernacular equivalent) continued to be seen as an appropriate designation for a widow, 'singlewoman' was largely, although not exclusively, applied to the never married. This chapter contends that, while in theory the Statute only applied to certain kinds of legal documents, in practice it had an impact on a wide range of documents over the course of the fifteenth century and beyond. This argument has implications for early modern evidence too, for which it has either been argued that 'singlewoman' referred to the never married only, or that it (and 'singleman') encompassed a wide range of conditions as there was little interest in marking out the never married from the widowed in public documents before the late seventeenth century.[2]

The earliest uses of the vernacular term 'singlewoman' being applied to a named individual date from the early fifteenth century (after the Statute of Additions), although there are many more examples from the late fifteenth and early sixteenth centuries. Some have associated the appearance of the term with the existence of a group 'who passed their lives unmarried' or to '[t]he increasing importance of matrimony

---

[1] On the complex matter of medieval names see e.g. Postles, *Surnames of Devon*, esp. pp. 109–229; C. Clark, 'Socio-economic Status and Individual Identity: Essential Factors in the Analysis of Middle English Personal Naming', in D. Postles (ed.), *Naming, Society and Regional Identity* (Oxford: Leopard's Head Press, 2002), pp. 99–121.

[2] Froide, *Never Married*, pp. 159–60; Pelling, 'Finding Widowers', pp. 40–1.

for women as job opportunities for the single female diminished'.³ Yet support for the contention that the term's appearance and increased usage is connected to the Statute can be found through comparison with the use of other personal designations. D. A. L. Morgan, for example, has argued that it was a result of the Statute of Additions that 'gentleman' as a personal designation 'established itself in English social vocabulary in a widening range of documentation, both public and private'.⁴ Others have found that the use of additions in a range of records increased after 1413.⁵

The Statute of Additions set out that the 'Estate or Degree, or Mystery' of defendants was to be given in all original writs and appeals concerning personal actions and in all indictments in which process of outlawry lay. The place of residence was also to be stated, both measures to ensure that there was less possibility of incorrect identification of a defendant.⁶ One result of the statute was that there was some debate in the king's courts as to what were acceptable additions, which is recorded in the texts now known as 'year-books';⁷ when Sir Robert Brooke (d. 1558) compiled his abridgment of the year-books, he had sixty-seven entries under the heading of 'Addicions'.⁸ In 1432, for example, there was a discussion regarding a particular woman as to whether *vidua* or 'singlewoman' was sufficient as her addition, with Justice Martin arguing that they both were. This suggests that 'singlewoman' here meant 'unmarried'.⁹ The term had not yet gained widespread acceptance, though, as in 1437 it was ruled that the indictment of Joan

---

³ Poos, *Rural Society*, p. 157; Goldberg, *Women, Work, and Life Cycle*, p. 278; discussed in Ch. 1, 'Marriage' above.

⁴ D. A. L. Morgan, 'The Individual Style of the English Gentleman', in M. Jones (ed.), *Gentry and Lesser Nobility in Late Medieval Europe* (Gloucester: Alan Sutton, 1986), p. 16. He also states that its adoption as an addition in 1413 was preceded by 'its increasing frequency in English form as a general word of social reference' pre-1413, as was also the case with 'single woman': ibid., p. 29 n. 5.

⁵ See e.g. Swanson, *Medieval Artisans*, p. 4. Prof. Mark Ormrod has found that after 1415 additions become more prevalent in the Register of the Corpus Christi guild of Boston, Lincs. (personal communication in 2000, citing BL MS Harley 4795).

⁶ *Statutes of the Realm*, ed. A. Luders *et al.*, ii, p. 171 (1 Hen. V, ch. 5).

⁷ On the 'year-books' see Baker, *Introduction to English Legal History*, pp. 204–5.

⁸ Robert Brooke, *La graunde abridgement* ([London: Richard Tottyl], 1576); on this text see Baker, *Introduction to English Legal History*, p. 212.

⁹ Year Books, Michaelmas Term, 10 Hen. VI, p. 21, pl. 70, in [*Le primier part des ans ore nouelment peruse, etc.*] (London: Company of Stationers, 1609; STC 9616). The case is noted in Anthony Fitzherbert, *La graunde abridgement* ([London]: Richard Tottell, [1565]), fo. 15, tit. Addicion, pl. 5, and Brooke, *Graunde abridgement*, tit. Addicions, pl. 64. I owe the original reference and those in nn. 11, 13 below to J. H. Baker, 'Male

Botiller 'sengilwoman', before the justices of the peace in Cambridge, was insufficient because 'sengilwoman' did not meet the criteria of the Statute of Additions.[10] Yet that debate appears to have been won by 1468, when Justice Littleton tried to argue that 'servant' was a valid addition on the grounds that, although it was not a degree or mystery, it was a condition *like* 'singlewoman'; the consensus was that 'servant' was unsuitable because it applied to men who could be knights, squires, yeomen, or grooms.[11] Similar statements are made in printed guides to the law published in the late sixteenth century: 'widow' and 'singlewoman' are listed as 'good additions of estate or degree', and 'servant' is rejected as too vague.[12] The terms 'virgin' or 'maid' do not appear in these guides as suitable additions, although one year-book case refers to the term 'maid' in a discussion of additions.[13]

One would thus expect to find the term 'singlewoman' used in the king's courts after 1413. Phillipa Maddern found that the clerks of the King's Bench in the period 1422–42 identified women by the descriptors 'widow' and 'wife of . . .', and more rarely, 'singlewoman', 'spinster', and 'gentlewoman'.[14] It is the wider impact of the Statute of Additions that is of concern here, though. The earliest uses yet found of 'singlewoman' as a personal designation outside such legal records occur in the 1430s and 1440s, around the period when the term was being debated as a suitable addition in the law courts; we have seen that

and Married Spinsters', *American Journal of Legal History*, 21 (1977), p. 258 n. 14. Baker views the addition 'singlewoman' as a translation of *femme sole*: ibid., p. 258.

[10] TNA: PRO, JUST 3/7/4, m. 3r: 'sengilwoman intendi non potest addicio pro formam statuti de addicionibus'. I owe both the reference and the transcription to the generosity of Dr Emma Hawkes.

[11] Year Books, Trinity Term, 7 Edw. IV, p. 10, pl. 1 ('il est un condicion, come est de singlewoman'), in *Les ans ou reports del raigne du roye Edvvard le quart, novelment revien et corrigee en divers lieux, etc.* (London: I. More, 1640; STC 9769).

[12] W. Lambard, *Eirenarcha: or of The Office of the Justices of Peace* (facsimile of London: Ra: Newbery and H. Bynneman, 1581; Amsterdam: Theatrum Orbis Terrarum, 1970), pp. 387–8; William West, *Of symboleography the second part* (London: Thomas Wight and Bonham Norton, 1597; STC (2nd edn) 25277), 'Of the forme of Indictments', EEBO <http://gateway.proquest.com/openurl?ctx_ver=Z39.88–2003& res_id=xri:eebo&rft_id=xri:eebo:citation:99839058> (1 Sept. 2005).

[13] The case discusses whether 'singlewoman' or 'servant' was the suitable addition for a woman who was neither 'maid, widow, ne wife': Trinity Term, 14 Edw. 4, p. 7v, pl. 12 in *Les ans ou reports*. Brooke understood the first term as 'virgin': Brooke, *Graunde abridgement*, tit. Addicions, pl. 56.

[14] See P. C. Maddern, *Violence and Social Order: East Anglia 1422–1442* (Oxford: Clarendon, 1992), pp. 40–1. Some of the women designated as 'spinster' were married so it is doubtless being used as an occupational term; I am grateful to Prof. Maddern for elaborating on her findings in a personal communication (25 Mar. 1999).

the term 'singleman' was used as a personal designation in the Stratford guild register from 1435.[15] But it seems that it was only in the late fifteenth and early sixteenth centuries that the term 'singlewoman' was more widely used, a period by which it seemed to have gained legal acceptance as an addition.[16] It generally operated in place of variants of the category 'maiden', rather than 'widow', which was widely held as an appropriate addition. After initial discussion of two early usages of the term 'singlewoman' as a personal designation, the focus will be on records pertaining to the city of York. The advantage of such an approach, and of using York, is that a variety of texts can be used both so that chronological gaps are covered and the breadth of the new usage can be established. Texts considered include the Freemen's Register, the House Books (minute books of the city council), and the Chamberlains' Account Books. York's substantial series of testaments and its subsidy return of 1524 are then compared with similar texts from elsewhere, in order to broaden the scope of enquiry.

EARLY EXAMPLES OF 'SINGLEWOMAN'

The earliest example that the *Middle English Dictionary* cites of the term 'singlewoman' being used as a personal description is from an inquisition record for the subsidy of 1431.[17] The 1431 subsidy was a complicated land-tax levied by parliament and, as such, offers a link between the state's idea of how people should be identified and its application beyond the courts.[18] The Exchequer asked inquisitions to obtain contributors' names, place of abode, and 'of what estate, degree, craft, mystery or condition that they be'.[19] It thus replicates many of the requirements

[15] See Ch. 4, 'Maidens and single men' above.
[16] For example, this appears to be the case for the Court of Chancery, although petitions can only be approximately dated. The earliest examples I have found are in two petitions to the Bishop of Bath who was Chancellor in 1433–43 and 1467–72. One of the petitions can be linked to the later period by its reference to Humfrey Hayford as Sheriff of London (1464–8, 1470–80). The next example found is from 1473–5. TNA: PRO, C 1/46/47, C 1 46/134, C 1/48/43.
[17] *MED*, sengle (adj.) 2.
[18] See Given-Wilson *et al.* (eds.), *Parliament Rolls*, x, pp. 449–51; H. C. M. Lyte (ed.), *Inquisitions and Assessments Relating to Feudal Aids*, 6 vols. (London: Her Majesty's Stationery Office, 1899–1920), i, p. xxviii; H. L. Gray, 'Incomes from Land', *English Historical Review*, 49 (1934), p. 608.
[19] Given-Wilson *et al.* (eds.), *Parliament Rolls*, x, p. 450.

of the 1413 Statute, although here it also explicitly allows for a person's 'condition'.[20] According to the inquisition made for the hundred of Pershore (Worcestershire), Sibyl de la Bere 'sengilwoman' was taxed at 10s., the amount for half a knight's fee or ten librates of land held by other tenures, in Birtsmorten.[21] Persons assessed in 1431 were, under the requirements of the subsidy, owners of at least a tenth of a knight's fee or its equivalent. Thus the classifications encountered in the records generally reflect the privileged positions of those assessed. In the hundred of Pershore most taxpayers are classified by a social status: the men are classified as *armiger* (esquire: 16), *comes* (earl: 5), *dominus* (lord: 1), and *dux* (duke: 1); the two other women taxed are labelled *domina* (lady) and *vidua* respectively.[22] The 1432 discussion in the year-books indicated that the term 'singlewoman' could be applied to a widow, but its use here alongside *vidua* perhaps makes that less likely. Other sources do suggest that Sibyl de la Bere was probably a never-married woman.

According to Thomas Habington, who compiled a survey of Worcester in the early seventeenth century, Sibyl only acquired the land in 'Brutes Morton' in 1431, from one John Nansan.[23] She was also perhaps the same Sibyl de la Bere who, with her three sisters (all orphaned daughters of the knight Richard de la Bere), petitioned Chancery between 1449 and 1453 about manorial profits in neighbouring Herefordshire. The youngest was said to be nineteen years old, but all the sisters were presumably unmarried as they claimed that the money was intended for their future marriages.[24] Another Chancery petition, from 1465–71 or possibly 1480–3, again with a Hereford connection, refers to Sibyl de la Bere as deceased; her nephew, Kynarde, was petitioning for the return of some goods detained by Sibyl's executor.[25] If this is the same woman, and the chronology suggests it is possible, Sibyl was still known by her

[20] See Littleton's comment above about 'singlewoman' as a 'condition'.
[21] Lyte (ed.), *Inquisitions and Assessments*, v, p. 327. A knight's fee was originally an estate, usually a manor, granted to a feudal vassal for military service of one knight, but by this date the military service aspect had lapsed. See M. Hicks, *Bastard Feudalism* (London: Longman, 1995), p. 227.
[22] Lyte (ed.), *Inquisitions and Assessments*, v, pp. 326–7.
[23] See *A Survey of Worcestershire by Thomas Habington*, ed. J. Amphlett, 2 vols., Worcestershire Historical Society, 5 (Oxford: J. Parker, 1893–5), i, p. 120. Nansan himself only acquired Birtsmorten from Edward Ruyhale's trustees in 1424–5, according to evidence from the Feet of Fines, while the return for the 1428 subsidy has it as still held by a Richard Ruyhle and his heirs, as it was in 1346: J. W. Willis-Bund *et al.*, *The Victoria History of the County of Worcester*, 5 vols. (Westminster: A. Constable, 1901–26), iv, p. 31, n. 30; Lyte (ed.), *Inquisitions and Assessments*, v, pp. 323, 306.
[24] TNA: PRO, C 1/19/132.   [25] TNA: PRO, C 1/31/445.

maiden name when she died (and by this date in England women often adopted their husband's surnames).[26]

Another early example of the term 'singlewoman' as a personal designation can be found in one of York's civic records for 1446–7. It occurs in the city's earliest surviving Chamberlains' Account Book relating to a payment made by 'Johanna Ingleby singlewoman' for admission to the freedom of the city.[27] This example differs from the previous one where the assessors were required to state the person's condition. Presumably the designation was added in order to further identify the person in question, although the same woman is classified in a variety of ways in the one text. The Chamberlains' Account Books are ordered by year and note, in one section, the payments of those who were admitted to the freedom in that year, and, in another section headed 'arrears', the payments by those who had become free in previous years.[28] The reference to 'Johanna Ingleby singlewoman' is in the first of these sections for 1446–7, and she is recorded as paying 3s. 4d. Payments of the same amount are also noted as having been made by 'Johanna Ingleby gentilman' and 'Johanna Ingleby' (no status given).[29] Thus, in the year of her entry Joan Ingleby paid 10s.[30] What is significant here, though, is the lack of consistency in how she is classified. While the

---

[26] On women's names and marriage see e.g. Postles, *Surnames of Devon*, esp. p. 244; J. M. Bennett, 'Spouses, Siblings and Surnames: Reconstructing Families from Medieval Village Court Rolls', *Journal of British Studies*, 23 (1983), p. 40.

[27] York City Archives (YCA), CC 1, p. 11. More early examples could undoubtedly be uncovered. I am aware of two early examples from Norwich, one in a surety to keep the peace recorded in one of the Mayor's Court Books (1443–4) and one in the city's Register of the Freedom (1446): Norfolk Record Office, Norwich City Records, Case 16, shelf a, 1, p. 133 (I owe the reference to Dr Jeremy Goldberg); J. L'Estrange, *Calendar of the Freemen of Norwich from 1317 to 1603*, ed. W. Rye (London, 1888), viii, p. 9.

[28] See J. Muggleston, 'Some Aspects of the Two Late Medieval Chamberlains' Account Books of York', *Yorkshire Archaeological Journal*, 67 (1995), p. 134.

[29] YCA, CC 1, p. 11. The rest of those who entered the freedom and made fines in 1446–7 were men and the majority are classified by occupation, although some are not assigned a designation: ibid., pp. 11–13.

[30] According to Muggleston, each person who entered the freedom was generally expected to pay £1 in total but some took at least eight years to settle the balance and it was not uncommon for a citizen to make more than one payment during a year: Muggleston, 'Some Aspects', pp. 136–7; aliens and those described as 'gentle' paid more, and those admitted by patrimony paid nothing: ibid., p. 138. In the following year a 'Johanna Ingleby' can be found in the section headed 'arrears', again paying 3s. 4d.: YCA, CC 1, p. 47. There are no entries in her name in the following six years: ibid., pp. 103–9; CC 1/A, fos. 13–16v, 50–3, 77–80, 99–102, 120–2v. See also P. M. Stell, 'Paying for the Freedom of the City of York in the Fifteenth Century: the Standar' Maioris', *York Historian*, 18 (2001), 7–12.

term 'senglewoman' was initially used, when the other payments were made either a different status was used or no designation at all, despite all the entries being on the same page. This suggests that they were written as and when the payments were made. Kittell, on finding similar inconsistency in the classification of women in the documentary record for medieval Douai, commented that, at the local level, the classification process usually involved interaction between the person being labelled, the person responsible for the record in an official capacity, and a scribe, notwithstanding that these people might already be known to each other.[31] Such factors perhaps led to a variety of personal designations being applied to the same individual at different points, as happened with Joan Ingleby.

The Freemen's Register confirms that one 'Johanna Monkton alias... Ingylby' entered the franchise in 1446–7 but the term 'senglewoman' is not used here, nor is any other status.[32] It is possible to associate this Joan Ingleby with the widow of the same name who died in 1478.[33] Although this was thirty-two years later, James Raine comments that this woman, who had outlived her son, 'seems to have lived to a great age'.[34] The testator is styled 'Domina' in her will and described as the widow of the knight, William Ingleby. Such a person was likely to have been referred to as 'gentil', if not usually as 'gentilman'. The testator also made a bequest to the Monkton nunnery, a connection that might pertain to the byname 'Monkton' which was used in the Freemen's Register. It thus appears that, in these early examples of 'singlewoman' as a personal designation, in one case it is applied to a never-married woman and in the other to a widow.

YORK'S CIVIC RECORDS c. 1475–c. 1540

The records for late fifteenth- and early sixteenth-century York reveal many more examples of the term, for example in the city's House

[31] Kittell, 'Construction of Women's Social Identity', pp. 217–18.

[32] YCA, D 1, fo. 124r. Collins mistakenly gives her forename as 'Juliana': F. Collins (ed.), *Register of the Freemen of the City of York*, 2 vols., Surtees Society, 96, 102 (Durham: Andrews & Co., 1897–1900), i, p. 164.

[33] Borthwick Institute of Historical Research, York (BIHR), Prob. Reg. 5, fos. 133v–134r.

[34] J. Raine *et al.* (eds.), *Testamenta Eboracensia*, 6 vols., Surtees Society, 4, 30, 45, 53, 79, 106 (London: J. B. Nichols, 1836–1919), iii, p. 243n.; Raine gives an extract from the will too.

Books from 1478, in the Freemen's Register from 1482, again in the Chamberlain's Account Books but from 1520, in a testament dated 1519–20, and in the 1524 subsidy. There are problems in placing too much significance on the first occurrence of the term in some of these records. For example, although there was the 1446–7 example of Joan Ingleby classified as 'singlewoman' in the Chamberlains' Account Books, these records only survive in full for the period 1446–54, just as the arrears section for 1480–2, and then intermittently from 1520 onwards. Similarly, the House Books only survive from 1476. The Freemen's Register, though, begins in 1273 and runs uninterrupted from 1289 to 1671. York also has a full series of testamentary records from the fourteenth century, with a noticeable lacuna only for 1409–25.[35] Taken together these texts suggest an increased use of the term 'singlewoman' as a personal designation in the fifteenth and early sixteenth centuries. Analysis of the Freemen's Register further suggests that use of the term is linked in part to changes in record keeping (as it was in writs after the Statute of Additions) rather than, for example, to the increasing economic importance of marriage for women.[36]

The first use of the term 'singlewoman' in the Freemen's Register was in 1482 and it is used a further seven times before 1550: four times before 1500, once in 1503, and twice in the early 1530s.[37] The uses of the term seem to occur in phases, with 1482–95 being a notable one.[38] 1482 was also the first year in which entrants' names were listed according to which of the three ways the freedom had been acquired: by purchase, by patrimony, or through apprenticeship.[39] The term was used in the second section, of those who entered *per patres*: 'Agnes

[35] The registers of the peculiar jurisdiction of the Dean and Chapter survive in unbroken sequence from 1321, and the fuller registers of the Exchequer and Prerogative Court date from 1389, although these contain the lacuna: Goldberg, *Women, Work and Life Cycle*, p. 362; F. Collins (ed.), *Index of Wills in the York Registry, 1389 to 1514*, YASRS, 6 ([Worksop]: Yorkshire Archaeological and Topographical Association, 1889).

[36] Cf. Goldberg, *Women, Work and Life Cycle*, p. 278; discussed in Ch. 1, 'Marriage' above.

[37] D 1, fos. 153 [1483], 161v [1489], 162v [1490], 166 [1495], 171v [1503], 187v [1530], 189v [1534]; Collins (ed.), *Register of the Freemen*, i, pp. 206, 214, 215, 220, 227, 250, 253.

[38] See Collins (ed.), *Register of the Freemen*, i, pp. 204–20.

[39] See ibid., pp. 203–5. The change here is the separate listing of those who joined via an apprenticeship, as those who entered by patrimony had been listed in the main register since 1432–3. Lists of those who entered by patrimony do survive from 1397 onwards but they were initially recorded on stray parchment sheets: R. B. Dobson, 'Admissions to the Freedom of the City of York in the Later Middle Ages', *Economic History Review*, 2nd ser., 26 (1973), p. 8.

Hall, syngilwoman, filia Johannis Hall, sledman'.[40] Agnes was the only woman recorded for this year. The first use of the term 'singlewoman' can therefore be linked with the greater detail in the recording of those who entered the freedom in 1482. Although the tripartite division of names only continues until 1487, those who inherited the freedom from their father continue to be recorded in the register and it is in this section that the term is predominantly found. Six of the eight uses of the term occur in the *per patres* sections, including all of the pre–1500 examples. Of the women who enter by patrimony in the period 1482–95, all except two are classified by the term (and one of these two is mistakenly described as *filius*). Similarly, of the four women who purchase the freedom in this period, three are classified as *vidua*. The category of 'widow' is rarely used in the Register (before 1482 *vidua* was used once in 1441, and 'wydowe' in 1464), so again this suggests a period in which there was an increased interest in personal designations.[41] It seems likely that at least six of the eight women classified by the term 'singlewoman' (those who entered by patrimony) were never married in that they share surnames with their fathers.[42] The term was perhaps more likely to be applied to the never married if *vidua* was also considered a suitable designation for the Register in this period.

Uses of the term in the early sixteenth-century Chamberlains' Account Books also occur alongside the category 'widow'.[43] The term is used in the annual sections concerning stallage (the payment for permission to use a vending stall at a market or fair). Entries are generally in Latin until 1535–6, although designations are sometimes in the vernacular. The term 'singlewoman' is used in 1520 and 1521, although not in the years

---

[40] D 1, fo. 151v; Collins (ed.), *Register of the Freemen*, i, p. 204. As Palliser comments, 'Collins made no attempt to deal with the complications produced by the overlapping of different dating systems (regnal, mayoral, chamberlains' and A.D. years) used in the register, but from 1375 . . . it is clear that . . . Collins' dates are just over one year out': D. M. Palliser, 'The York Freemen's Register 1273–1540: Amendments and Additions', *York Historian*, 12 (1995), p. 21.

[41] See D 1, fo. 120: 'Agnes Barowe vid' filia Laurencii de Dordragh', although it is recorded as 'widow' in Collins (ed.), *Register of the Freemen*, i, p. 158; ibid., p. 183: 'Alicia Hurtskye, wydowe'.

[42] There are a few examples where women who entered *per patres* are identified as widows, and a few where the women have different surnames from their fathers and had perhaps married. See ibid., pp. 155 (Johanna Burton), 158 (Agnes Barowe), 182 (Margeria Rycroft and Johanna Smerethwayte), 197 (Elena Brompton), 242 (Isabella Spexston).

[43] The Books run up to 1642 but I have examined those up to 1539: YCA, CC 1 [1446–50]; CC 1/A [1448–54, 1480–2]; CC 2 [1520–5]; CC 3 (1) [1526–9]; CC 3 (2) [1535–6]; CC 3 (3) [1538–9].

1522–8. The next surviving account book is for 1535–6, then 1538–9; in both these books 'singlewoman' is used. Other classifications include *uxor, vidua,* and 'wydo', but occupational statuses are also used, and some women have no classification.[44] For example, in 1520 eleven women are named in the stallage section: 'Johanna Roly singylwoman' (although this entry is crossed through), three women described as widows (two in Middle English, one in Latin), three with occupational designations, and four with no classification.[45] Classifications are also still not applied consistently to individuals in this text: Isabel Hyndiner was labelled as 'servaunt' in 1535–6, but as 'syngylwoman' in 1538–9.[46] Margaret Bland, classified as 'syngylwoman' in 1535–6 and in 1538–9 when paying to rent a market stall, is perhaps the Margaret Bland 'vytteler' (a seller of food and drink) who entered the freedom in 1541.[47] Although not enough is known about the individual women labelled 'singlewoman' to prove they were never married, that so many other women named alongside them are described as widows suggests that this is indeed a possibility.[48]

In the city's House Books there is some evidence that the personal designation 'singlewoman' might be applied to a widowed woman in the late fifteenth century, although there are also indications that, because the category 'widow' continues to be used as a personal designation, 'singlewoman' is more often applied to the never married. The House Books are civic registers that include royal business that affected the city, municipal activities, local law and its enforcement, and some craft guild business, and they survive for the period 1476–1642.[49] In the first six books (1476–90) the term 'singlewoman' is used seven times, twice to refer to the same woman.[50] Of particular interest are a couple of

---

[44] YCA, CC 2, fos. 20, 57, 97, 143, 187, 228; CC 3 (1), pp. 35, 131, 231; CC 3 (2), p. 93; CC 3 (3) fo. 20.

[45] YCA, CC 2, fo. 20.

[46] YCA, CC 3 (2), p. 93; CC 3 (3) fo. 20; and see the discussion of Joan Ingleby above.

[47] Collins (ed.), *Register of the Freemen,* i, p. 260.

[48] Cf. the argument re. *sola* and *vidua* in Ch. 3, 'The Bishop's Lynn poll tax' above.

[49] See L. C. Attreed (ed.), *The York House Books 1461–1490,* 2 vols. (Stroud: Alan Sutton, 1991), p. xi; A. F. Johnston and M. Rogerson (eds.), *York,* 2 vols., Records of Early English Drama (Toronto: University of Toronto Press, 1979), p. xviii.

[50] Joan Armourer, classified as 'singlewoman' in the House Books in 1489–90, can perhaps be linked to an entry in the Freemen's Register for 1489: 'Johanna Armorer, singlewoman, filia Rogeri Armorer, armorer': YCA, B 2–4, fo. 173v; D 1, fo. 161v; Attreed (ed.), *York House Books,* p. 684; Collins (ed.), *Register of the Freemen,* i, p. 214). For the other usages, see B 1, fo. 120 (Elizabeth More), B 2–4, fos. 122v ([. . .]

examples where the term's use can be compared to that of the category 'widow'.

In two bonds to keep the peace from January 1490 Joan Guy and Christine Guy agree not to do damage to one William Mankha. Joan is classified by the Latin *vidua*, Christine by the Middle English 'singlewoman'.[51] In the record of their arrest they are assigned these same designations, although here *vidua* is interlined, as is a description of Christine as Joan's daughter.[52] The contrasting use of *vidua* to describe a mother and 'singlewoman' to describe her daughter suggests that the latter was used here for a never-married woman. There is a similar example in Nottingham's Borough Court Book: in 1496 Elizabeth Spenser and Alice Spenser, both labelled 'singlewoman', brought separate actions against Emma Spenser, classified as *vidua*, regarding the detention of certain goods.[53] Although Emma is not identified as their mother this seems probable when other details are considered. Elizabeth's action refers to 'diverse images of alabaster' and the draft (written on the back) identifies them as 'lying in her shop'. The deceased owner of this shop was one John Spencer, imagemaker.[54] He can be further linked to the John Spencer of Nottingham who died intestate, leaving a widow called Emmota (a variant of Emma), according to an administration entered in the Probate Registers of York's Exchequer Court in May 1495.[55] Both actions to Nottingham's Borough Court by Elizabeth and Alice Spenser refer to 'half of a third part' of various objects such as a salt-cellar, perhaps representing their joint claim to a third of John's goods as his children; such practice, known as *legitim*, was a local custom only by this date but one place it did survive was in the province of York (which included Nottingham).[56] The use of the vernacular term 'singlewoman' in these

---

Johnson), 173v (Joan Whitecroft); Attreed (ed.), *York House Books*, pp. 201, 309, 685, and the two examples discussed below.

[51] YCA, B 6, fo. 172v; Attreed (ed.), *York House Books*, p. 682.

[52] YCA, B 6, fo. 173v: 'filiam eiusdem Johanne'. See also Attreed (ed.), *York House Books*, p. 685. These arrests are said to take place during the mayoralty of John Harper (Feb. 1489 to Feb. 1490) and this is the penultimate entry.

[53] W. H. Stevenson *et al.* (eds.), *Records of the Borough of Nottingham*, 8 vols. (London: Bernard Quaritch, 1882–1952), iii, pp. 38–41.

[54] Ibid., p. 39, n. 8. He is referred to in a Court Book entry of 1495: Nottinghamshire Archives and Southwell Diocesan Record Office, CA 1375, p. 9.

[55] BIHR, Prob. Reg. 5, fo. 461.

[56] See R. H. Helmholz, '*Legitim* in English Legal History', in R. H. Helmholz, *Canon Law and the Law of England* (London: Hambledon, 1987), pp. 254–6.

Latin records, then, again seems to mark out the never married from the widowed.[57]

A second set of related entries from the York House Books contains another example of the inconsistent application of personal designations in this period. In September 1488 Matilda Metcalf, labelled *vidua*, brought a suit leading to the arrest of Hugh Litster.[58] In November of the same year it was ordered that Matilda Metcalf, labelled 'singlewoman', be arrested at the suit of one Alice Litster.[59] It seems likely that the Matilda of both instances was the same woman given that her opponents share the same surname.[60] An error seems unlikely in that in the first example Matilda initiated the suit, and in the second a mistake in the addition would have made the writ invalid. There does appear to be a similar case of a woman referred to as 'singlewoman' in one context and as a widow in another in Coventry's records: Margery Cutler was classified as 'Single Woman' in Coventry's military survey of 1522, but in the city's 'census' of 1523 she is labelled 'wyddo'.[61] There are no other examples in these records, though, of a woman being labelled both as a widow and as 'singlewoman'.[62] However, in Coventry's 'census' there are a number of examples of men who appear to be widowers (for example, listed with children) classified as 'singleman'.[63] The term 'widower' is also used in this text (although in the listing for a different ward), but it is a category that was rarely applied in premodern records, in contrast to that of

[57] For other uses of the term in these records see Stevenson *et al.* (eds.), *Records of the Borough of Nottingham*, iii, pp. 36, 328.

[58] YCA, B 2–4, fo. 197; Attreed (ed.), *York House Books*, p. 406.

[59] YCA, B 2–4, fo. 189v; Attreed (ed.), *York House Books*, p. 396.

[60] It might also be the same Matilda Metcalf who is called a bawd (*pronuba*) in one of York's wardmote courts in 1494. See T. Andrew, 'The Fifteenth Century Wardmote Court Returns for York', MA diss. (York, 1997), p. 77.

[61] M. H. M. Hulton (ed.), *Coventry and its People in the 1520s*, Publications of the Dugdale Society, 38 ([Stratford-upon-Avon]: Dugdale Society in association with the Shakespeare Birthplace Trust, 1999), pp. 70 (Cross Cheaping 71), 139 (Cross Cheaping 65). I make this identification not just by name (Hulton transcribes it as Butler for 1522), but also on the basis of the ward she is listed under and approximately where in that listing, as they appear to be ordered topographically.

[62] Phythian-Adams argues that this happens in a number of cases but I have only found examples of women described as a widow in one record, without a designation in another: C. Phythian-Adams, *Desolation of a City: Coventry and the Urban Crisis of the Late Middle Ages* (Cambridge: Cambridge University Press, 1979), p. 201.

[63] See e.g. Hulton (ed.), *Coventry and its People*, pp. 138 (Henry Dave), 141 (Thomas Fyssher), 142 (William Fesycion). See also Phythian-Adams, *Desolation of a City*, pp. 201–2.

'widow'.[64] Coventry's records will be discussed further below, but one might conclude on the basis of the evidence discussed so far that, because the category 'widow' was still seen as an appropriate classification, the term 'singlewoman' was largely applied to the never married, although it was not necessarily confined to that meaning. In contrast, because 'widower' was not such an established classification, the term 'singleman' perhaps could be more widely applied to widowed men.[65]

FROM THE MEDIEVAL TO THE EARLY MODERN

York's subsidy return of 1524–5 and a testament dated 1519–20 also use the term 'singlewoman', and both appear to use it for never-married women, as we shall see. But Coventry's military survey of 1522 (a survey which is linked to Parliament's tax request of 1523) perhaps suggests that 'singlewoman' might still be an applicable term for a widow.[66] The intention here, then, is to compare York's subsidy return and testament with those from other places in order to broaden the scope of enquiry. Froide argues that a shift occurred in the second half of the sixteenth century, when court, probate, and administrative records used terms such as 'singlewoman', *soluta*, and 'spinster', rather than the terms 'maiden' and 'virgin', which 'assumed virginity, youth, or eventual marriage'.[67] But the contention here is that any such change should not be pinned down to a particular period or be seen as one-way, as it occurred in different records, in different places, at different times, and in some texts there is evidence of a change *from* 'singlewoman' *to* 'maiden'.

Of the women recorded in the 1524 subsidy return for York and Ainsty, thirty-nine are described by name only, forty-one are classified as

[64] See e.g. Hulton (ed.), *Coventry and its People*, pp. 143 (John Tayler), 144 (Walter Sweyrod). See also Pelling, 'Finding Widowers', pp. 38–42, 49.

[65] In the Stratford guild register it seems to have been used for the never married only, but this was perhaps because men were more likely to join the guild earlier in life. See Ch. 4, 'Maidens and single men' above.

[66] On the 1522 muster (and its relationship to the subsidy), see J. J. Goring, 'The General Proscription of 1522', *English Historical Review*, 86 (1971), 681–705; J. Cornwall, 'A Tudor Domesday: The Musters of 1522', *Journal of the Society of Archivists*, 3 (1965–9), 19–24. For the 1523 subsidy request, see *Statutes of the Realm*, ed. A. Luders, iii, pp. 230–41.

[67] Froide, *Never Married*, pp. 159–60.

widows (either in Middle English or in Latin), one as 'maistress', and two by the term 'singlewoman'.[68] The two women described by the latter term appear to be young, unmarried women. The first, Emmota Cotes 'singylwoman', was taxed 3s. 6d. on her 'chylds porcon' of £7.[69] This refers to a sum of money bequeathed to her by her father.[70] The second use of the term is also in an entry concerning a child's portion: Robert Jonson was taxed 20s. on his goods worth £20, but he was also to pay 2s. for 'yᵉ child's porcon of Jennet Dobytson singylwoman', which was worth £4.[71] Robert Jonson was probably Jennet's guardian, with control of her money; this is suggested in other references to child's portions in the subsidy, where the named person is said to have someone's portion 'in his hands'.[72] They are not the only women assessed in relation to a child's portion, but the others are just listed by name with no personal designation.[73]

The term 'singlewoman' (and, indeed, 'singleman') is used in a number of other returns (both the returns for the subsidy approved by Parliament in 1523 and those for the 1522 military survey, as the latter also list women and children who had real or personal wealth). In most of the cases where the term 'singlewoman' is used in a return, it is used in close proximity to the term 'widow'.[74] It therefore perhaps functions in place of variants of the category 'maiden', which some other returns do use.[75] For example, of the twenty-eight women listed in the Oxford tax return of 1524, twenty-four are classified as widows, three have no status, and one is described as 'mayden'.[76] More tellingly, in the 1522

[68] E. Peacock, 'Subsidy Roll for York and Ainsty', *Yorkshire Archaeological and Topographical Journal*, 4 (1877), 170–201.

[69] Ibid., p. 176.

[70] In York it was the custom that a third of a deceased man's property went to his children; discussed above p. 134.

[71] Peacock, 'Subsidy Roll', p. 179.

[72] For example Richard Hutchonson is said to have 'a child's porcon in his hands' and Richard Scadlock's portion is said to be 'in the hands of John Webster': ibid., pp. 183, 200.

[73] Ibid., pp. 177 (x 3), 178, 181, 193, 195.

[74] See e.g. J. Cornwall (ed.), *The County Community Under Henry VIII: The Military Survey, 1522, and Lay Subsidy, 1524–5, For Rutland*, Rutland Record Society Record Series, 1 (Oakham: Rutland Record Society, 1980), p. 51; J. Pound (ed.), *The Military Survey of 1522 for Babergh Hundred*, Suffolk Records Society, 28 (Woodbridge: Boydell Press, 1986), pp. 28, 90, 96, 113; S. H. A. Hervey (ed.), *Suffolk in 1524*, Suffolk Green Books, 10 (Woodbridge: G. Booth, 1910), p. 183.

[75] Cf. the anomalous use of *puella* in a late fourteenth-century tax return: see Ch. 3 above.

[76] J. E. T. Rogers (ed.), *Oxford City Documents, Financial and Judicial, 1268–1665*, Oxford Historical Society, 18 (Oxford: Clarendon Press, 1891), pp. 63–75.

return for Buckinghamshire, in the section concerned with Beaconsfield, people are listed under the headings 'Wedowes', 'Maydens', and 'Single men'.[77] The first two are also categories that are applied to named individuals elsewhere in this return.[78] That women are subdivided into maidens and widows, but men are just 'single' is reminiscent of the use of *solus* in the Bishop's Lynn poll tax return of 1379.[79]

The Coventry returns present a more complex picture, in part because the 1522 military survey can be compared not only with the subsidy returns of 1524 and 1525 but also with the city's own 'census' of 1523.[80] Unlike other musters, the 1522 survey incorporated a comprehensive valuation of wealth, both real and personal.[81] The text of Coventry's 1522 survey appears to be a copy made for local reference, but the original classification was perhaps undertaken by different people for different wards (the city was divided into ten wards), as it was in 1523.[82] Most women in Coventry's 1522 survey are described as widows (one might expect widows to make up a large proportion as the survey only included females with assets). Of the other women listed, some have no designation, four are labelled 'singlewoman', one as 'Maiden', and there is the odd occupational status (most men are classified in this way).[83] The four usages of the term 'singlewoman' relate to women who lived in four different wards. All occur in close proximity to uses of the category 'widow', whereas the term 'maiden' is used for a woman in a fifth ward.

The 1523 text differs in a number of ways. It was a municipal project, rather than a state one, which set out to record 'The names of men and wyfes hoswlyng people and children', a title that is written at the head of each sheet in the same hand. Each ward's listing is on a new sheet and written by a different scribe.[84] A typical entry might read 'John Spenser and hys wife ii prentes ii chyldern', with only the designated householder named.[85] While in this entry John Spenser is

[77] A. C. Chibnall (ed.), *The Certificate of Musters for Buckinghamshire in 1522*, Buckinghamshire Record Society, 17 (London: Her Majesty's Stationery Office, 1973), p. 250.

[78] See e.g. ibid., pp. 228, 259.

[79] See Ch. 3, 'The Bishop's Lynn poll tax return' above.

[80] All these texts are in Hulton (ed.), *Coventry and its People*. For further discussion of the 1523 text, see Phythian-Adams, *Desolation of a City*, pp. 291–3.

[81] Cornwall, 'Tudor Domesday', p. 19.

[82] Hulton (ed.), *Coventry and its People*, p. 2.

[83] See e.g. ibid., pp. 70 (Margaret Butler), 80 (Agnes Couper), 87 (Joan Goodlade), 108 (Katerene Grenesmyth), 109 (Agnes Welles).

[84] See ibid., pp. 3, 128. See also Phythian-Adams, *Desolation of a City*, pp. 291–2.

[85] Hulton (ed.), *Coventry and its People*, p. 128 (Much Park Street, 3).

given no personal designation, and this is the norm, particularly for married men, it is in the listings for Cross Cheaping and Broadgate that some men are described by the term 'singleman', whilst it is in the one for Spon Street that the category 'widower' is used.[86] The term 'singlewoman' also occurs in the Cross Cheaping listing, but in those for Much Park, Broadgate, and Gosford Street the category 'maid' is used as a personal designation.[87] Just as the term 'singleman' might be used by one scribe where another might use the term 'widower', a scribe might similarly opt for 'maid' over 'singlewoman'. In the 1524 return for an instalment of the subsidy most women are classified as *vidua*, but the terms *virgo* and 'virgen' are also used.[88] The 1525 return labels most women as widows, and some wards include few other designations.[89] Taken together, the Coventry records do suggest that, with the notable exception of Margery Cutler, the term 'singlewoman' seems to have generally operated in place of the category 'maiden'.[90]

A study of testamentary records suggests regional differences in the use of the categories 'single woman' and 'maiden' but no clear-cut, chronological transition from one set of terms to another. In York's series of testaments personal designations are often not given, although those that do often use appostives such as 'daughter of', 'former wife of', 'servant of'.[91] The term 'singlewoman' is first used for a testator's status in 1519–20: 'Margaret Vicares single woman doghter of Sr. Symonis Vicares'. She was a never-married woman, probably young (her father and step-mother were still alive at the time of the will's making), but of marriageable age (she makes a bequest to a man 'that shuld have bene my husbound').[92] There are later examples of the

---

[86] Ibid., pp. 137–42, 143–4, 150.

[87] Ibid., pp. 130, 139, 153, 172. The term 'maid' is also used in the survey as a noun for female servants, who are unnamed; e.g. the entry 'Annes Barker hyr sister maydes' can be compared with the nearby entries 'Herre Tyllot and uxor jorneyman and a meyd' and 'Annes Jonson hyr modyr wydoys': ibid., p. 130.

[88] Ibid., pp. 211, 212, 226.

[89] For example compare the listing for Much Park Street ward, where most men have an occupational designation and all four women are classified as *vidua*, with that for Cross Cheaping, where the only people with a designation are the seven women identified as *vidua*: ibid., pp. 177–9, 182–5.

[90] For Margery Cutler see p. 135 above.

[91] I have examined the wills of York women up to 1520 in the registers of the Exchequer and Prerogative Court: BIHR, Prob. Reg. 1–9.

[92] Prob. Reg. 9, fol. 92v. For a discussion of Margaret and the Vicars family: Raine (ed.), *Testamenta Eboracensia*, iii, p. 122n.; C. O. Steer 'The Parish Elites of St Michael's, Spurriergate, York and their Clergy, 1500–1550', MA diss. (York, 1997), pp. 19–25, 56, 68.

term's use but marital statuses are not consistently given.[93] The use of the term *puella* in Agnes Kilburn's testament of 1477 is similarly rare in this series. That it is recorded in the register immediately before the testament of 'Elena Willumson . . . vidua', suggests a temporary interest in recording a precise marital status, as widows are more usually described as 'once the wife of . . .'.[94] Phillips argues that references in Kilburn's will to a servant and to quantities of cloth suggest that she was probably not a young maiden but an older, never-married woman.[95] Indeed, *puella* is used in a variety of legal records to refer to such women, suggesting that in these contexts it signified singleness rather than youth.[96]

A study of London's testaments does suggest a trend in the use of the categories 'single woman' and 'maiden', but *from* 'single woman' *to* 'maiden' in the late fifteenth century. Whilst the term 'singlewoman' is used in eleven London testaments in the period 1450–1550 (all in the period 1450–81 with the exception of one in 1548),[97] the vernacular term 'maiden' is first used in 1456, but there are seven usages between 1480 and 1550, and five more before 1570;[98] the Latin *puella* is also used in a testament dated 1493.[99] In London's late sixteenth- and early seventeenth-century Consistory Court depositions the most frequent designations given to women were those of *uxor*, *vidua*, and *puella*. Loreen Giese notes that other terms appear in the

---

[93] See e.g. F. Collins (ed.), *Index of Wills in the York Registry, A.D. 1514 to 1553*, YASRS, 11 ([Worksop]: Yorkshire Archæological and Topographical Association, 1891), pp. 58, 102, 144, 212. See also C. Cross, 'Northern Women in the Early Modern Period: The Female Testators of Hull and Leeds 1520–1650', *Yorkshire Archaeological Journal*, 59 (1987), pp. 85, 93.

[94] Prob. Reg. 5, fo. 18.   [95] Phillips, 'Four Virgins' Tales', p. 94.

[96] For example in the Rolls of Ladies, Boys, and Girls, drawn up for Henry II in 1185, it is used for a 50-year-old woman, and in a York cause paper of 1519 it is applied to a deponent aged 'thirty years and more': *Rotuli de Dominabus et Pueris et Puellis de XII Comitatibus [1185]*, ed. J. H. Round, Pipe Roll Society, 35 (London, 1913; reprinted Vaduz, 1966), p. 83; BIHR, CP G 119. For later examples, see L. L. Giese, *London Consistory Court Depositions, 1586–1611: List and Indexes*, London Record Society, 32 (London: London Record Society, 1995), p. xxvi.

[97] Guildhall Library, London (GL), MSS 9171/5 fos. 15v, 339v, /6 fos. 6v, 11v, 45v, 46v, 272v, 318v, /8 fos. 34v, 66v, /12, fo. 6v.

[98] GL, MSS 9171/5 fo. 196v, /6 fo. 283v, /7 fo. 14, /8 fo. 259, /10 fos. 78, 129, 226v, /11 fo. 40, /13 fo. 69, /14 fo. 43, /15 fos. 126, 147, 322. This is similar to the pattern identified in T-Y. J. Woo, 'Medieval Single Women in London', MA diss. (London, 2001), Appendix 1, but in that the descriptors from the 19th-century calendar are used, which blurs the picture with its own use of the term 'spinster'.

[99] GL, MS 9171/8 fo. 94v; this term is also used in the court's Act Book in 1554: GL, MS 9168/11 fo. 32v.

body of the deposition (usually written in English), although not in the biographical information about the witness (usually written in Latin), such as *virgo* and 'spinster', and it is here that there is 'a rare instance' of the term 'single woman'.[100] This qualifies Froide's thesis, that terms such as 'singlewoman', *soluta*, and 'spinster' replaced those of 'maiden' and 'virgin' in the second half of the sixteenth century. Margaret Pelling found that in marriage licences dated between 1558 and 1699 'the terms "singlewoman" and "singleman" were apparently used to cover a range of conditions'. She argues that there was little interest in distinguishing between the never married and the widowed until, 'at the earliest', the late seventeenth century.[101] A rare exception is the 1570 Norwich census of the poor, which uses the category of 'never-married', but only in relation to women.[102] Such early modern findings suggest caution in identifying chronological trends in the use of classifications.

Although this survey is by no means exhaustive, the findings are nevertheless suggestive. It seems that the term 'singlewoman' as a personal designation was used more frequently from the mid-fifteenth century onwards and that it was largely applied to the never married. This does not mean, though, that the term was *intended* to mark out such a group. It has been argued that as 'widow' continued to be seen as an appropriate designation for widowed women, 'singlewoman' was, by default, applied largely to the never married and perhaps then acquired that association. A brief study of the term 'spinster' suggests a parallel development, although fuller analysis is beyond the scope of this book.

The term 'spinster' originally referred to a spinner and Maddern found it used in this way, and so applied to married women, in the early fifteenth-century King's Bench records.[103] William West's *Symboleography*, a printed guide to the law first published in 1594,

---

[100] Giese, *London Consistory Court Depositions*, pp. xxvi–xxvii; see also pp. xv–xvi. Froide suggests that the change affected the classification of women in the diocese of Winchester's consistory court, but no specific references are given: Froide, *Never Married*, pp. 156, 159.

[101] Pelling, 'Finding Widowers', pp. 40–1. She argues that this was the case with parish registers until the Marriage Act of 1754. For the use of the term 'singlewoman' in such a text, see the Register of Baptisms, Marriages, and Burials for St Saviour's Church, Southwark, 1538–63: London Metropolitan Archives, P92/SAV/356a, e.g. fos. 63v, 64r, 65v.

[102] Pelling, 'Finding Widowers', p. 50.

[103] See n. 14 above. See also Ch. 3, 'Widows' above, for the extensive use of 'spinner' as a personal designation in the Derby poll tax return of 1379.

discusses suitable additions and states that 'spinster' was an acceptable one, as was 'every other addition of any lawfull occupations'.[104] This reading of 'spinster' as an occupational designation is supported by year-book entries for 1525, 1540, and 1553, which reveal that the term could still be applied to married women and, as one justice argued, could also be applied to men who were worsted spinners. The justices' concern was rather that the indictment of a woman as 'A.B., wife of J.B., yeoman', was insufficient as the wife had no addition of her own.[105] However, in other sixteenth-century records which did not require an addition by law, the term 'spinster' perhaps functioned as, if not yet a marital designation, a default status for those who were neither married nor widowed, although it is still possible to find the odd example of a married woman classified as a spinster. For example, women are generally described as wives, widows, or spinsters in Sussex's coroners' inquests, and similarly in the wills enrolled in Knaresborough's court rolls.[106] In the early seventeenth century one lexicographer claimed that 'spinster' was the correct term at law for 'maids unmarried', as did law dictionaries from the middle of the seventeenth century.[107] Yet when this shift took place is unclear as the compiler of another glossary, Henry Spelman (d. 1641), also stated in the early seventeenth century that it

[104] West, *Of symboleography*, 'Of the forme of Indictments'.

[105] These debates are discussed in Baker, 'Male and Married Spinsters', pp. 255–7, and see also J. S. Cockburn, 'Early-modern Assize Records as Historical Evidence', *Journal of the Society of Archivists*, 5 (1974–7), p. 223. I have read the relevant accounts in James Dyer, *Les reports des divers select matters & resolutions* (London: John Streater and Henry Twyford, 1672), under Easter 31–2 Henry VIII and Trinity 7 Edward VI. Baker's thesis is more convincing than those of C. Z. Wiener, 'Is a Spinster an Unmarried Woman?', *American Journal of Legal History*, 20 (1976), 27–31, and V. C. Edwards, 'The Case of the Married Spinster: An Alternative Explanation', *American Journal of Legal History*, 21 (1977), 260–5.

[106] R. F. Hunnisett (ed.), *Sussex Coroners' Inquests 1455–1558*, Sussex Record Society, 74 (Lewes: Sussex Record Society, 1985). Some of those labelled 'spinster' are further identified as servants: ibid., nos. 72, 97, 167. For Knaresborough, see F. Collins (ed.), *Wills & Administrations from the Knaresborough Court Rolls*, 2 vols., Surtees Society 104, 110 (Durham: Andrews & Co., 1902–5), i, pp. 1–70 (for the years 1507–55); I have checked TNA: PRO, DL 30/491/ various and DL/30/492/ various. For an example of a married woman classified as 'spinster' see R. F. Hunnisett (ed.), *Calendar of Nottinghamshire Coroners' Inquests 1485–1558*, Thoroton Society Record Series, 25 (Nottingham: Thoroton Society, 1969), no. 207. See also S. J. Stevenson, 'The Rise of Suicide Verdicts in South-East England, 1530–1590: The Legal Process', *Continuity and Change*, 2 (1987), pp. 61–2.

[107] John Minsheu, *Hegemon eis tas glossas: id est, Ductor in linguas, The guide into tongues* (London: John Browne, 1617), p. 482; see also, Baker, 'Male and Married Spinsters', p. 258.

was a term applied to all women.[108] Perhaps, as with 'singlewoman', the shift in meaning was not universal, which led to inconsistencies between texts and over a chronological period.

The contention of this chapter is that the appearance of the term 'singlewoman' as a personal designation in the fifteenth century was linked to the Statute of Additions of 1413, which attempted to standardize such designations in legal writs and appeals, and subsequent debates in the king's courts where justices argued about what were acceptable additions for women. From these debates it appears that 'singlewoman' was considered suitable for any unmarried woman but, as *vidua* was also approved, it was largely used for the never married (and in preference to the term 'maid'). Although other records need not have followed the strict guidelines of this statute, it does appear, as Morgan has argued regarding the term 'gentleman', that 'singlewoman' as a personal designation 'established itself in English social vocabulary in a widening range of documentation', and this as a result of a state project of standardization in the form of the implementation of the Statute of Additions.[109]

---

[108] Henry Spelman, *Aspilogia*, in Edward Bysshe, *Nicolai Vptoni de stvdio militari, libri quatuor. Iohan de Bado Aureo, Tractatvs de armis, Henrici Spelmanni Aspilogia* (London: R. Norton, 1654), p. 115 ['hodie omnes fœminæ *Spinsters* dictæ sunt']; see also Henry Spelman, *Glossarium archaiologicum* (London: Alice Warren, 1664), p. 521 ['Spinster. Quare foeminæ nobiliores sic hodie dictæ sunt in rescriptis fori judicalis']; I owe the references to Baker, 'Male and Married Spinsters', p. 257 nn. 6, 9.

[109] Morgan, 'Individual Style', p. 16.

Conclusion: Cultural Intersections

Classification is a political act in that it entails value-laden choices about where divisions should be drawn, and about what those divisions mean. Is it better to be on one side of a dividing line or the other? Certain groups in certain situations have this power to classify and the choices made might have implications for individuals, from how much penance one should do, to how much tax one should pay. The choices made might also have an important but less direct effect in terms of creating a shared identity for a group, which affects how they are perceived by others. Different behaviour was undoubtedly expected of 'maidens' than of 'young men' or of 'wives'.

The power of classification, though, resides as much in language, in dominant cultural ideas that influence and inflect language use, as with individual classifiers. The selection of a particular category can have meaning, whether the classifier is conscious or not of why he chooses the category or what its effect might be. Key factors affecting the cultural construction of categories include dominant religious and legal ideas in particular historical contexts, but we have also seen how the specific intentions of particular texts affect how categories are deployed. This study evokes a sense of the interpenetration of medieval culture, through its analysis of the intersection of influential cultural discourses and more specific discourses. A focus on the troubling and disruptive category 'single woman', a category with the potential both to encompass every unmarried woman (as in the legal construct *femme sole*) or to be excluded from the dominant schema of maid-wife-widow, offers a way into the complex process of social classification in late medieval England, both at the level of the interpretive scheme, which deals with abstract groups, and at the level of the labelling of named individuals.

The ubiquity of the maid-wife-widow model in part stems from the similarities shared by two different models: a life-stage model of maid-wife-widow and a hierarchical model of virgin-widow-wife, based on discussions of chastity in the writings of the early church fathers. Not only do the two models intersect with each other, in part prompted by a society that placed a higher premium on female chastity, but they are also elaborated upon, with the result that the categories of 'virgin' and 'widow' are subdivided into types of virgin and widow. Furthermore, the models intersect with other forms of classification, thus allowing for the category 'single woman' to be used alongside the categories 'virgin' and 'widow'. For example, in the pastoral manuals that divide the active sin of lechery into fourteen degrees, the most important social division is between the religious and the secular, followed by bonds of kinship. It is after these divisions are taken into account that marital and sexual status are raised, 'single' or 'married' for men but, for women, 'wife', 'virgin', 'vowed widow', 'common woman', and 'single woman'. The 'single woman' is here the unmarried woman who was not a virgin, not vowed to chastity, nor a commercial prostitute. The category is produced not only by a desire to be all-encompassing in the classification of sinners, but also by particular concerns with vows and bonds of kinship or marriage, which affect the seriousness of the sin of lechery. In the discussions of chastity as seven states, life-stage is also taken into account so that the 'single woman' is the *never-married* woman who was not a virgin nor vowed to chastity. Although the categorization is produced by a different set of concerns, those of sexual sin and rehabilitation through penance, the result is that the category 'single woman' in both traditions is inflected with associations of sexual activity, with the notable exception of *Ayenbite*, which uses 'sengle wifman' to denote a virgin in its discussion of lechery.

Although such inflections need not be carried into other contexts, the moral associations of the categories 'virgin'/'maid' and 'widow', acquired through their use in an overarching and widely accepted discourse about chastity, do influence their use in other discourses or inflect their meaning. When Stratford's Guild Register began to use the vernacular term 'sengilman' in the fifteenth century, as discussed in Chapter 4, it continued to use the categories 'virgin'/'maid' and 'widow' to label female guild entrants. One does not have to look to the religious concerns of parish guilds to explain such a practice, as they are categories that, for example, also appear in property deeds and in tax returns. Further, parish guild ordinances use categories in different ways to reflect the different concerns of those texts. The 1388–9 return for the London guild of St Anne's Chantry uses the category 'single man' to warn unmarried, male members about the consequences of fornication. The returns that use the category 'single woman', though, all do so in relation to the different responsibilities that she had in contrast to the married woman, predominantly that of paying for herself. Here we can see the influence of another dominant cultural force, the law. The common law position, which saw adult, unmarried women as 'in their own power', in contrast to the married woman who was generally 'covered' by her husband, resulted in a binary division that was invoked in a number of contexts in which money or public decision-making was a factor. It can also be seen, for example, in the schedule for the poll tax of 1379.

Again, though, the binary division of women as *femmes soles* or *femmes covertes* intersected with other forms of classification. In the Bishop's Lynn poll tax return of 1379, all female taxpayers could have been viewed as *femmes soles*, or as *sola* to use the language of the return, but some are more specifically labelled as *puella* or *vidua*. Further, most of the women described as *sola* also have an occupational designation, whereas none of those classified as *puella* or *vidua* are described in that way. While the category 'widow' did have fiscal significance in that it could be used to signal that the woman was assessed according to her former husband's status (as it is in the tax schedule), it is applied more generally here because the category 'widow' has a wider cultural significance. (Indeed, in the Derby poll tax return of 1379 two women are described as 'poor little widows', even though the classifiers had decided that they were not poor enough to be exempted from the tax, as others clearly were.) It is the use of the term *puella* to describe daughters living at home, though, which suggests that, even in terms of economic responsibility, the binary division of women as *femmes soles* or *femmes covertes* is too simplistic. All females listed in the return were old enough to be liable for the tax, but the labelling of most of the daughters who still lived at home as *puella*, whereas all servants in other households are labelled *sola*, suggests that it was not just age which made someone a social adult, but one's position in a household, as an independent worker rather than a dependent daughter. For the legal treatise *Bracton*, a woman became of age 'whenever she can and knows how to order her house and do the things that belong to the arrangement and management of a house'.[1]

The law had an effect on classification in another way: its attempt at standardization. While the Statute of Additions of 1413 did not seek to standardize the use of personal designations in all types of record, some of

---

[1] *Bracton*, ed. Woodbine, ii, p. 250.

the terms that the king's justices agreed were 'proper' under the Statute, such as 'singlewoman', became established in a wider range of texts such as civic records and testaments from the mid-fifteenth century. The term 'singlewoman' appears to have largely replaced variants of 'maid', probably because 'widow' was also approved by the justices as an addition. Yet, one should not see this as an evolution in the use of terms, but rather as a trend that occurred in different records, in different places, at different times and which could just as easily be reversed, as it was in London's testaments which adopted 'singlewoman' *c*.1450 but then shifted to the term 'maiden' *c*.1480. Just as the category 'widow' had a wider cultural significance, so too did 'maiden', which accounts for its continued existence.

The category 'single woman' has been shown to interact with those of 'maiden' and 'widow', whatever language is used, from the thirteenth century and (although beyond the period of the book's focus) into the seventeenth century. It is thus unlikely that one can tie the emergence of the Middle English 'singlewoman' as a personal designation in the fifteenth century to an increased concern with unmarried women or to numbers of women who spent their lives unmarried, as Goldberg and Poos have suggested. The Middle English 'sengle woman' (that is, the noun rather than the descriptor) first appears in the fourteenth century in, for example, pastoral manuals and guild returns, because of increased use of Middle English, rather than because the concerns about unmarried women and sexual sin or economic liability were new. Such concerns earlier produced terms like *sola* and *femme sole*. A study of the relational use of categories in specific contexts, though, can reveal, *which* types of unmarried woman a text was particularly concerned with and why, which also allows for changing historical circumstances. Indeed, many of the texts discussed in this study were produced as an indirect consequence of particular social and political developments, such as wars with France, the Peasants' Revolt of 1381, heightened fear of heresy, and an increase in bureaucracy both at central and local government levels. Yet, even when the creation or use of the category 'single woman' was the by-product of other concerns, that category can still have meaning, whether intended by the classifiers or not.

One contention of this study is that no single example should be taken as representative; we cannot assume that because a category has a certain meaning in one context that it will have the same meaning in another context. Taken as a whole, though, the study illustrates the interconnectedness of medieval culture, the complex relationship between representation and social reality, and the competing and overlapping nature of social categories. The 'single woman'—whether an umbrella category for all unmarried women, any never-married woman, or an anomaly that sits outside the dominant schema of maid-wife-widow—presents various paths through the labyrinthine world of social classification in late medieval England.

Bibliography

MANUSCRIPT SOURCES

London

Guildhall Library, Department of Manuscripts
    MS 9168/11: Commissary Court of London, Act book
    MSS 9171/5, /6, /7, /8, /10, /11, /12, /13, /14, /15: Commissary Court of London, Probate registers
London Metropolitan Archives
    Archives of St Saviour's Church, Southwark
    P92/SAV/356a: Register of Baptisms, Marriages, and Burials
The National Archives: Public Record Office, Kew
    C 1/1–356 various: Chancery Proceedings (Early)
    C 47/38–46: Guild returns
    DL 30/491–2 various: Knaresborough manor court rolls
    E 179/ various: Subsidy rolls
    EXT 6/99/ various: Subsidy rolls

Nottingham

Nottinghamshire Archives and Southwell Diocesan Record Office
    CA 1375: Nottingham Borough Court Book

Stratford-upon-Avon

Shakespeare Birthplace Trust Records Office, Stratford-upon-Avon
    MS BRT 1/1: Register of the Guild of the Holy Cross

York

Borthwick Institute of Historical Research, York
    CP G 119: York Consistory Court, Cause paper
    Prob. Reg. 1–9: Probate registers, Exchequer Court
York City Archives, York
    B 1, 2–4, 6: Corporation House (or Minute) Books
    CC 1, 1/A, 2, 3 (1), 3 (2), 3 (3): Chamberlains' Account Books
    D 1: Register of admissions to the Freedom of the City

PRINTED PRIMARY SOURCES

Alan of Lille, *The Art of Preaching*, trans. G. R. Evans (Kalamazoo, MI: Cistercian Publications, Inc., 1981).

Andrew, T., 'The Fifteenth Century Wardmote Court Returns for York', MA diss. (York, 1997), pp. 51–97.

The Anonimalle Chronicle, 1333 to 1381, ed. V. H. Galbraith (Manchester: Manchester University Press, 1927).

Les Ans ou reports del raigne du roye Edvvard le quart, novelment revien et corrigee en divers lieux, etc. (London: I. More, 1640; STC 9769).

Aquinas, St Thomas, *Summa Theologiae*, 60 vols. (London: Blackfriars in conjunction with Eyre & Spottiswoode, 1964–75).

Arnold, M. S. (ed.), *Select Cases of Trespass from the King's Courts, 1307–1399*, 2 vols., Selden Society, 100, 103 (London: Selden Society, 1985–7).

'Assessment Roll of the Poll-tax for Howdenshire, Etc., in the Second Year of the Reign of King Richard II (1379)', *Yorkshire Archaeological Journal*, 9 (1886), 129–62.

Attreed, L. C. (ed.), *The York House Books 1461–1490*, 2 vols. (Stroud: Alan Sutton, 1991).

St Augustine, 'Of Holy Virginity', in St Augustine, *On the Holy Trinity, Doctrinal Treatises, Moral Treatises*, A Select Library of Nicene and Post-Nicene Fathers of the Christian Church, iii, ed. P. Schaff (Edinburgh: T. & T. Clark, 1956; reprint of Buffalo, NY: Christian Literature Company, 1887).

The Babees Book, ed. F. J. Furnivall, EETS o.s. 32 (London: N. Trübner & Co., 1868).

Barron, C. M., and Wright, L., 'The London Middle English Guild Certificates of 1388–9', *Nottingham Medieval Studies*, 39 (1995), 108–45.

Bartlett, N. (ed.), *The Lay Poll Tax Returns for the City of York in 1381* (London: A. Brown & Son, 1953).

Bateson, M. (ed.), *Borough Customs*, 2 vols., Selden Society, 18 & 21 (London: Bernard Quaritch, 1904–6).

—— (ed.), *Cambridge Gild Records*, Cambridge Antiquarian Society, 8th ser., 39 (London: George Bell and Sons, 1903).

—— *et al.* (eds.), *Records of the Borough of Leicester*, 7 vols. ([S.I.], 1899–1974) (London: C. J. Clay & Sons, 1901).

Beadle, R. (ed.), *The York Plays* (London: Edward Arnold, 1982).

Benson, L. D. (ed.), *The Riverside Chaucer*, ed. L. D. Benson, 3rd edn. (Oxford: Oxford University Press, 1987).

Book for a Simple and Devout Woman: A Late Middle English Adaptation of Peraldus's Summa de Vitiis et Virtutibus and Friar Laurent's Somme le Roi, ed. F. N. M. Diekstra (Groningen: Egbert Forsten, 1998).

The Book of Vices and Virtues: A Fourteenth Century English Translation of the Somme le Roi of Lorens D'Orléans, ed. W. N. Francis, EETS, o.s. 217 (London: Oxford University Press, 1942).

Bracton on the Laws and Customs of England, ed. George E. Woodbine, trans. S. E. Thorne, 4 vols. (Cambridge, MA: Belknap Press, 1968).

Brooke, R., *La graunde abridgement* ([London: Richard Tottyl], 1576).

Bysshe, E., *Nicolai Vptoni de stvdio militari, libri quatuor. Iohan de Bado Aureo, Tractatvs de armis, Henrici Spelmanni Aspilogia* (London: R. Norton, 1654).

Casagrande, C. (ed.), *Prediche alle donne del secolo XIII: Testi di Umberto da Romans, Gilberto da Tournai, Stefano di Borbone* (Milan: Bompiani, 1978).

Caxton, W., *The book was compiled [and] made atte requeste of kynge Phelyp of Fraunce* (Westminster: William Caxton, 1485; STC (2nd edn.) 21429), accessed via EEBO.

Chibnall, A. C. (ed.), *The Certificate of Musters for Buckinghamshire in 1522*, Buckinghamshire Record Society, 17 (London: Her Majesty's Stationery Office, 1973).

Collins, F. (ed.), *Register of the Freemen of the City of York*, 2 vols., Surtees Society, 96, 102 (Durham: Andrews & Co., 1897–1900).

_____ (ed.), *Wills & Administrations from the Knaresborough Court Rolls*, 2 vols., Surtees Society 104, 110 (Durham: Andrews & Co., 1902–5).

Cornwall, J. (ed.), *The County Community Under Henry VIII: The Military Survey, 1522, and Lay Subsidy, 1524–5, For Rutland*, Rutland Record Society Record Series, 1 (Oakham: Rutland Record Society, 1980).

St Cyprian, 'The Dress of Virgins', in *Saint Cyprian: Treatises*, trans. R. J. Deferrari (Washington, DC: Catholic University of America Press in association with Consortium Books, 1958).

Dan Michel's Ayenbite of Inwyt *or Remorse of Conscience,* ed. R. Morris, and rev. P. Gradon, 2 vols., EETS, o.s. 23, 278 (Oxford: Oxford University Press, 1965–79).

Dobson, R. B. (ed.), *The Peasants' Revolt of 1381* (London: Macmillan, 1970).

Dyer, J., *Les Reports des divers select matters & resolutions* (London: John Streater and Henry Twyford, 1672).

Fasciculus Morum: A Fourteenth-Century Preacher's Handbook, ed. and trans. S. Wenzel (University Park, PA: Pennsylvania State University Press, 1989).

Fenwick, C. C. (ed.), *The Poll Taxes of 1377, 1379 and 1381*, Records of Social and Economic History, new ser., 3 vols. (Oxford: Oxford University Press for the British Academy, 1998–2006).

Fitzherbert, A., *La graunde abridgement* ([London]: Richard Tottell, [1565]).

Given-Wilson, C. *et al.* (eds.), *The Parliament Rolls of Medieval England, 1275–1504*, 16 vols. (London: Boydell Press, 2005).

Goldberg, P. J. P. (ed.), *Women in England c. 1275–1525* (Manchester: Manchester University Press, 1995).

Guibert de Tournai, *Sermones* (Louvain: Johannes de Westfalia, c. 1481–3).

Hali Meiðhad, ed. B. Millett, EETS, o.s. 284 (London: Oxford University Press, 1982).

Hardy, W. J. (ed.), *Stratford-on-Avon Corporation Records: The Guild Accounts* (Stratford-upon-Avon: reprinted from the Stratford-upon-Avon Herald [1886]).

Hervey, S. H. A. (ed.), *Suffolk in 1524*, Suffolk Green Books, 10 (Woodbridge: G. Booth, 1910).

Hobhouse, E. (ed.), *Church-Wardens' Accounts of Croscombe, Pilton, Patton, Tintinhull, Morebath, and St. Michael's, Bath*, Somerset Record Society, 4 ([London]: Somerset Record Society, 1890).

Horrox, R. (ed.), *The Black Death* (Manchester: Manchester University Press, 1994).

Hulton, M. H. M. (ed.), *Coventry and its People in the 1520s*, Publications of the Dugdale Society, 38 ([Stratford-upon-Avon]: Dugdale Society in association with the Shakespeare Birthplace Trust, 1999).

Hunnisett, R. F. (ed.), *Calendar of Nottinghamshire Coroners' Inquests 1485–1558*, Thoroton Society Record Series, 25 (Nottingham: Thoroton Society, 1969).

——— (ed.), *Sussex Coroners' Inquests 1455–1558*, Sussex Record Society, 74 (Lewes: Sussex Record Society, 1985).

Jacob's Well: An Englisht Treatise on the Cleansing of Man's Conscience, ed. A. Brandeis, Part 1, EETS, o.s. 115 (London: Kegan Paul, Trench, Trübner & Co., 1900).

St Jerome, *Jerome: Letters and Select Works*, A Select Library of Nicene and Post-Nicene Fathers of the Christian Church, second ser., 6, ed. P. Schaff and H. Wace (Edinburgh: T. & T. Clark, 1996; reprint of Buffalo, NY: Christian Literature Company, 1892).

Johnston, A. F. and Rogerson, M. (eds.), *York*, 2 vols., Records of Early English Drama (Toronto: University of Toronto Press, 1979).

Jones, P. E. (ed.), *Calendar of Plea and Memoranda Rolls, Preserved Among the Archives of the Corporation of the City of London at the Guildhall, A.D. 1437–1457* (Cambridge: Cambridge University Press, 1954).

Knighton's Chronicle 1337–1396, ed. G. H. Martin (Oxford: Clarendon Press, 1995).

Lambard, W., *Eirenarcha: or of The Office of the Justices of Peace* (facsimile of London: Ra. Newbery and H. Bynneman, 1581; Amsterdam: Theatrum Orbis Terrarum, 1970).

The Lay Folks' Catechism, ed. T. F. Simmons and H. E. Nolloth, EETS, o.s. 118 (London: K. Paul, Trench, Trübner & Co., 1901).

Leggett, J. I., 'The 1377 Poll Tax Returns for the City of York', *Yorkshire Archaeological Journal*, 43 (1971), 128–46.

L'Estrange, J., *Calendar of the Freemen of Norwich from 1317 to 1603*, ed. W. Rye (London, 1888).

A Litil Tretys On the Seven Deadly Sins by Richard Lavynham, ed. J. P. W. M. van Zutphen (Rome: Institutum Carmelitanum, 1956).

The Little Red Book of Bristol, ed. F. B. Bickley, 2 vols. (Bristol: W. Crofton Hemmons, 1900).

Lloyd, E. (ed.), 'Poll Tax Returns for the East Riding 4 Ric. II', *Yorkshire Archaeological Journal*, 20 (1909), 318–52.

Lyte, H. C. M. (ed.), *Inquisitions and Assessments Relating to Feudal Aids*, 6 vols. (London: Her Majesty's Stationery Office, 1899–1920).

Minsheu, J., *Hegemon eis tas glossas: id est, Ductor in linguas, The guide into tongues* (London: John Browne, 1617).

Myers, A. R. (ed.), *English Historical Documents [IV], 1327–1485* (London: Eyre & Spottiswoode, 1969).

A Myrour to Lewde Men and Wymmen: A Prose Version of the Speculum Vitae, *ed. from B. L. MS Harley 45*, ed. V. Nelson (Heidelberg: Carl Winter, 1981).

On the Properties of Things: John Trevisa's Translation of Bartholomæus Anglicus De Proprietatibus Rerum. *A Critical Text*, ed. M. C. Seymour *et al.*, 3 vols. (Oxford, 1975–88).

Owen, D. M. (ed.), *The Making of King's Lynn: A Documentary Survey*, Records of Social and Economic History, new ser., 9 (London: Oxford University Press for the British Academy, 1984).

Peacock, E., 'Subsidy Roll for York and Ainsty', *Yorkshire Archaeological and Topographical Journal*, 4 (1877), 170–201.

Pound, J. (ed.), *The Military Survey of 1522 for Babergh Hundred*, Suffolk Records Society, 28 (Woodbridge: Boydell Press, 1986).

[*Le primier part des ans ore nouelment peruse, etc.*] (London: Company of Stationers, 1609; STC 9616).

Raine, J. *et al.* (eds.), *Testamenta Eboracensia*, 6 vols., Surtees Society, 4, 30, 45, 53, 79, 106 (London: J. B. Nichols, 1836–1919).

The Register of John Waltham, Bishop of Salisbury, 1388–1395, ed. T. C. B. Timmins, Canterbury and York Society, 80 (Woodbridge: Boydell Press, 1994).

The Register of the Gild of the Holy Cross, the Blessed Mary and St. John the Baptist . . . of Stratford-upon-Avon, ed. J. H. Bloom (London: Phillimore and Co., 1907).

Riley, H. T. (ed.), *Munimenta Gildhallae Londiniensis; Liber Albus, Liber Custumarum et Liber Horn*, 3 vols. (London: Longman, Brown, Green, Longman, and Roberts, 1859–62).

Robert of Brunne's Handlyng Synne, ed. F. J. Furnivall, 2 parts, EETS, o.s. 119, 123 (London: Kegan Paul, Trench, Trübner & Co., 1901–3).

Rogers, J. E. T. (ed.), *Oxford City Documents, Financial and Judicial, 1268–1665*, Oxford Historical Society, 18 (Oxford: Clarendon Press, 1891).

'Rolls of the Collectors in the West-Riding of the Lay-Subsidy (Poll Tax) 2 Richard II', *Yorkshire Archaeological Journal*, 5, 6, 7 (1879–84); vol. 5: 1–51, 241–66, 417–32; vol. 6: 1–44, 129–71, 287–342; vol. 7: 6–31, 145–86.

Rotuli de Dominabus et Pueris et Puellis de XII Comitatibus [1185], ed. J. H. Round, Pipe Roll Society, 35 (London, 1913; reprinted Vaduz, 1966).

Sellers, M. (ed.), *York Memorandum Book*, 2 parts, Surtees Society, 120 & 125 (Durham: Andrews & Co., 1912–15).

Shakespeare, W., *Measure for Measure*, ed. N. W. Bawcutt (Oxford: Clarendon Press, 1991).

Smeltz, J. W., '*Speculum Vitae*: An Edition of British Museum Manuscript Royal 17.C.viii', Ph.D. thesis (Duquesne, PA, 1977).

Smith, J. T., and Smith L. T. (eds.), *English Gilds*, EETS, o.s. 40 (London: N. Trübner & Co., 1870).

Spelman, H., *Aspilogia*, in E. Bysshe, *Nicolai Vptoni de stvdio militari, libri quatuor. Iohan de Bado Aureo, Tractatvs de armis, Henrici Spelmanni Aspilogia* (London: R. Norton, 1654).

―――― *Glossarium archaiologicum* (London: Alice Warren, 1664).

Statutes of the Realm, ed. A. Luders *et al.*, 11 vols. ([London]: [George Eyre and Andrew Strahan], 1810–28).

Stevenson, W. H. *et al.* (eds.), *Records of the Borough of Nottingham*, ed. *et al.*, 8 vols. (London: Bernard Quaritch, 1882–1952).

A Survey of Worcestershire by Thomas Habington, ed. J. Amphlett, 2 vols., Worcestershire Historical Society, 5 (Oxford: J. Parker, 1893–5).

Thomas, A. H. (ed.), *Calendar of Early Mayor's Court Rolls, Preserved Among the Archives of the Corporation of the City of London at the Guildhall, A.D. 1298–1307* (Cambridge: Cambridge University Press, 1924).

―――― (ed.), *Calendar of Plea and Memoranda Rolls, Preserved Among the Archives of the Corporation of the City of London at the Guildhall, Rolls A1a–A9, A.D. 1323–1364* (Cambridge: Cambridge University Press, 1926).

―――― (ed.), *Calendar of Plea and Memoranda Rolls, Preserved Among the Archives of the Corporation of the City of London at the Guildhall, A.D. 1364–1381* (Cambridge: Cambridge University Press, 1929).

―――― (ed.), *Calendar of Plea and Memoranda Rolls, Preserved Among the Archives of the Corporation of the City of London at the Guildhall, A.D. 1413–1437* (Cambridge: Cambridge University Press, 1943).

Thomas de Chobham, *Thomae de Chobham summa confessorum*, ed. F. Broomfield (Louvain: Béatrice Nauwelaerts, [1968]).

Warren, F. E., 'Gild of St. Peter in Bardwell', *Proceedings of the Suffolk Institute of Archaeology and Natural History*, 11 (1901), 81–110.

West, W., *Of symboleography the second part* (London: Thomas Wight and Bonham Norton, 1597; STC (2nd edn.) 25277), accessed via EEBO.

The Westminster Chronicle 1381–1394, ed. L. C. Hector and B. F. Harvey (Oxford: Clarendon Press, 1982).

SECONDARY WORKS

Amtower, L., and Kehler, D. (eds.), *The Single Woman in Medieval and Early Modern England: Her Life and Representation* (Tempe, AZ: Arizona Center for Medieval and Renaissance Studies, 2003).

_____ 'Introduction', in L. Amtower and D. Kehler (eds.), *The Single Woman in Medieval and Early Modern England: Her Life and Representation* (Tempe, AZ: Arizona Center for Medieval and Renaissance Studies, 2003), pp. ix–xx.

Arnold, J. H., *Inquisition and Power: Catharism and the Confessing Subject in Medieval Languedoc* (Philadelphia, PA: University of Pennsylvania Press, 2001).

_____ *Belief and Unbelief in Medieval Europe* (London: Hodder Arnold, 2005).

Arnould, E. J., *Le Manual des péchés: étude de literature religieuse anglo-normande (XIIIᵐᵉ siècle)* (Paris: Librairie E. Droz, 1940).

Aston, M. E., 'Lollardy and Sedition, 1381–1431', *Past and Present*, 17 (1960), 1–44.

Bailey, M., 'Demographic Decline in Late Medieval England: Some Thoughts on Recent Research', *Economic History Review*, new ser., 49 (1996), 1–19.

Bainbridge, V. R., *Gilds in the Medieval Countryside: Social and Religious Change in Cambridgeshire c. 1350–1558* (Woodbridge: Boydell Press, 1996).

Baker, J. H., 'Male and Married Spinsters', *American Journal of Legal History*, 21 (1977), 255–9.

_____ *Manual of Law French* ([Amersham]: Avebury Publications, 1979).

_____ *An Introduction to English Legal History*, 3rd edn. (London: Butterworth's, 1990).

Baldwin, J. W., *Masters, Princes and Merchants: The Social Views of Peter the Chanter and His Circle*, 2 vols. (Princeton, NJ: Princeton University Press, 1970).

Bardsley, S., 'Women's Work Reconsidered: Gender and Wage Differentiation in Late Medieval England', *Past and Present*, 165 (1999), 3–29.

Barron, C. M., 'The Parish Fraternities of Medieval London', in C. M. Barron and C. Harper-Bill (eds.), *The Church in Pre-Reformation Society: Essays in Honour of F. R. H. Du Boulay* (Woodbridge: Boydell Press, 1985), pp. 13–37.

_____ 'The "Golden Age" of Women in Medieval London', *Reading Medieval Studies*, 15 (1989), 35–58.

Barry, J., and Melling, J., 'The Problem of Culture: An Introduction', in J. Melling and J. Barry (eds.), *Culture in History: Production, Consumption and Values in Historical Perspective* (Exeter: University of Exeter, 1992), pp. 3–27.

Beattie, C., 'A Room of One's Own? The Legal Evidence for the Residential Arrangements of Women Without Husbands in Late Fourteenth- and Early Fifteenth-Century York', in N. J. Menuge (ed.), *Medieval Women and the Law*, (Woodbridge: Boydell Press, 2000), pp. 41–56.

_____ 'The Problem of Women's Work Identities in Post Black Death England', in J. Bothwell *et al.* (eds.), *The Problem of Labour in Fourteenth-Century England* (Woodbridge: York Medieval Press, 2000), pp. 1–19.

Beattie, C., 'Meanings of Singleness: The Single Woman in Late Medieval England', D.Phil. thesis (York, 2001).

—— 'Single Women, Work and Family: The Chancery Dispute of Jane Wynde and Margaret Clerk', in M. Goodich (ed.), *Voices from the Bench: the Narratives of Lesser Folk in Medieval Trials* (New York, NY: Palgrave Macmillan, 2006), pp. 177–202.

Bennett, J. M., 'Spouses, Siblings and Surnames: Reconstructing Families from Medieval Village Court Rolls', *Journal of British Studies*, 23 (1983), 26–46.

—— 'Medieval Women, Modern Women: Across the Great Divide', in D. Aers (ed.), *Culture and History 1350–1600: Essays on English Communities, Identities, and Writing* (London: Harvester Wheatsheaf, 1992), pp. 147–75.

—— 'Writing Fornication: Medieval Leyrwite and its Historians', *Transactions of the Royal Historical Society*, 6th ser., 13 (2003), 131–62.

—— and A. M. Froide (eds.), *Singlewomen in the European Past 1250–1800* (Philadelphia, PA: University of Pennsylvania Press, 1999).

—— and A. M. Froide, 'A Singular Past', in J. M Bennett and A. M. Froide (eds.), *Singlewomen in the European Past 1250–1800* (Philadelphia, PA: University of Pennsylvania Press, 1999), pp. 1–37.

Benson R. L., and Constable, G., with Lanham, C. D. (eds.), *Renaissance and Renewal in the Twelfth Century* (Oxford: Clarendon Press, 1982).

Bériou, N., 'Autour de Latran IV (1215): La Naissance de la confession moderne et sa diffusion', in Groupe de la Bussière (eds.), *Pratiques de la confession: Des Pères du desert à Vatican II* (Paris: CERF, 1983), pp. 73–93.

Bernau, A., Salih, S., and Evans, R. (eds.), *Medieval Virginities* (Cardiff: University of Wales Press, 2003).

Biller, P., *The Measure of Multitude: Population in Medieval Thought* (Oxford: Oxford University Press, 2000).

Bird, J., 'The Religious's Role in a Post-Fourth-Lateran World: Jacques de Vitry's *Sermones ad status* and *Historia occidentalis*', in C. Muessig (ed.), *Medieval Monastic Preaching* (Leiden: Brill, 1998), pp. 209–29.

Bossy, J., 'The Social History of Confession in the Age of the Reformation', *Transactions of the Royal Historical Society*, 5th ser., 25 (1975), 21–38.

Bowker G. C., and Star, S. L., *Sorting Things Out: Classification and its Consequences* (Cambridge, MA: MIT Press, 1999).

Boyle, L. E., 'The Summa for Confessors as a Genre and its Religious Intent', in C. Trinkaus and H. A. Oberman (eds.), *The Pursuit of Holiness in Late Medieval and Renaissance Religion* (Leiden: Brill, 1974), pp. 126–30.

—— 'The Fourth Lateran Council and Manuals of Popular Theology', in T. J. Heffernan (ed.), *The Popular Literature of Medieval England* (Knoxville, TN: University of Tennessee Press, 1985), pp. 30–43.

—— 'The Inter-Conciliar Period 1179–1215 and the Beginnings of Pastoral Manuals', in F. Liotta (ed.), *Miscellanea Rolando Bandinelli, Papa Alessandro III* (Siena: Accademia senese degli intronati, 1986), pp. 45–56.

Brand, P., 'The Languages of the Law in Later Medieval England', in D. A. Trotter (ed.), *Multilingualism in Later Medieval Britain* (Cambridge: D. S. Brewer, 2000), pp. 63–76.

Bremmer, J., and van den Bosch, L. (eds.), *Between Poverty and the Pyre: Moments in the History of Widowhood* (London: Routledge, 1995).

Brooke, C. N. L., *The Medieval Idea of Marriage* (Oxford: Oxford University Press, 1989).

Brown, E. A. R., 'Georges Duby and the Three Orders', *Viator*, 17 (1986), 51–64.

Brown, P., *The Body and Society: Men, Women, and Sexual Renunciation in Early Christianity* (New York, NY: Columbia University Press, 1988).

Brundage, J. A., *Law, Sex, and Christian Society in Medieval Europe* (Chicago, IL: University of Chicago Press, 1987).

—— 'Widows as Disadvantaged Persons in Medieval Canon Law', in L. Mirrer (ed.), *Upon My Husband's Death: Widows in the Literature and Histories of Medieval Europe* (Ann Arbor, MI: University of Michigan Press, 1992), pp. 193–206.

Burke, P., 'The Language of Orders in Early Modern Europe', in M. L. Bush (ed.), *Social Orders and Social Classes in Europe since 1500: Studies in Social Stratification* (London: Longman, 1992), pp. 1–12.

Carlier, M., and Soens, T. (eds.), *The Household in Late Medieval Cities, Italy and Northwestern Europe Compared* (Louvain-Apeldoorn: Garant, 2001).

Carlin, M., *Medieval Southwark* (London: Hambledon Press, 1996).

Carlson, C. L., and Weisl, A. J. (eds.), *Constructions of Widowhood and Virginity in the Middle Ages* (Houndmills: Macmillan, 1999).

Carruthers, L. M., 'The Liturgical Setting of *Jacob's Well*', *English Language Notes*, 24/4 (June 1987), 11–24.

—— 'Where did *Jacob's Well* Come from? The Provenance and Dialect of MS Salisbury Cathedral 103', *English Studies*, 71 (1990), 335–40.

—— ' "Know thyself": Criticism, Reform and the Audience of Jacob's Well', in J. Hamesse *et al.* (eds.), *Medieval Sermons and Society: Cloister, City, University* (Louvain-La-Neuve: Fédération Internationale des Instituts d'Études Médiévales, 1998), pp. 219–40.

Cartlidge, N., ' "Alas, I go with chylde": Representations of Extra-marital Pregnancy in the Middle English Lyric', *English Studies*, 5 (1998), 395–414.

Casagrande, C., 'The Protected Woman', trans. C. Botsford, in C. Klapisch-Zuber (ed.), *A History of Women in the West: II. Silences of the Middle Ages* (Cambridge, MA: Belknap Press, 1992), pp. 70–104.

Cavallo, S. and Warner, L. (eds.), *Widowhood in Medieval and Early Modern Europe* (Harlow: Pearson Education Ltd, 1999).

Clark, C., 'Socio-economic Status and Individual Identity: Essential Factors in the Analysis of Middle English Personal Naming', in D. Postles (ed.), *Naming, Society and Regional Identity* (Oxford: Leopard's Head Press, 2002), pp. 99–121.

Cloke, G., *'This Female Man of God': Women and Spiritual Power in the Patristic Age, AD 350–450* (London: Routledge, 1995).

Cockburn, J. S., 'Early-modern Assize Records as Historical Evidence', *Journal of the Society of Archivists*, 5 (1974–7), 215–31.

Collins, F. (ed.), *Index of Wills in the York Registry, 1389 to 1514*, YASRS, 6 ([Worksop]: Yorkshire Archaeological and Topographical Association, 1889).

—— (ed.), *Index of Wills in the York Registry, A.D. 1514 to 1553*, YASRS, 11 ([Worksop]: Yorkshire Archæological and Topographical Association, 1891).

Constable, G., 'The Orders of Society', in G. Constable, *Three Studies in Medieval Religious and Social Thought* (Cambridge: Cambridge University Press, 1995), pp. 249–360.

Cornwall, J., 'A Tudor Domesday: The Musters of 1522', *Journal of the Society of Archivists*, 3 (1965–9), 19–24.

Corti, M., 'Models and Antimodels in Medieval Culture', *New Literary History*, 10 (1979), 339–66.

Crespo, B., 'Historical Background of Multilingualism and its Impact on English', in D. A. Trotter (ed.), *Multilingualism in Later Medieval Britain* (Cambridge: D. S. Brewer, 2000), pp. 23–35.

Crick, J., 'Men, Women and Widows: Widowhood in Pre-Conquest England', in S. Cavallo and L. Warner (eds.), *Widowhood in Medieval and Early Modern Europe* (Harlow: Pearson Education Ltd., 1999), pp. 24–36.

Cross, C., 'Northern Women in the Early Modern Period: The Female Testators of Hull and Leeds 1520–1650', *Yorkshire Archaeological Journal*, 59 (1987), 83–94.

Crouch, D. J. F., *Piety, Fraternity and Power: Religious Gilds in Late Medieval Yorkshire 1389–1547* (Woodbridge: York Medieval Press, 2000).

Darnton, R., *The Great Cat Massacre and Other Episodes in French Cultural History* (Harmondsworth: Penguin, 1985).

Davis, I., Müller, M., and Rees Jones, S. (eds.), *Love, Marriage, and Family Ties in the Later Middle Ages* (Turnhout: Brepols, 2003).

Davis, N. Z., *Society and Culture in Early Modern France* (Cambridge: Polity Press, 1987).

D'Avray, D. L., *The Preaching of the Friars: Sermons Diffused From Paris Before 1300* (Oxford: Clarendon Press, 1985).

—— and M. Tausche, 'Marriage Sermons in *ad status* Collections of the Central Middle Ages', *Archives d'histoire doctrinale et littéraire du Moyen Age*, 47 (1981), 71–119.

Dedek, J. F., 'Premarital Sex: The Theological Argument from Peter Lombard to Durand', *Theological Studies*, 41 (1980), 643–67.

Dillard, H., *Daughters of the Reconquest: Women in Castilian Town Society, 1100–1300* (Cambridge: Cambridge University Press, 1984).

Dobson, R. B., 'Admissions to the Freedom of the City of York in the Later Middle Ages', *Economic History Review*, 2nd ser., 26 (1973), 1–21.

Donahue, C., Jr., 'What Causes Fundamental Legal Ideas? Marital Property in England and France in the Thirteenth Century', *Michigan Law Review*, 78 (1979), 59–88.

—— 'Female Plaintiffs in Marriage Cases in the Court of York in the Later Middle Ages: What Can We Learn from the Numbers?', in S. S. Walker (ed.), *Wife and Widow in Medieval England* (Ann Arbor, MI: University of Michigan Press), pp. 183–213.

Douglas, A., 'Salisbury Women and the Pre-Elizabethan Parish', in C. M. Rousseau and J. T. Rosenthal (eds.), *Women, Marriage, and Family in Medieval Christendom: Essays in Memory of Michael M. Sheehan, C.S.B.* (Kalamazoo, MI: University of Western Michigan Press, 1998), pp. 79–117.

Duby, G., *Medieval Marriage: Two Models from Twelfth-Century France*, trans. E. Forster (Baltimore, MD: Johns Hopkins University Press, 1978).

—— *The Three Orders: Feudal Society Imagined*, trans. A. Goldhammer (Chicago, IL: University of Chicago Press, 1980).

—— *The Knight, the Lady and the Priest: The Making of Modern Marriage in Medieval France*, trans. B. Bray (London: Allen Lane, 1983).

Duffy, E., *The Stripping of the Altars: Traditional Religion in England c. 1400–c. 1580* (New Haven, CT: Yale University Press, 1992).

Dunn, A., *The Great Rising of 1381* (Stroud: Tempus, 2002).

Durkheim, E., and Mauss, M., *Primitive Classification*, trans. R. Needham, 2nd edn. (London: Cohen & West, 1969).

Edwards, V. C., 'The Case of the Married Spinster: An Alternative Explanation', *American Journal of Legal History*, 21 (1977), pp. 260–5.

Eiden, H., 'Joint Action against "Bad" Lordship: The Peasants' Revolt in Essex and Norfolk', *History*, 83 (1998), 5–30.

Elliott, D., *Proving Woman: Female Spirituality and Inquisitorial Culture in the Later Middle Ages* (Princeton, NJ: Princeton University Press, 2004).

Evans, R., 'Virginities', in C. Dinshaw and D. Wallace (eds.), *The Cambridge Companion to Medieval Women's Writing* (Cambridge: Cambridge University Press, 2003), pp. 21–39.

Farmer, S., ' "It Is Not Good That [Wo]man Should Be Alone": Elite Responses to Singlewomen in High Medieval Paris', in J. M Bennett and A. M. Froide (eds.), *Singlewomen in the European Past 1250–1800* (Philadelphia, PA: University of Pennsylvania Press, 1999), pp. 82–105.

—— 'The Beggar's Body: Intersections of Gender and Social Status in High Medieval Paris', in S. Farmer and B. H. Rosenwein (eds.), *Monks & Nuns, Saints & Outcasts: Religion in Medieval Society. Essays in Honor of Lester K. Little* (Ithaca, NY: Cornell University Press, 2000), pp. 153–71.

—— *Surviving Poverty in Medieval Paris: Gender, Ideology, and the Daily Lives of the Poor* (Ithaca, NY: Cornell University Press, 2002).

Farmer, S., 'Introduction', in S. Farmer and C. B. Pasternack (eds.), *Gender and Difference in the Middle Ages* (Minneapolis, MN: University of Minnesota Press, 2003), pp. ix–xxvii.

Farnhill, K., *Guilds and the Parish Community in Late Medieval East Anglia, c. 1470–1550* (Woodbridge: York Medieval Press, 2001).

Fauve-Chamoux, A., 'Présentation', *Annales de Démographie Historique* (Paris: La Haye, 1981), 207–13.

Federico, S., 'The Imaginary Society: Women in 1381', *Journal of British Studies*, 40 (2001), 159–83.

Fenwick, C. C., 'The English Poll Taxes of 1377, 1379 and 1381: A Critical Examination of the Returns', Ph.D. thesis (London, 1983).

Fleming, P., *Family and Household in Medieval England* (Houndmills: Palgrave, 2001).

Foucault, M., *The History of Sexuality, Volume 1: An Introduction*, trans. R. Hurley (Harmondsworth: Penguin Books, 1990).

Fox, L., *The Borough Town of Stratford-upon-Avon* (Stratford-upon-Avon: Corporation of Stratford-upon-Avon, 1953).

French, K. L., ' "To Free Them From Binding": Women in the Late Medieval English Parish', *Journal of Interdisciplinary History*, 27 (1996–7), 387–412.

—— 'Maidens' Lights and Wives' Stores: Women's Parish Guilds in Late Medieval England', *Sixteenth Century Journal*, 29 (1998), 399–425.

—— *The People of the Parish: Community Life in a Late Medieval Diocese* (Philadelphia, PA: University of Pennsylvania Press, 2001).

Froide, A. M., 'Marital Status as a Category of Difference: Singlewomen and Widows in Early Modern England', in J. M Bennett and A. M. Froide (eds.), *Singlewomen in the European Past 1250–1800* (Philadelphia, PA: University of Pennsylvania Press, 1999), pp. 236–69.

—— *Never Married: Singlewomen in Early Modern England* (Oxford: Oxford University Press, 2005).

Gastle, B. W., ' "As if she were single": Working Wives and the Late Medieval English *Femme Sole*', in K. Robertson and M. Uebel (eds.), *The Middle Ages at Work: Practicing Labor in Late Medieval England* (New York, NY: Palgrave, 2004), pp. 41–64.

Gerchow, J., 'Gilds and Fourteenth-Century Bureaucracy: The Case of 1388–9', *Nottingham Medieval Studies*, 40 (1996), 109–48.

Giese, L. L., *London Consistory Court Depositions, 1586–1611: List and Indexes*, London Record Society, 32 (London: London Record Society, 1995).

Given-Wilson, C., *The English Nobility in the Late Middle Ages: The Fourteenth-Century Political Community* (London: Routledge & Kegan Paul, 1987).

Goldberg, P. J. P., 'Female Labour, Service and Marriage in the Late Medieval Urban North', *Northern History*, 22 (1986), 18–38.

_____ 'Urban Identity and the Poll Taxes of 1377, 1379, and 1381', *Economic History Review*, new ser., 43 (1990), 194–216.

_____ *Women, Work, and Life Cycle in a Medieval Economy: Women in York and Yorkshire c. 1300–1520* (Oxford: Clarendon Press, 1992).

_____ 'Craft Guilds, The Corpus Christi Play and Civic Government', in S. Rees Jones (ed.), *The Government of Medieval York: Essays in Commemoration of the 1396 Royal Charter* (York: Borthwick Institute of Historical Research, 1997), pp. 141–63.

_____ 'Masters and Men in Later Medieval England', in D. M. Hadley (ed.), *Masculinity in Medieval Europe* (London: Longman, 1999), pp. 56–70.

_____ 'What Was a Servant?', in A. Curry and E. Matthew (eds.), *Concepts and Patterns of Service in the Later Middle Ages* (Woodbridge: Boydell Press, 2000), pp. 1–20.

_____ 'Household and the Organisation of Labour in Late Medieval Towns: Some English Evidence', in M. Carlier and T. Soens (eds.), *The Household in Late Medieval Cities, Italy and Northwestern Europe Compared* (Louvain-Apeldoorn: Garant, 2001), pp. 59–70.

_____ 'Coventry's "Lollard" Programme of 1492 and the Making of Utopia', in R. Horrox and S. Rees Jones (eds.), *Pragmatic Utopias: Ideals and Communities, 1200–1630* (Cambridge: Cambridge University Press, 2001), pp. 97–116.

_____ *Medieval England: A Social History, 1250–1550* (London: Arnold, 2004).

_____ 'Migration, Youth and Gender in Later Medieval England', in P. J. P. Goldberg and F. Riddy (eds.), *Youth in the Middle Ages* (Woodbridge: York Medieval Press, 2004), pp. 85–99.

_____ and Riddy, F. (eds.), *Youth in the Middle Ages* (Woodbridge: York Medieval Press, 2004).

Goring, J. J., 'The General Proscription of 1522', *English Historical Review*, 86 (1971), 681–705.

Gray, H. L., 'Incomes from Land', *English Historical Review*, 49 (1934), 607–39.

Gregg, J. Y., 'The Exempla of "Jacob's Well": A Study in the Transmission of Medieval Sermon Stories', *Traditio*, 33 (1977), 359–80.

Groupe de la Bussière (eds.), *Pratiques de la confession: Des pères du desert à Vatican II* (Paris: CERF, 1983).

Hallissy, M., *Clean Maids, True Wives, Steadfast Widows: Chaucer's Women and Medieval Codes of Conduct* (Westport, CT: Greenwood Press, 1993).

Hanawalt, B. A., 'Remarriage as an Option for Urban and Rural Widows in Late Medieval England', in S. S. Walker (ed.), *Wife and Widow in Medieval England* (Ann Arbor, MI: University of Michigan Press), pp. 141–64.

_____ 'The Widow's Mite: Provisions for Medieval London Widows', in L. Mirrer (ed.), *Upon My Husband's Death: Widows in the Literature and Histories of Medieval Europe* (Ann Arbor, MI: University of Michigan Press), pp. 21–45.

Hanawalt, B. A., and McRee, B. R., 'The Guilds of *homo prudens* in Late Medieval England', *Continuity and Change*, 7 (1992), 163–79.

Haskett, T. S., 'The Medieval English Court of Chancery', *Law and History Review*, 14 (1996), 245–313.

Heffernan, T. J. (ed.), *The Popular Literature of Medieval England* (Knoxville, TN: University of Tennessee Press, 1985).

Helmholz, R. H., '*Legitim* in English Legal History', in R. H. Helmholz, *Canon Law and the Law of England* (London: Hambledon, 1987), pp. 247–62.

___ 'Married Women's Wills in Later Medieval England', in S. S. Walker (ed.), *Wife and Widow in Medieval England* (Ann Arbor, MI: University of Michigan Press), pp. 165–82.

Herlihy, D., *Medieval Households* (Cambridge, MA: Harvard University Press, 1985).

Hicks, M., *Bastard Feudalism* (London: Longman, 1995).

Homans, G. C., *English Villagers of the Thirteenth Century* (New York, NY: Norton, 1941).

Houser, R. E., *The Cardinal Virtues: Aquinas, Albert, and Philip the Chancellor* (Toronto: Pontifical Institute of Mediaeval Studies, 2004).

Howell, M., 'The Properties of Marriage in Late Medieval Europe: Commercial Wealth and the Creation of Modern Marriage', in I. Davis, M. Müller, and S. Rees Jones (eds.), *Love, Marriage, and Family Ties in the Later Middle Ages* (Turnhout: Brepols, 2003), pp. 17–61.

Hudson, A., *Lollards and their Books* (London: Hambledon Press, 1985).

Hufton, O., 'Women Without Men: Widows and Spinsters in Britain and France in the Eighteenth Century', *Journal of Family History*, 9 (1984), 355–76.

Hunter, D. G., 'Resistance to the Virginal Ideal in Late-Fourth-Century Rome: The Case of Jovinian', *Theological Studies*, 48 (1987), 45–64.

Jansen, K. L., 'Mary Magdalen and the Mendicants: The Preaching of Penance in the Late Middle Ages', *Journal of Medieval History*, 21 (1995), 1–25.

___ *The Making of the Magdalen: Preaching and Popular Devotion in the Later Middle Ages* (Princeton, NJ: Princeton University Press, 2000).

Jewell, H. M., *English Local Administration in the Middle Ages* (Newton Abbot: David & Charles, 1972).

Jussen, B., 'On Church Organisation and the Definition of an Estate: The Idea of Widowhood in Late Antique and Early Medieval Christianity', *Tel Aviver Jahrbuch für deutsche Geschichte*, 22 (1993), 25–42.

___ *Der Name der Witwe: Erkundungen zur Semantik der Mittelalterlichen Busskultur*, Veröffentlichungen des Max-Planck-Instituts für Geschichte, 158 (Göttingen: Vandenhoeck and Ruprecht, 2000).

___ ' "Virgins-Widows-Spouses": On the Language of Moral Distinction as Applied to Women and Men in the Middle Ages', *History of the Family*, 7 (2002), 13–32.

Justice, S., *Writing and Rebellion: England in 1381* (Berkeley and Los Angeles, CA: University of California Press, 1994).

——— 'Inquisition, Speech, and Writing: A Case from Late Medieval Norwich', in R. Copeland (ed.), *Criticism and Dissent in the Middle Ages* (Cambridge: Cambridge University Press, 1996), pp. 289–322.

Karras, R. M., 'Two Models, Two Standards: Moral Teaching and Sexual Mores', in B. A. Hanawalt and D. Wallace (eds.), *Bodies and Disciplines: Intersections of Literature and History in Fifteenth-Century England* (Minneapolis, MN: University of Minnesota Press, 1996), pp. 123–38.

——— 'Sex and the Singlewoman', in J. M Bennett and A. M. Froide (eds.), *Singlewomen in the European Past 1250–1800* (Philadelphia, PA: University of Pennsylvania Press, 1999), pp. 127–45.

——— *Sexuality in Medieval Europe: Doing Unto Others* (New York, NY: Routledge, 2005).

Keen, M., *English Society in the Later Middle Ages, 1348–1500* (London: Penguin, 1990).

Kellaway, W., 'John Carpenter's *Liber Albus*', *Guildhall Studies in London History*, 3 (1978), 67–84.

Kelly, K. C., *Performing Virginity and Testing Chastity in the Middle Ages* (London: Routledge, 2000).

Kermode, J., *Medieval Merchants: York, Beverley and Hull in the Later Middle Ages* (Cambridge: Cambridge University Press, 1998).

Kerr, M. H., 'Husband and Wife in Criminal Proceedings in Medieval England', in C. M. Rousseau and J. T. Rosenthal (eds.), *Women, Marriage, and Family in Medieval Christendom: Essays in Memory of Michael M. Sheehan, C.S.B.* (Kalamazoo, MI: Medieval Institute Publications, 1998), pp. 211–51.

Kittel, R., 'Women Under the Law in Medieval England', in B. Kanner (ed.), *The Women of England from Anglo-Saxon Times to the Present: Interpretive Bibliographical Essays* (London: Mansell Information Publishing, 1980), pp. 124–37.

Kittell, E. E., 'The Construction of Women's Social Identity in Medieval Douai: Evidence from Identifying Epithets', *Journal of Medieval History*, 25 (1999), 215–27.

Klapisch-Zuber, C., 'Plague and Family Life', in M. Jones (ed.), *The New Cambridge Medieval History*, 6, pp. 124–54.

Kowaleski, M., 'Women's Work in a Market Town: Exeter in the Late Fourteenth Century', in B. A. Hanawalt (ed.), *Women and Work in Preindustrial Europe* (Bloomington, IN: Indiana University Press, 1986), pp. 145–64.

——— 'Singlewomen in Medieval and Early Modern Europe: The Demographic Perspective', in J. M Bennett and A. M. Froide (eds.), *Singlewomen in the European Past 1250–1800* (Philadelphia, PA: University of Pennsylvania Press, 1999), pp. 38–81.

——— and J. M. Bennett, 'Crafts, Gilds, and Women in the Middle Ages: Fifty Years After Marian K. Dale', in J. M. Bennett *et al.* (eds.), *Sisters and*

Workers in the Middle Ages (Chicago, IL: University of Chicago Press, 1989), pp. 11–25.

Kurath, H. *et al.* (eds.), *The Middle English Dictionary* (Ann Arbor, MI: University of Michigan Press, 1956–).

Labarge, M. W., *Women in Medieval Life* (1986; repr. London: Penguin, 2001).

Lambert, J. M., *Two Thousand Years of Gild Life* (Hull: A. Brown and Sons, 1891).

Lambert, S., 'Crusading or Spinning', in S. B. Edgington and S. Lambert (eds.), *Gendering the Crusades* (Cardiff: University of Wales Press, 2001), pp. 1–15.

Latham, R. E., *Revised Medieval Latin Word-List from British and Irish Sources* (London: Oxford University Press for the British Academy, 1965).

Le Goff, J., 'A Note on Tripartite Society, Monarchical Ideology, and Economic Renewal in Ninth- to Twelfth-Century Christendom', in J. Le Goff, *Time, Work, and Culture in the Middle Ages*, trans. A. Goldhammer (Chicago, IL: University of Chicago Press, 1980), pp. 53–7.

Lévi-Strauss, C., *Structural Anthropology*, trans. C. Jacobson and B. G. Schoepf (London: Allen Lane, 1968).

Leyser, H., *Medieval Women: A Social History of Women in England 450–1500* (London: Phoenix Giant, 1996).

Litchfield, R. B., 'Single People in the Nineteenth-Century City: A Comparative Perspective on Occupations and Living Situations', *Continuity and Change*, 3 (1988), 83–100.

Lochrie, K., *Covert Operations: The Medieval Uses of Secrecy* (Philadelphia, PA: University of Pennsylvania Press, 1999).

Loengard, J. S., '"Legal History and the Medieval Englishwoman" Revisited: Some New Directions', in J. T. Rosenthal (ed.), *Medieval Women and the Sources of Medieval History* (Athens, GA: University of Georgia Press, 1990), pp. 210–36.

—— 'Common Law for Margery: Separate But Not Equal', in L. E. Mitchell (ed.), *Women in Medieval Western European Culture* (New York, NY: Garland Publishing, Inc., 1999), pp. 117–30.

Longère, J., 'La Femme dans la théologie pastorale', in E. Privat (ed.), *La femme dans la vie religieuse du Languedoc (XIIIe–XIVe S.)* (Toulouse: Privat, 1988), pp. 127–52.

McCarthy, C., *Marriage in Medieval England: Law, Literature and Practice* (Woodbridge: Boydell Press, 2004).

McIntosh, M. K., *Controlling Misbehavior in England, 1370–1600* (Cambridge: Cambridge University Press, 1998).

—— *Working Women in English Society, 1300–1620* (Cambridge: Cambridge University Press, 2005).

—— 'The Benefits and Drawbacks of *Femme Sole* Status in England, 1300–1630', *Journal of British Studies*, 44 (2005), 410–38.

McNamara, J. A., *A New Song: Celibate Women in the First Three Christian Centuries* (New York, NY: Institute for Research in History and Haworth Press, Inc., 1983).

McRee, B. R., 'Religious Gilds and Regulation of Behavior in Late Medieval Towns', in J. Rosenthal and C. Richmond (eds.), *People, Politics and Community in the Later Middle Ages* (Gloucester: Alan Sutton, 1987), pp. 108–22.

—— 'Religious Gilds and Civil Order: The Case of Norwich in the Late Middle Ages', *Speculum*, 67 (1992), 69–97.

McSheffrey, S., 'Conceptualizing Difference: English Society in the Late Middle Ages', *Journal of British Studies*, 36 (1997), 134–9.

Maddern, P. C., *Violence and Social Order: East Anglia 1422–1442* (Oxford: Clarendon, 1992).

Mann, J., *Chaucer and Medieval Estates Satire: The Literature of Social Classes and the* General Prologue *to the* Canterbury Tales (Cambridge: Cambridge University Press, 1973).

Marks, R., 'Two Illuminated Guild Registers from Bedfordshire', in M. P. Brown and S. McKendrick (eds.), *Illuminating the Book: Makers and Interpreters. Essays in Honour of Janet Backhouse* (London: The British Library and University of Toronto Press, 1998), pp. 121–41.

Martin, H., 'Confession et contrôle social à la fin du moyen âge', in Groupe de la Bussière (eds.), *Pratiques de la confession: Des pères du desert à Vatican II* (Paris: CERF, 1983), pp. 117–36.

Mate, M. E., *Daughters, Wives and Widows After the Black Death: Women in Sussex, 1350–1535* (Woodbridge: Boydell Press, 1998).

—— *Women in Medieval English Society* (Cambridge: Cambridge University Press, 1999).

Mattingley, J., 'The Medieval Parish Guilds of Cornwall', *Journal of the Royal Institution of Cornwall*, new ser., 10 (1989), 290–329.

Mirrer, L. (ed.), *Upon My Husband's Death: Widows in the Literature and Histories of Medieval Europe* (Ann Arbor, MI: University of Michigan Press, 1992).

Mohl, R., *The Three Estates in Medieval and Renaissance Literature* (New York, NY: Columbia University Press, 1933).

Morey, A., *Bartholomew of Exeter, Bishop and Canonist: A Study in the Twelfth Century* (Cambridge: Cambridge University Press, 1937).

Morgan, D. A. L., 'The Individual Style of the English Gentleman', in M. Jones (ed.), *Gentry and Lesser Nobility in Late Medieval Europe* (Gloucester: Alan Sutton, 1986), pp. 15–35.

Muggleston, J., 'Some Aspects of the Two Late Medieval Chamberlains' Account Books of York', *Yorkshire Archaeological Journal*, 67 (1995), 133–46.

Murray, J., 'The Absent Penitent: The Cure of Women's Souls and Confessors' Manuals in Thirteenth-Century England', in L. Smith and J. H. M. Taylor (eds.), *Women, the Book, and the Godly: Selected Proceedings of the St Hilda's Conference, 1993, vol. 1* (Cambridge: D. S. Brewer, 1995), pp. 13–25.

____ 'Gendered Souls in Sexed Bodies: The Male Construction of Female Sexuality in Some Medieval Confessors' Manuals', in P. Biller and A. J. Minnis (eds.), *Handling Sin: Confession in the Middle Ages* (Woodbridge: York Medieval Press, 1998), pp. 79–93.

Nelson, J. L., 'Women and the Word in the Earlier Middle Ages', in W. J. Sheils and D. Wood (eds.), *Women in the Church: Papers Read at the 1989 Summer Meeting and the 1990 Winter Meeting of the Ecclesiastical History Society*, Studies in Church History, 27 (Oxford: Basil Blackwell, 1990), pp. 53–78.

Newhauser, R., *The Treatise on Vices and Virtues in Latin and the Vernacular*, Typologie des sources du moyen âge occidental, 68 (Turnhout: Brepols, 1993).

Newman, B., 'Flaws in the Golden Bowl: Gender and Spiritual Formation in the Twelfth Century', in B. Newman, *From Virile Woman to WomanChrist: Studies in Medieval Religion and Literature* (Philadelphia, PA: University of Pennsylvania Press, 1995), pp. 19–45.

Oexle, O. G., 'Perceiving Social Reality in the Early and High Middle Ages: A Contribution to a History of Social Knowledge', in B. Jussen (ed.), *Ordering Medieval Society: Perspectives on Intellectual and Practical Modes of Shaping Social Relations*, trans. P. Selwyn (Philadelphia, PA: University of Pennsylvania Press, 2001), pp. 92–143.

Ormrod, W. M., ' "In Bed With Joan of Kent": The King's Mother and the Peasants' Revolt', in J. Wogan-Browne *et al.* (eds.), *Medieval Women: Texts and Contexts in Late Medieval Britain* (Turnhout: Brepols, 2000), pp. 277–92.

____ 'The Use of English: Language, Law, and Political Culture in Fourteenth-Century England', *Speculum*, 78 (2003), 750–87.

Palliser, D. M., 'The York Freemen's Register 1273–1540: Amendments and Additions', *York Historian*, 12 (1995), pp. 21–7.

Pantin, W. A., *The English Church in the Fourteenth Century* (Cambridge: Cambridge University Press, 1955).

Payer, P. J., 'Foucault on Penance and the Shaping of Sexuality', *Studies in Religion*, 14 (1985), 313–20.

____ *The Bridling Of Desire: Views of Sex in the Later Middle Ages* (Toronto: University of Toronto Press, 1993).

____ 'Confession and the Study of Sex in the Middle Ages', in V. L. Bullough and J. A. Brundage (eds.), *Handbook of Medieval Sexuality* (New York, NY: Garland Publishing, Inc., 1996), pp. 3–31.

Payling, S. J., 'Social Mobility, Demographic Change, and Landed Society in Late Medieval England', *Economic History Review*, new ser., 45 (1992), 51–73.

Pelling, M., 'Finding Widowers: Men Without Women in English Towns Before 1700', in S. Cavallo and L. Warner (eds.), *Widowhood in Medieval and Early Modern Europe* (Harlow: Pearson Education Ltd., 1999), pp. 37–54.

Peters, C., 'Single Women in Early Modern England: Attitudes and Expectations', *Continuity and Change*, 12 (1997), 325–45.

_____ *Patterns of Piety: Women, Gender and Religion in Late Medieval and Reformation England* (Cambridge: Cambridge University Press, 2003).

Phillips, K. M., 'Maidenhood as the Perfect Age of Woman's Life', in K. J. Lewis, N. J. Menuge, and K. M. Phillips (eds.), *Young Medieval Women* (Stroud: Sutton Publishing, 1999), pp. 1–24.

_____ 'Four Virgins' Tales: Sex and Power in Medieval Law', in A. Bernau, S. Salih, and R. Evans (eds.), *Medieval Virginities* (Cardiff: University of Wales Press, 2003), pp. 80–101.

_____ *Medieval Maidens: Young Women and Gender in England, 1270–1540* (Manchester: Manchester University Press, 2003).

_____ 'Desiring Virgins: Maidens, Martyrs and Femininity in Late Medieval England', in P. J. P. Goldberg and F. Riddy (eds.), *Youth in the Middle Ages* (Woodbridge: York Medieval Press, 2004), pp. 45–59.

Phythian-Adams, C., *Desolation of a City: Coventry and the Urban Crisis of the Late Middle Ages* (Cambridge: Cambridge University Press, 1979).

Pollock, F., and Maitland, F. W., *The History of English Law Before the Time of Edward I*, 2nd edn., 2 vols. (Cambridge: Cambridge University Press, 1911).

Poos, L. R., *A Rural Society after the Black Death: Essex 1350–1525* (Cambridge: Cambridge University Press, 1991).

Postles, D., *The Surnames of Devon* (Oxford: Leopard's Head Press, 1995).

Raymo, R. R., 'Works of Religious and Philosophical Instruction', in A. E. Hartung (ed.), *A Manual of the Writings in Middle English 1050–1500*, 10 vols. (New Haven, CT: Connecticut Academy of Arts & Sciences, 1967–98), 7, pp. 2255–378, 2467–582.

Rigby, S. H., *English Society in the Later Middle Ages: Class, Status and Gender* (Houndmills: Macmillan, 1995).

_____ *Chaucer in Context: Society, Allegory, and Gender* (Manchester: Manchester University Press, 1996).

_____ 'Gendering the Black Death: Women in Later Medieval England', *Gender and History*, 12 (2000), 745–54.

_____ 'Introduction: Social Structure and Economic Change in Late Medieval England', in R. Horrox and W. M. Ormrod (eds.), *A Social History of England, 1200–1500* (Cambridge: Cambridge University Press, 2006), pp. 1–30.

Roberts, A., 'Helpful Widows, Virgins in Distress: Women's Friendship in French Romance of the Thirteenth and Fourteenth Centuries', in C. L. Carlson and A. J. Weisl (eds.), *Constructions of Widowhood and Virginity in the Middle Ages* (Houndmills: Macmillan, 1999), pp. 25–47.

Rosser, G., 'Going to the Fraternity Feast: Commensality and Social Relations in Late Medieval England', *Journal of British Studies*, 33 (1994), 430–46.

—— 'Workers' Associations in English Medieval Towns', in P. Lambrechts and J-P. Sosson (eds.), *Les Métiers au moyen âge: aspects économiques et sociaux* (Louvain-la-Neuve: Institut d'Études Médiévales de l'Université Catholique de Louvain, 1994), pp. 283–305.

—— 'Crafts, Guilds and the Negotiation of Work in the Medieval Town', *Past and Present*, 154 (1997), 3–31.

—— 'Communities of Parish and Guild in the Late Middle Ages', in S. J. Wright (ed.), *Parish, Church and People: Local Studies in Lay Religion 1350–1750* (London: Hutchinson, 1998), pp. 29–55.

Rousseau, C. M., and Rosenthal, J. T. (eds.), *Women, Marriage, and Family in Medieval Christendom: Essays in Memory of Michael M. Sheehan, C.S.B.* (Kalamazoo, MI: University of Western Michigan Press, 1998).

Rusconi, R., 'De la Prédication à la confession: transmission et contrôle de modèles de comportement au XIIIᵉ siècle', in *Faire Croire: Modalités de la diffusion et de la réception des messages religieux du XIIᵉ au XVᵉ siècle* (Rome: ecole Française de Rome, 1981), pp. 67–85.

—— '*Ordinate confiteri*: La confessione dei peccati nelle "summae de casibus" e nei manuali per i confessori (metà XII–inizi XIV secolo)', in *L'Aveu: Antiquité et moyen-âge*, Actes de la table ronde organisée par l'ecole Française de Rome avec le concours du CNRS et de l'Université de Trieste, Rome 28–30 Mars 1984 (Rome: Ecole Française de Rome, 1986), pp. 297–313.

Rushforth, G. M., *A Short Guide to the Painted Windows in the Church of St. Neot, Cornwall* (London: SPCK, 1937).

Salih, S., *Versions of Virginity in Late Medieval England* (Cambridge: D. S. Brewer, 2001).

Salisbury, J. E., *Church Fathers, Independent Virgins* (London: Verso, 1991).

Sanok, C., 'Performing Feminine Sanctity in Late Medieval England: Parish Guilds, Saints' Plays, and the *Second Nun's Tale*', *Journal of Medieval and Early Modern Studies*, 32 (2002), 269–303.

Scott, J. C., *Seeing Like a State: How Certain Schemes to Improve the Human Condition Have Failed* (New Haven, CT: Yale University Press, 1998).

Scott, J. W., 'A Statistical Representation of Work: *La Statistique de l'Industrie à Paris*, 1847–1848', in J. W. Scott, *Gender and the Politics of History* (New York, NY: Columbia University Press, 1988), pp. 113–38.

—— 'Deconstructing Equality-versus-Difference: Or, The Uses of Poststructuralist Theory for Feminism', *Feminist Studies*, 14 (1988), 33–50.

—— 'The Evidence of Experience', *Critical Inquiry*, 17 (1991), 773–97.

Sedinger, T., 'Working Girls: Status, Sexual Difference, and Disguise in Ariosto, Spenser, and Shakespeare', in L. Amtowler and D. Kehler (eds.), *The Single Woman in Medieval Europe and Early Modern England: Her Life and Representation* (Tempe, AZ: Arizona Center for Medieval and Renaissance Studies, 2003), pp. 167–91.

Shahar, S., *The Fourth Estate: A History of Women in the Middle Ages*, rev. edn. (London: Routledge, 2003).

Shaw, J., 'The Influence of Canonical and Episcopal Reform on Popular Books of Instruction', in T. J. Heffernan (ed.), *The Popular Literature of Medieval England* (Knoxville, TN: University of Tennessee Press, 1985), pp. 44–60.

Sheehan, M. M., 'The Influence of Canon Law on the Property Rights of Married Women in England', in M. M. Sheehan, *Marriage, Family, and Law in Medieval Europe: Collected Studies*, ed. J. K. Farge (Cardiff: University of Wales Press, 1996), pp. 16–30.

Smith, R. M., 'Some Reflections on the Evidence for the Origins of the "European Marriage Pattern" in England', in C. Harris *et al.* (eds.), *The Sociology of the Family: New Directions for Britain* (Keele: University of Keele, 1979), pp. 74–112.

——— 'Hypothèses sur la nuptialité en Angleterre aux XIIe–XIVe siècles', *Annales: Economies, Sociétés, Civilisations*, 38 (1983), 107–36.

——— 'Geographical Diversity in the Resort to Marriage in Late Medieval Europe: Work, Reputation, and Unmarried Females in the Household Formation Systems of Northern and Southern Europe', in P. J. P. Goldberg (ed.), *Woman is a Worthy Wight: Women in English Society c. 1200–1500* (Stroud: Alan Sutton, 1992; reprinted as *Women in Medieval English Society*, 1997), pp. 16–59.

Sokol, B. J., and Sokol, M., *Shakespeare, Law, and Marriage* (Cambridge: Cambridge University Press, 2003).

Spiegel, G. M., 'History, Historicism, and the Social Logic of the Text in the Middle Ages', *Speculum*, 65 (1990), 59–86.

Steer, C. O., 'The Parish Elites of St Michael's, Spurriergate, York and their Clergy, 1500–1550', MA diss. (York, 1997).

Stell, P. M., 'Paying for the Freedom of the City of York in the Fifteenth Century: The Standar' Maioris', *York Historian*, 18 (2001), 7–12.

Stevenson, S. J., 'The Rise of Suicide Verdicts in South-East England, 1530–1590: The Legal Process', *Continuity and Change*, 2 (1987), 37–85.

Stoertz, F. H., 'Young Women in France and England, 1050–1300', *Journal of Women's History*, 12/4 (2001), 22–46.

Stone, L. W., and Rothwell, W. (eds.), *Anglo-Norman Dictionary* (London: Modern Humanities Research Association, 1977–92).

Strohm, P., *Social Chaucer* (Cambridge, MA: Harvard University Press, 1989).

Strohm, P., *Hochon's Arrow: The Social Imagination of Fourteenth-Century Texts* (Princeton, NJ: Princeton University Press, 1992).

Swanson, H., 'The Illusion of Economic Structure: Craft Guilds in Later Medieval English Towns', *Past and Present*, 121 (1988), 29–48.

—— *Medieval Artisans: An Urban Class in Late Medieval England* (Oxford: Basil Blackwell, 1989).

Swanson, J., 'Childhood and Childrearing in *ad status* Sermons by Later Thirteenth Century Friars', *Journal of Medieval History*, 16 (1990), 309–31.

Taylor, C. (ed.), *Joan of Arc: La Pucelle* (Manchester: Manchester University Press, 2006).

Tentler, T. N., 'The Summa for Confessors as an Instrument of Social Control', in C. Trinkhaus and H. A. Oberman (eds.), *The Pursuit of Holiness in Late Medieval and Renaissance Religion* (Leiden: Brll, 1974), pp. 103–26.

—— 'Response and Retraction', in C. Trinkhaus and H. A. Oberman (eds.), *The Pursuit of Holiness in Late Medieval and Renaissance Religion* (Leiden: Brll, 1974), pp. 131–7.

—— *Sin and Confession on the Eve of the Reformation* (Princeton, NJ: Princeton University Press, 1977).

Thurston, B. B., *The Widows: A Women's Ministry in the Early Church* (Minneapolis, MN: Fortress Press 1989).

Trinkaus, C., and Oberman, H. A., (eds.), *The Pursuit of Holiness in Late Medieval and Renaissance Religion*, (Leiden: Brill, 1974).

Trotter, D. A. (ed.), *Multilingualism in Later Medieval Britain* (Cambridge: D. S. Brewer, 2000).

Tuck, J. A., 'The Cambridge Parliament, 1388', *English Historical Review*, 84 (1969), 225–43.

—— 'Nobles, Commons and the Great Revolt of 1381', in R. H. Hilton and T. H. Aston (eds.), *The English Rising of 1381* (Cambridge: Cambridge University Press, 1984), pp. 194–212.

Tucker, P., 'The Early History of the Court of Chancery: A Comparative Study', *English Historical Review*, 115 (2000), 791–811.

Walker, S. S., 'Proof of Age of Feudal Heirs in Medieval England', *Mediaeval Studies*, 35 (1973), 306–23.

—— (ed.), *Wife and Widow in Medieval England* (Ann Arbor, MI: University of Michigan Press, 1993).

Watkins, S. C., 'Spinsters', *Journal of Family History*, 9 (1984), 310–25.

Wenzel, S., *Verses in Sermons: Fasciculus Morum and its Middle English Poems* (Cambridge, MA: Mediaeval Academy of America, 1978).

Westlake, H. F., *The Parish Gilds of Mediæval England* (London: Society for Promoting Christian Knowledge, 1919).

Wiener, C. Z., 'Is a Spinster an Unmarried Woman?', *American Journal of Legal History*, 20 (1976), 27–31.

Willis-Bund, J. W. *et al.*, *The Victoria History of the County of Worcester*, 5 vols. (Westminster: A. Constable, 1901–26), iv.

Witte, J., Jr., *From Sacrament to Contract: Marriage, Religion, and Law in the Western Tradition* (Louisville, KY: Westminster John Knox Press, 1997).

Wogan-Browne, J., *Saints' Lives and Women's Literary Culture, c. 1150–1300: Virginity and its Authorizations* (Oxford: Oxford University Press, 2001).

Woo, T-Y. J., 'Medieval Single Women in London', MA diss. (London, 2001).

Woods, M. C., and Copeland, R., 'Classroom and Confession', in D. Wallace (ed.), *The Cambridge History of Medieval English Literature* (Cambridge: Cambridge University Press, 1999), pp. 376–406.

Index

additions (personal designations) 2–3,
  5–6, 33, 38, 65–6, 73–93,
  113–14, 115–18, 124–43
  Statute of Additions (1413) 124–6,
    131, 143, 146–7
adultery 47–8, 53, 112–13
age 2, 8 n. 18, 9, 10, 37, 63, 64, 88,
  98, 122, 140, 146
  of legal responsibility 24, 25–6
  of marriage 33, 69, 117
  of reason 19, 58–9
  of servants 36, 75 n. 51, 81
  social adulthood 81, 146
  taxable age 63–4, 71, 85, 146
  vetula (old) 83, 87
  see also youth
Alan of Lille 21, 22
Albertus Magnus (Albert the Great) 19,
  59
Alexander of Hales 54
Alphabetum narrationum 43
Anglo-Norman 20, 26 n. 55, 47, 55, 67
Ambrose 15, 18, 19
Amtower, Laurel 8
Aquinas, Thomas 19, 41 n. 8
aristocracy 4–5
  see also nobility
Artificers' Act (1363) 91
Athanasius 18 n. 16
Augustine (of Hippo) 15, 18, 19
Ayenbite of Inwyt 42, 44, 49, 51–9,
  61, 145
  see also *Somme le Roi* (the
    Somme-tradition)
aynlepi 54

Bainbridge, Virginia 102, 106–7
Baldwin, John 15
Barron, Caroline 102
Bartholomew of Exeter 54, 55 n. 66
Bennett, Judith 8
Bible 4, 88–9
  Ephesians 106
  Luke 88–9
  Mark 89 n. 96
  Matthew 15

Bishop's Lynn 66, 72–86, 89 n. 101,
  92–3, 138, 146
Black Death 33–5
bodies 19–20, 41 n. 11, 43, 45, 51,
  59, 93–4, 112
  see also virginity
Bonaventure 19
Book of Vices and Virtues 42, 44 n. 24,
  49, 52–3, 56, 57 n.71, 58–9
  see also *Somme le Roi* (the
    Somme-tradition)
Bracton 111, 146
Bristol 115
Brooke, Robert (Sir) 125, 126 n. 13
Buckinghamshire 138
bureaucracy 6 n. 13, 38, 100, 147
bynames 72 n. 42, 78–9, 81 n. 68, 89,
  108, 130

Cambridge Parliament, *see*
  government
Cambridgeshire 102, 121
Carlin, Martha 87
Caxton, William 44 n. 24
  see also *Ryal Book*
celibacy 18
  see also chastity
Chancery 100
  court of, 30–31, 127 n. 16, 128
chastity:
  religious discourse of 14–24, 40, 50,
    55–61, 144–5
  vow of 14, 18, 19, 20, 52, 53
  see also models (virgin-widow-spouse
    model)
chronicles 62–3, 67, 93, 95
  Anonimalle Chronicle 63 n. 5, 67
  Westminster Chronicle 100
  see also Knighton, Henry
church fathers (early) 15, 16–19, 144
  see also Ambrose; Athanasius;
    Augustine; Cyprian; Jerome
church wardens' accounts 119, 121
civic records 26–9, 31, 33, 37–8, 127,
  129–36, 138–9, 141
class 9

class (*cont.*)
  see also social status
classificatory schemes, *see* additions;
    models
clergy 18, 44, 56, 60, 96, 108
  prelates 42
  priests 40, 60, 98
Collins, Patricia Hill 9
common women, *see* prostitution
communities 18, 64, 94
La Compileison 20, 58
concubines 48–9
confession 44–6, 59–61
  confessors 39, 45
  confessors' manuals 45, 46–7
  conscience 44, 45
Constable, Giles 3
continent 57 n. 71
  see also chastity
Coventry 135–6, 138–9
  'census' of 1523: 135, 138–9
coverture 25–8, 32, 35, 70, 99, 106,
    110, 111–12, 119, 122, 146
  see also guardianship
Croscombe (Somerset) 121
Cutler, Margery 135, 139
Cyprian (of Carthage) 17

daughters 60, 62, 77, 82, 83, 85 n. 81,
    87, 92, 93, 109, 134
  'daughter' 66, 72, 73, 77, 79–82,
    84, 87, 91–2, 111, 116–17,
    121, 131–2, 139
  as financially dependent 69, 81–2,
    94, 146
  as workers 92
demography 8 n. 18, 33, 55
  see also population levels
Derby 71, 83, 87–91, 93, 146
Douai 5, 130
Duby, Georges 4

economic status 67–9, 74, 75, 81–2,
    87–8, 92
economy 33–6
estate 3, 5, 7, 65, 67–9, 75, 77, 96,
    125–6, 127
  see also models (three-orders model)
exempla 43, 45, 59–60

Farmer, Sharon 8, 9

Fasciculus Morum 40–1, 47–9, 51
Federico, Sylvia 64 n. 8, 94
femme coverte 25, 105, 146
  see also coverture
femme sole 10, 69–70, 92, 126 n. 9,
    146, 147
  as a legal construct 15, 33, 24–31,
    70, 99, 105, 107, 122, 144
Fenwick, Carolyn 65, 70 n. 27, 71, 75,
    78, 85
fornication (*fornicacio*) 40, 41 n. 8,
    47–50, 54–5, 112–13, 145
Foucault, Michel 46
franciscans, *see* mendicant orders
fraternities, *see* guilds
French 10, 51
  law French 25 n. 51
  see also Anglo-Norman
French, Katherine 119, 120
friars, *see* mendicant orders
Froide, Amy 8, 136, 141

gender 2, 7, 9, 37, 94 n. 111, 111
    n. 76, 121
Gerchow, Jan 100–1, 107
Giese, Loreen 140–1
Goldberg, P. J. P. 33, 35, 37, 147
government:
  Cambridge Parliament (1388) 97,
    100, 102
  Commons 71, 100
  Exchequer 63, 65, 67, 71–2, 75,
    127
  Richard II's third parliament (1379)
    67, 70
  the state 100, 101, 127, 138, 143
  see also Chancery
guardianship 25–6, 137
Guibert of Tournai 21–2
guilds:
  account books 99, 113–15, 118
  in Cambridge 102, 103, 106–8,
    112, 119 n. 114
  craft guilds 97, 100, 101 n. 21, 102
    n. 24, 104, 133
  founders 107, 108, 109, 110–12
  of the Holy and Undivided Trinity,
    Luton, 114, 121
  of the Holy Cross,
    Stratford-upon-Avon 99,
    113–19, 121, 122, 127, 136
    n. 65, 145

of the Holy Trinity and St Leonard, Lancaster 103, 111, 112 n. 77, 113
of the Holy Trinity, Coventry 114
in Kingston-upon-Hull 103, 106, 108–12, 119 nn. 113–14
lights 97, 116–20
in London 102, 103–6, 112–13, 119 n. 113, 145
maidens' groups 98, 119–22
membership 97–8, 99, 101–5, 107–22, 145
ordinances 96, 99–100, 101–2, 103–10, 112–13, 145
of St Christopher, Norwich 96, 101
of St Peter in Bardwell, Suffolk 114
returns (1388–9) 37, 96–7, 98–113, 118–19, 122, 147
registers 99, 113–19, 121, 122, 125 n. 5, 127
'sisters' 96–7, 98–9, 102–4, 106–11, 113, 120
wives' groups 98, 119–22
young men's groups 119–21, 122

Habington, Thomas 128
Hampshire 88
Hanawalt, Barbara 102, 106 n. 44
Handlyng Synne 47
Hebrew 13
  law code 89
Herefordshire 128
  Hereford 128
heresy 37, 39, 147
  Lollardy 37, 101
hierarchies 15–19, 22, 32, 57–8, 67–8, 96–7, 101, 120
households 72–3, 74 n. 46, 79–80, 81 n. 70, 82, 84, 87, 88, 92, 111, 146
  householders 72, 75, 76, 78, 82, 85, 87, 121, 138
  and marriage 22, 33, 36
  and work 32, 35
Howdenshire 83, 91–2
Hull; *see* Kingston-upon-Hull

Ingleby, Joan 129, 130, 131
interpretive schemes 2–5, 6, 50, 55, 68, 99, 124, 144

Jacob's Well 41–5, 47–53, 56–7, 59–61

see also *Somme le Roi* (the *Somme*-tradition)
Jerome 15, 18, 19, 59
Jovinian 18
Jussen, Bernhard 13

Karras, Ruth 40, 48–9, 55 n. 66, 57
Kehler, Dorothea 8
King's Bench 126, 141
king's courts, *see* law
Kingston-upon-Hull 71–2
kinship 41, 48, 54, 94, 109–10, 111, 145
  see also relational status
Kittell, Ellen 5, 130
Knaresborough 142
Knighton, Henry 62–4, 66, 93–5
Kowaleski, Maryanne 34

labour, *see* work
Lateran Council III (1179) 17
Lateran Council IV (1215) 17, 20
law 24–32, 111, 124–6, 140–3, 146, 146–7
  canon law 25 n. 48, 43 n. 20, 89
  common law 24 n. 46, 24–6, 30, 70, 106, 146
  customary law 24 n. 46, 26–8, 31, 32
  justices of the peace 125–6
  king's courts 28 n. 61, 124–6, 143, 147
  see also Chancery; coverture
Lay Folks' Catechism 54
lechery (*luxuria*) 40–3, 47–61, 145
  incest (*incestus*) 47–8, 49, 60
  rape (*raptus*) 47–8, 59 n. 82
  sacrilege 47
  sodomy (*sodomia*) 41, 47–8, 49, 59
  violation of virgins (*stuprum*) 47–8, 49, 52–3
  see also adultery; fornication; prostitution
legal status 9, 13, 24–32, 111
  see also coverture; *femme sole*; guardianship
Leicestershire 67 n. 22, 88
Lévi-Strauss, Claude 93
Liber Albus 26–8, 31
life-stages 8, 14, 15–16, 20, 22–3, 51, 58, 97, 145
Lincoln 26 n. 55

Lollardy, *see* heresy
London 26–9, 31, 102, 103–6,
   112–13, 115, 127 n. 16, 145,
   147
lust, *see* lechery

McNamara, Jo Ann 18
McRee, Ben 102, 106 n. 44
Maddern, Phillipa 126, 141
maidens 94, 117
   category 'maid(en)' 8, 16 n. 9, 42,
      43, 51, 52–3, 54, 80–1, 96,
      119–23, 138, 142
   'maid(en)' as a personal
      designation 99, 113–14, 126,
      136, 137–9, 140–1, 143, 147
   maidenhood 23, 52–3, 58
   pucelle 53–4, 61
   puella 16 n. 9, 22, 62–3, 66, 74,
      76–7, 79–83, 85, 93–4, 114,
      116, 140, 146
   see also models
Manuel des péchés 47, 55
marital status 2, 7, 37, 65–6, 68–70,
   71, 72, 73–81, 82–7, 91–3, 98,
   104–5, 109, 115–18, 122, 145
marriage 1, 29, 31–6, 50–1, 54, 58,
   69, 122, 128, 131, 139, 145
   and chastity 15, 17–18, 19–21, 32,
      56, 58
   and guild membership 103, 107–9,
      112, 116–19
   marriage licences 141
   married persons 21, 48, 49, 50,
      69–70, 71, 74–5
   northwest European marriage
      pattern 33–4, 35
   and property 25, 32, 98
   remarriage 13–14, 24, 29, 34, 58,
      109
   as sacrament 32, 47
   and sex 32, 98
   and women's names 129
   and work 32–3
   see also never married; married
      women
married women 22, 25–8, 31, 32, 35,
   51, 64 n. 8, 70, 72, 73, 75, 105,
   107–9, 111, 118
   'wife' 22, 40, 42, 50–1, 69–70, 72,
      91, 96, 106, 111, 119–22, 126,
      138, 142, 145

Mattingley, Joanna 120, 121 n. 131
mendicant orders 17, 21, 45
Middle English, *see* multilingualism
Middle English Dictionary (MED) 127
military survey 135, 136
models:
   maid-wife-widow model 1, 2, 3, 7,
      8, 15–23, 144–5, 148
   single/married binary 75, 105, 122,
      146
   three-orders model 3, 5, 7, 8
   virgin-widow-spouse model
      (hierarchical) 15–23, 32, 53,
      57–8, 144–5
   see also interpretive schemes
Morebath (Devon) 121
Morgan, D. A. L. 125, 143
multilingualism 10, 15
   Latin 10, 13, 15, 25 n. 51, 26 n. 55,
      54–5, 80 n. 67, 89, 113–14,
      116, 123, 132–5, 136–7
   Middle English 10, 15, 26 n. 55, 33,
      51, 54–5, 80–1, 89, 99, 103,
      113–14, 116, 127, 133–4,
      136–7, 147
   see also French
muster, *see* military survey
Myrour to Lewde Men and Wymmen 42,
   43 n. 23, 49, 51–3, 56–9, 61
   see also *Somme le Roi* (the
      Somme-tradition)

never married 33–34, 56–7, 59, 70,
   79, 124, 141
   v. ever married 121
   men 75–6, 99
   women 8, 10, 36–37, 40, 49, 55–6,
      57, 76–7, 82, 86, 89, 92–3,
      116, 121, 128, 130, 132–6,
      139–40, 141, 143, 145, 147,
      148
nobility 5, 37, 67–9, 72, 96, 128
   'gentleman' as a personal
      designation 125, 129, 143
   'gentlewoman' as a personal
      designation 126
   noblewomen 69, 128
Norfolk 63, 66, 69 n. 25, 71 n. 33, 75
   n. 50;
   see also Bishop's Lynn
Norwich 96, 101, 103 n. 81, 129 n.
   27, 141

Nottingham 134–5
nuns 40, 43, 130
see also religious women

occupational status 7, 9, 37, 65–6,
   68–9, 71, 72–93, 96–7, 115,
   124, 126 n. 14, 127, 129 n. 29,
   133, 138, 139 n. 89, 142, 146
Oexle, Otto 2, 4
onlepi, *see* aynlepi
Oxford 137

parishes 45, 70, 98, 102, 107 n. 48,
   114, 119–22, 145
parish registers 141 n. 101
pastoral literature 17, 40–61, 145, 147
Payer, Pierre 19, 41 n. 12, 47, 54, 55
   n. 66
Peasants' Revolt (1381) 37, 62, 94,
   100, 101, 147
Pelling, Margaret 141
penance 40, 41 n. 11, 44–7, 57,
   59–61, 145
see also confession
Peraldus, William 48 n. 42
personal designations, *see* additions
Peters, Christine 119–21
Phillips, Kim 23, 140
poll taxes 62–95
   1377 tax 64 n. 8, 67, 70, 71–2, 73,
      74–5, 79, 82, 92
   1379 tax (schedule) 4, 37, 65,
      66–75, 77–9, 81, 86, 88, 92,
      96, 146
   1379 tax (returns) 71, 72–93, 138
   1380–1 tax 62–5, 71, 87, 93–4
Poos, L. R. 33, 37, 147
population levels 34–5
poverty 30, 64, 65, 88–9, 110, 113
   n. 80, 146
preaching 17, 39, 44–5, 47
see also sermons
property deeds 23–4, 119, 145
prostitution 47
   'common woman' 42, 49, 50, 51,
      53, 145
   meretrix 48–9
   prostitutes 1, 8, 40–1, 48–9, 51,
      60, 61
   repentant prostitutes 60 n. 84, 61
puella, see maidens

Raine, James 130
relational status 5, 66, 72–4, 77, 80,
   83–5, 87, 91–2, 115, 116–17,
   139
   'mother of' 77, 87 n. 86, 88, 91
   'sister of' 84, 111, 116, 139 n. 87
   see also daughters; servants
religious women 42, 56, 57 n. 71
reputation 94, 98
respectability 81, 123
Rigby, S. H. 9
Rosser, Gervase 98
Ryal Book 44 n. 24, 51 n. 47

St Paul 106
St Neot (Cornwall) 120
Salisbury 83–7, 92
Scott, Joan 65 n. 15
scribes 6, 74, 100–1, 104 n. 18, 115,
   116, 117, 130, 138–9
   chanceries 100–1
sermons 3, 23, 43, 45
   ad status 21–2
servants 8, 33, 36, 75–6, 78, 81–2,
   86, 92, 140, 142 n. 106, 146
   category 'servant' 66, 72, 73, 75,
      76–7, 80, 84–5, 87, 90–2,
      126, 133, 139, 142 n. 106
   'maidservant' 80–1, 139 n. 87
sex 32, 39–42, 46–61, 93–4,
   112–13, 145
sexual status 7, 9, 37, 145
sexualities 9, 113
   women as passive 50 n. 47, 111,
      113
sin 39, 43 n. 20, 45, 47, 50, 53, 60 n.
   83, 61, 145
   seven deadly sins 41 n. 11, 43, n. 21,
      44, 47
   sexual 21, 40, 46, 47, 54–5, 60,
      145, 147
see also lechery
single man 2, 42, 49, 50, 54–5, 57, 69,
   99, 103, 107, 108–10, 112–13,
   119, 120–1, 138, 145
   'bachelor' 121
   nonmaritatus 115, 117
   as a personal designation 33, 99,
      113–14, 116, 117–18, 123,
      124, 127, 135–6, 137, 139,
      141, 145
   solus 66, 73–7, 82, 85, 138

single man (*cont.*)
    see also youth (young men)
single woman:
    as economically and legally
        independent 26, 28–9, 31,
        69–70, 99, 105, 107, 108, 111,
        112, 122, 145–6
    as a personal designation 33, 37–8,
        114, 124–43
    as sexually active 40–1, 48–9, 51, 56,
        57, 59–61, 145
    sola 10, 66, 73–4, 76–80, 82–6,
        92, 146, 147
    soluta 40, 54, 136, 141
    as 'to-be-married woman' 108, 119,
        122
    as woman alone 29–31, 32, 99, 110,
        111, 122
    as woman without a husband 107,
        110
    as worker 76–7, 82–3, 110–11,
        146
social status 2, 7, 9, 37, 68–9, 71–2,
    96–7, 114, 124, 128
    see also aristocracy; economic status;
        estate; urban groups
Somme le Roi 41–2, 44, 47, 49, 51 n.
    47, 52 n. 52, 53–4, 61
    the *Somme*-tradition 47–61
Southwark 87–8
Speculum Vitae 42–4, 49, 51–54,
    56–7, 61
    see also *Somme le Roi* (the
        Somme-tradition)
Spelman, Henry 142–3
spinster:
    as occupational designation 78, 87,
        89–91, 93, 126, 141–2
    as unmarried woman 136, 140
        n. 98, 141–3
standardization 38, 124, 143, 146–7
Stratford-upon-Avon
    see guilds
Strohm, Paul 62
subsidies:
    1428 subsidy 128 n. 23
    1431 subsidy 127–8
    1524–5 subsidy 127, 131, 136–9
    see also military survey; poll taxes
summae 4, 17
Sussex 71, 74 n. 46, 142

tax returns 119, 145, 147
    see also poll taxes; subsidies
testaments 24, 25 n. 48, 33, 127, 130,
    131, 136, 139–40, 142, 147
    legitim 134, 137
theological treatises 3, 17, 19, 20, 21
    n. 87, 23
three-orders, *see* models
Thurston, Bonnie 13

universities 16, 19, 23
    University of Paris 17, 19
urban groups 4–5, 67–8, 96

vernacular 10, 37, 55, 99, 116, 123,
    124, 132, 134, 140
    see also French; multilingualism
vidua, see widows
virginity 16 n. 9, 19–21, 24, 50, 51,
    52–3, 57 n. 71, 58–9, 60 n. 84,
    61, 64, 80 n. 67, 81, 93–4, 117,
    119, 121, 122, 123
    see also chastity
virgins 8, 14, 15, 17–22, 39, 43, 47,
    51, 52, 56, 58–9, 80, 145
    category 'virgin' 2, 13, 14, 16,
        19–23, 40, 121, 126, 136, 139,
        141, 145
    virgo 16 n. 9, 22, 114, 115–17,
        121, 139, 141
    see also maidens; models
vowesses 52 n. 50
    see also widows (vowed)

wages 35, 82, 106
West, William 141–2
widowers 76, 109, 135–6
    category 'widower' 51 n. 47, 76,
        135–6, 139
    probable widowers 75–6, 85, 135
widows 10, 16, 24, 28–31, 34, 48–9,
    52, 55, 69, 76, 78–9, 82, 85–7,
    92, 121, 124, 130, 132 n. 42, 138,
    140
    category 'widow' 2, 8, 13, 14–15,
        21–2, 23, 30, 40–1, 42, 43,
        50–1, 58, 68–9, 71, 72–3, 76,
        77–9, 81, 83, 86–8, 91, 92–3,
        96, 99, 113–14, 115–16, 122,
        126–7, 132, 133, 135–6,

136–9, 141, 142, 145, 146, 147
'poor widow' 30, 89
'poor little widow' 88–9, 146
probable widows 75–6, 78, 85
relicta 14
vidua 13–14, 52 n. 50, 66, 72 n. 42, 73–4, 76–7, 79, 82–8, 114, 115–16, 124, 125, 128, 132, 134, 139 n. 89, 140, 143, 146
vidua paupercula 83, 87–9, 93
vowed widows 14, 18, 49, 52, 53, 58, 145
widowhood 14, 19–20, 23–24, 52, 56, 58, 93
see also models
wills, *see* testaments
Winchelsea 28 n. 60
Wogan-Browne, Jocelyn 20, 60 n. 84
Worcestershire:
Birtsmorten 128
Worcester 26 n. 55, 28 n. 60, 128
work 27, 30–1, 32, 33–6, 37, 76–7, 82, 86, 87–8, 89–92, 103, 110–11, 124–5, 146

work identity 83, 93
see also occupational status

year-books 125–6, 128, 142
York 26 n. 55, 33, 35 n. 90, 127, 129–37, 139–40
Chamberlains' Account Books 127, 129–30, 131–3
freedom of 129, 130, 131–3
Freemen's Register 127, 130, 131–2, 133
House Books 127, 130–1, 133–4
Probate Registers, Exchequer Court 131 n. 85, 134
Yorkshire 78 n. 62, 81, 83
Ainsty 136
see also Howdenshire
youth 16 n. 9, 75, 76, 80–2, 110, 136
young men 64, 119–21, 122, 144
young women 22, 29 n. 66, 43, 52, 54, 61, 62–4, 93–4, 117, 119–22, 137, 139, 140
see also maidens